Securitization Revisited

This book seeks to interrogate how contemporary policy issues become 'securitized' and, furthermore, what the implications of this process are. A generation after the introduction of the concept of securitization to the security studies field, this book engages with how securitization and desecuritization 'works' within and across a wide range of security domains including terrorism and counterterrorism, climate change, sexual and gender-based violence, inter-state and intra-state conflict, identity, and memory in various geographic and social contexts. Blending theory and application, the contributors to this volume – drawn from different disciplinary, ontological, and geographic 'spaces' – orient their investigations around three common analytical objectives: revealing deficiencies in and through application(s) of securitization; considering securitization through speech-acts and discourse as well as other mechanisms; and exposing latent orthodoxies embedded in securitization research. The volume demonstrates the dynamic and elastic quality of securitization and desecuritization as concepts that bear explanatory fruit when applied across a wide range of security issues, actors, and audiences. It also reveals the deficiencies in restricting securitization research to an overly narrow set of issues, actors, and mechanisms.

This volume will be of great interest to scholars of critical security studies, international security, and International Relations.

Michael J. Butler is Associate Professor of Political Science and Director of the Leir Luxembourg Program at Clark University. His publications include *Deconstructing the Responsibility to Protect* (Routledge, forthcoming), *Selling a 'Just' War: Framing, Legitimacy, and U.S. Military Intervention* (Palgrave, 2012), and *International Conflict Management* (Routledge, 2009).

Routledge Critical Security Studies Series

Securitization Revisited

Contemporary Applications and Insights

Edited by Michael J. Butler

Routledge
Taylor & Francis Group
LONDON AND NEW YORK

First published 2020 by Routledge

2 Park Square, Milton Park, Abingdon, Oxon, OX14 4RN
605 Third Avenue, New York, NY 10017

Routledge is an imprint of the Taylor & Francis Group, an informa business

First issued in paperback 2020

British Library Cataloguing- in-Publication Data
A catalogue record for this book is available from the British Library

Library of Congress Cataloging- in-Publication Data
A catalog record has been requested for this book

ISBN: 978-0-367-15037-2 (hbk)
ISBN: 978-0-367-78523-9 (pbk)

Typeset in Times New Roman
by Wearset Ltd, Boldon, Tyne and Wear

Contents

Illustrations

Contributors

Katerina Antoniou is a lecturer at the University of Central Lancashire, Cyprus. She specializes in peacebuilding and conflict resolution research. She holds a PhD on international peacebuilding from the University of Central Lancashire. Her dissertation examined group membership and interaction among peacebuilding professionals in Cyprus. Additional research interests include securitization, social identity, intergroup contact, and dark tourism. Katerina has received training on higher education, cross-cultural facilitation, and conflict mediation. She has also been involved in a variety of non-formal education initiatives, including youth empowerment workshops and intercommunal activities, and is a Fulbright Alumna. She holds a BA in Political Science and Economics from Clark University, Massachusetts, and an MSc in International Relations Theory from the London School of Economics.

Mark A. Boyer is a Board of Trustees Distinguished Professor at the University of Connecticut and serves as Executive Director of the International Studies Association. Throughout his career as a scholar-teacher, he has actively sought the integration of teaching, research, and service in all his professional activities. In addition to an array of journal articles, his books include *International Cooperation and Public Goods* (Johns Hopkins University Press, 1993) and *Defensive Internationalism* (University of Michigan Press, 2005; co-authored with Davis B. Bobrow). His most recent, and ongoing, research project, *Adapting to Climate Change*, is currently under contract with the University of Michigan Press. His professional awards include the UConn Honors Program Faculty Member of the Year (2015), the International Studies Association's Ladd Hollist Award for Service to the Profession (2009), the UConn Provost's Outreach Award for Public Service (2006), the UConn Alumni Association's Award for Excellence in Teaching at the Graduate Level (2004), the UConn Chancellor's Information Technology Award (2001), the American Political Science Association's Rowman & Littlefield Award for Teaching Innovation (2000), a Pew Faculty Fellowship in International Affairs (1992) and an SSRC-MacArthur Fellowship from 1986–1988. He also served twice as editor for ISA journals: *International Studies Perspectives* (2000–2004) and *International Studies Review* (2008–2012; co-edited with Jennifer Sterling-Folker).

Michael J. Butler is Associate Professor in the Department of Political Science and Director of the Henry J. and Erna D. Leir Luxembourg Program at Clark University in Worcester, Massachusetts. In 2014–2015, he was a Fulbright Scholar at the Institute of International Studies, University of Wrocław (Poland). His research and teaching interests converge in the areas of conflict and security. He is the author of three books – *International Conflict Management* (Routledge, 2009), *Selling a 'Just' War: Framing, Legitimacy, and U.S. Military Intervention* (Palgrave Macmillan, 2012), and *Global Politics: Engaging a Complex World* (with M.A. Boyer and N.F. Hudson, McGraw-Hill, 2013) – with an additional monograph, *Deconstructing the Responsibility to Protect*, forthcoming (Routledge). He has published numerous articles in leading academic journals and has served on the editorial boards of *International Studies Review*, *Simulation & Gaming* and *International Studies Perspectives*. He is a member of the Governing Council of the International Studies Association-Northeast as well as a senior fellow at the Canadian Centre for the Responsibility to Protect (CCR2P) at the University of Toronto, and is series co-editor (with Shareen Hertel) of the International Studies Intensives book series (Routledge).

Blanca Camps-Febrer is Associate Professor of International Relations at the Autonomous University of Barcelona and the Ramon Llull University. She is a member of the IRMENA research group. She is also the Research Coordinator of the Observatory on Human Rights and Business in the Mediterranean Region (ODHE). Her research focuses on security and gender issues. More specifically, her work examines the counter-terrorist narratives in Morocco as a securitization strategy.

Alexandra Cosima Budabin is Senior Researcher at the Human Rights Center and Adjunct Professor in the Department of Political Science at the University of Dayton (U.S.A.). Her research explores non-state actors in the global governance of human rights, humanitarianism, and development. She is a co-investigator in the research project "Commodifying Compassion: Implications of Turning People and Humanitarian Causes into Marketable Things" (2016–2020), funded by the Danish Council for Independent Research.

Natalie Florea Hudson is Associate Professor in the Department of Political Science at the University of Dayton, where she also serves as the Director of the Human Rights Studies Program. She specializes in gender and international relations, the politics of human rights, human security, and international law and organization. Her book, *Gender, Human Security and the UN: Security Language as a Political Framework for Women* (Routledge, 2009) examines the organizational dynamics of women's activism in the United Nations system and how women have come to embrace, and been impacted by, the security discourse in their work for rights and equality.

Jarosław Jarząbek is Assistant Professor in the Institute of International Studies at the University of Wrocław. He obtained his PhD in Political Science in

2007 at the Faculty of Social Sciences, University of Wrocław. His research interest focuses on security studies and Middle Eastern studies, with publications on topics including regional security complexes, the politics of security and armed forces in the Middle East, political systems and international relations in the Middle East, the Israeli-Palestinian conflict, and development of the Palestinian national movement. In 2016, Jarząbek was a Fulbright scholar at the University of Central Florida in Orlando and is currently coordinator of the Erasmus Mundus Global Studies program at the University of Wrocław.

Neil Oculi received his PhD in Geography, as well as a Masters in International Studies at the University of Connecticut. Following completion of an undergraduate degree in Human Ecology at The College of the Atlantic, Neil studied farm management and rural development at the United World College in Venezuela. He has done field research in Venezuela, Mexico, Tanzania, and the Caribbean. Neil has been part of his country's delegation at the United Nations Framework Convention on Climate Change (UNFCCC). His research interests include the vulnerability of Small Island Development State (SIDS), climate change, climate change negotiations, modeling of sea level rise within SIDS, and hydro and hydraulic modeling of flood events within SIDS. He was born and raised in Saint Lucia.

Valérie Rosoux is Senior Research Fellow at the Belgian National Fund for Scientific Research (FNRS) and Professor at the Université catholique de Louvain. Since 2017, she has been an external Scientific Fellow at the Max Planck Institute, Luxembourg. In 2010–2011, she was a Jennings Randolph Senior Fellow at the United States Institute of Peace (USIP, Washington). As a post-doctoral researcher, she worked at The Johns Hopkins University School of Advanced International Studies (SAIS), the Center for International Studies and Research (CERI), Institut d'Études Politiques of Paris and the University Laval, Canada. Valérie Rosoux has a Licence in Philosophy and a PhD in International Relations. Since 2016, she has been a member of the Belgian Royal Academy. She is the author of several books and articles about post-war reconciliation and the uses of memory in international relations, the latest of which is *Negotiating Reconciliation in Peacemaking*, with Mark Anstey (Springer, 2017).

Roxanna Sjöstedt is Senior Lecturer of Political Science and the Director of Peace and Conflict Studies at Lund University. Her main areas of research are security studies, in particular securitization theory, international interventions, identity construction, and norm diffusion and socialization. She has published on these topics in leading outlets including: *Security Dialogue*, *Cooperation and Conflict*, *Foreign Policy Analysis*, the *Oxford Research Encyclopedia*, the *Journal of International Relations and Development*, and the *Journal of Peace Research*.

Siniša Vuković is Senior Lecturer in Conflict Management and Global Policy, and Associate Director of the Conflict Management Program at Johns

Hopkins University's School of Advanced International Studies (SAIS). He is also a visiting professor at the Institute of Security and Global Affairs, Leiden University, and at the Amsterdam University College, University of Amsterdam. He received a PhD (cum laude) in International Relations and Conflict Resolution from Leiden University. He is the recipient of numerous research grants, including "Rubicon" from the Netherlands Organization for Scientific Research (NWO). His research focuses on various forms of international conflict resolution, negotiation, and mediation. He has published in a range of scholarly and policy-oriented journals including: *Washington Quarterly, Cooperation and Conflict, Studies in Conflict and Terrorism, Millennium: Journal of International Studies, International Journal of Conflict Management, International Negotiation, Acta Politica, Foreign Affairs, Foreign Policy, World Economic Forum, Sustainable Security,* and *Policy Forum,* as well as contributing to several edited volumes. He is also the author of the book *International Multiparty Mediation and Conflict Management* (Routledge, 2015).

Zena Wolf is currently working as a research associate for U.S. Senator Elizabeth Warren's (D-MA) Presidential Campaign. Zena received a BA in Political Science (specializing in International Relations) in 2016, and a Master's degree in Public Administration (MPA) in 2017, both from Clark University. In 2017, she was a research intern at the Consortium on Gender, Security, and Human Rights in Boston, working on projects related to gender, security, and water infrastructure and access, as well as non-profit administration. In 2015–2016, she served as peer reviewer for *SURJ,* Clark's peer-reviewed undergraduate research journal. In 2017, Zena was a recipient of the Henry J. and Erna D. Leir Student Research Conference Participation Award, granted by the Leir Foundation.

Preface

The launch pad for this book was a three-day workshop convened in Remich, Luxembourg in the summer of 2017 under the auspices of the Henry J. and Erna D. Leir Luxembourg Program at Clark University, and supported by the generosity of the Leir Foundation. The contributing scholars came together with one express purpose in mind: to grapple, individually and collectively, with the concept of securitization in application. From that point to this, we have all sought not only to reveal as much as possible about what this crucial concept can tell us about the various security domains with which we are each concerned, but also to discern what these domains – and the actors, issues, policies, and processes subsumed within them – can tell us about the concept itself.

Although we come from different disciplinary, ontological, and geographic 'places,' we were able to collectively identify a set of common analytical concerns early on in this enterprise which have served as important intellectual guideposts for the journey. In the spirit of critical interrogation, we strive in this volume not only to underscore the important contribution of securitization to security studies and policy, but also to identify deficiencies revealed in its application(s), to push beyond speech-acts and discourse when examining securitization and desecuritization, and to expose any latent orthodoxies that might constrain securitization's explanatory power. And, in the spirit of reflexivity, we also strive to the extent possible to acknowledge and contend with our own roles in the process as scholars, practitioners, and citizens. Whether we have succeeded in realizing these ambitious goals is up to the reader to decide.

In closing, it bears mentioning that the path leading to this point, while not without its complications, has been a continual source of intellectual stimulation and personal fulfillment for the editor. This has everything to do with the brilliance, dedication, responsiveness, and most of all warmth and collegiality of the contributors. One would be hard-pressed to find a better group of scholars and people with whom to collaborate.

Acknowledgments

The editor as well as the contributors wish to extend our deepest gratitude to The Leir Foundation as well as the Henry J. and Erna D. Leir Luxembourg Program at Clark University for their generous support of the workshop 'Redefining Security, Revisited' convened in Remich, Luxembourg in July 2017. This event afforded us a wonderful and rare opportunity to engage in collaborative exchanges of the highest order in a truly idyllic setting – exchanges which proved to be catalytic for this volume.

The editor would also like to thank the Morton L. "Sonny" Lavine Foundation for its generous support in the preparation of this manuscript.

For numerous in-depth and thoughtful discussions of securitization and its applicability, the editor would also like to acknowledge and thank Padmini Dey, whose insights left a lasting imprint.

Lastly, the editor would be remiss in failing to acknowledge the assistance of the highly professional and responsive editorial staff at Routledge, including Ella Halstead, Bethany Lund Yates, and especially Andrew Humphrys, who saw merit in the project from the earliest stages.

Michael J. Butler
Clark University
Worcester, Massachusetts

Part I
Theoretical insights

Introduction

Revisiting securitization and the 'constructivist turn' in security studies

Michael J. Butler and Zena Wolf

Over a generation after Richard Ullman (1983) issued a clarion call for the redefinition of security, scholars and practitioners alike continue to seek a deeper understanding of the contingent processes that lead to specific constructions and interpretations of security and insecurity by agents engaged in the process of socialization and meaning-making – a process Ole Wæver (1995) labeled "securitization." This introductory chapter sets the stage for the range of applications and assessments of securitization contained in this book. It does so primarily by chronicling the larger shift in the security studies field toward critical approaches which, in turn, paved the way for the aforementioned 'constructivist turn' and in particular the development of securitization as a concept (C.A.S.E. Collective, 2006).[1]

This chapter situates the so-called 'constructivist turn' in relation to the emergence of critical security studies – a broader ontological shift itself explained by a convergence of social forces and intellectual factors detailed below. Following this origin story, we turn to a synthetic review of the scholarship concerning the 'constructivist turn' in security studies, and in particular what we consider to be its signal contribution: namely, the concept of securitization. This effort at providing a brief and synthetic intellectual history of securitization helps set the stage for the articulation of three common overarching concerns around which the inquiries and investigations advanced in this volume are oriented.

Both individually and collectively, those inquiries and investigations seek to contribute to a more robust understanding of securitization theory and practice. To that end, the contributions to this volume are motivated by two distinct but inter-related analytical objectives: namely, to examine how securitization works as a ***process***, as well as to assess its explanatory strengths and weaknesses as a ***concept***. These analytical objectives are not only related, but also mutually reinforcing. Indeed, when taking into account various security issues and actors, the contingent and specific dimensions of the securitization process have significant implications not only for political and policy outcomes, but for our very understanding of security (Williams, 2003).

Confronting a 'new' security environment

Theoretical insights in the social sciences are undoubtedly a by-product of pre-vailing intellectual and social-historical contexts, and the interplay between them (C.A.S.E. Collective, 2006). To this end, the end of the Cold War radically recast prevailing notions of the structure of the international system (Booth, 1997). Indeed, the dust from the Cold War had hardly settled before these and other emergent challenges led to proclamations of a post-Cold War "new security environment" (Kaplan, 1994; Buzan, 1991a). This structural transforma-tion in turn left scholars and policymakers alike without a singular, fixed account of the international security environment around which to base their analyses and actions. The resulting intellectual and policy vacuum stimulated greater recognition of the possibility of a 'new' security environment in which security actors, threats, and responses alike are subject to an ongoing social and political process of definition, redefinition, and contestation.

New actors, new threats

In reality, the emergence of a 'new' security environment was a gradual process stemming back decades. The point of origin of the concept itself remains the subject of continuing debate, but from our standpoint, the more meaningful con-versation is one that engages with *extant* structural dynamics producing, or perhaps revealing, a dizzying array of security challenges and unleashing a con-tested and politicized process to define and prioritize them. The extent to which these dynamics have led to a redefinition of the security landscape, elevating non-state actors and non-traditional 'threats' such as transnational terrorism, ethnic conflict, state failure, natural resource wars, ecological disasters, cyberat-tacks, abject poverty, and systematic discrimination and oppression on the con-temporary security agenda, is an important consideration underlying this volume (Krahmann, 2005; Matthews, 1989).

A particular target of most efforts to re-orient security studies to confront a 'new' security environment is the singular emphasis of realist theory on milita-rized interactions between competing states striving to advance national inter-ests. This emphasis is itself a by-product of realism's essential precept that the state is the central actor in international politics (Baldwin, 1997). The statist ori-entation of realism and its deliberate emphasis on power, order, and competing interests rendered the theory highly useful for describing security threats and proscribing security responses in a Cold War world in which these factors were predominant. However, given the elevation of social inequality, gender inequity, poverty and relative deprivation, resource scarcity and environmental degrada-tion, crime, health, external and internal migration, and the like within the 'new security environment,' the utility of a cognitive lens that places a premium on states, material interests, and military capabilities seems limited at best.

The degree to which non-state actors (NSAs) including multinational corpo-rations (MNCs), non-governmental organizations (NGOs), transnational terrorist networks, paramilitaries, private military contractors (PMCs), policy thinktanks, peace advocates, and the like have altered and eroded the power and influence traditionally enjoyed by nation-states is instructive in this regard. Consider, for instance, the emergence and significance of ISIS, and before that al-Qaeda, on the security agendas and policies of much of the international community; the role of NGOs such as the Coalition for an International Criminal Court in shaping international law and institutions; or the impacts of remittances from migratory workers to the economies of many developing countries. These and other similar examples point to two related components of structural change with great import for contemporary security thinking and practice: one, the rise to the fore of non-state actors as security actors; and two, the potential for that emergence of non-state actors to undermine state capacity in the security realm.

The 'dark side' of interdependence

Suppositions of a 'new security environment' are dependent not only on the emergence of new actors, but also on a recognition of new (or previously overlooked) sources of insecurity. From an empirical and policy standpoint, the emergence of 'new world disorder' (Zartman, 2008) in the Cold War's wake spawned a plethora of new (or previously overlooked) security threats and challenges. Included among these were the increasing frequency of intra-state conflicts, the rampant spread of small arms and light weapons (SALW), the simultaneous increase in both failing and predatory states, environmental degradation and population displacement, and the blossoming of transnational terrorism and crime.

At an abstract level, these sources of insecurity can be understood as unintended outcomes or 'negative externalities' produced by the complex interdependence animating the past several decades of globalization. The presumed or supposed benefits of such interdependence are oft-celebrated (Keohane & Nye, 2001; Friedman, 2007). Yet the depth and expanse of networked interactions between and among societies and individuals is not without its hazards. Most notable among these is the increased sensitivity and vulnerability of an ever-greater number of actors to a wide range of security threats (Baldwin, 1980). Indeed, to a very real extent, 'globalization' can be said to be the main impetus driving the emergence of a range of new or newly salient security threats and challenges.

Certainly, the political, social, economic, cultural, and ideational processes of globalization, as well as the backlash against these processes, pose a very real security challenge, in the form of a boiling over of frustrations about the transformations wrought by these processes into violence. Yet it is not just a turn to violence within, between, or across societies by globalization's 'discontents' that is important here. The increasing intensity and extensity of global interdependence has also created a degree of densely networked and weakly governed interconnectedness in commerce, transport, energy and natural resources, migration, and information technology that has raised both the profile and stakes of activities within these issue areas, wiping away the 'high' and 'low' politics dichotomy commonplace in a previous generation. At the core of the issue is the degree to which economic, social, and ecological processes are linked to political instability and volatility and, in turn, violence (Homer-Dixon, 1999).

The degree to which these mutually constitutive and reinforcing dynamics are gaining traction in the field of security studies is in turn fostering challenges to what were not so long ago considered to be discrete and mutually exclusive phenomena associated either with a 'security' or 'development' agenda, as opposed to the intersection or combination of the two (Collier, 2003). The evident and undeniable emergence of new security actors, threats, and challenges as briefly introduced here has had significant impact on the activities and agendas of security practitioners at the local, state, regional, and global level. Indeed, the story of the 'new security environment' is one in which, nearly three decades on from the end of the Cold War, security planning and postures remain in a seemingly perpetual state of flux.

The emergence of critical security studies

From an intellectual standpoint, the *extant* changes in the security arena described above inspired profound challenges to the conventional wisdom concerning the nature of security and how to provide it. As the impact and implications of actors and threats which were traditionally overlooked or marginalized became ever more real and profound, fundamental challenges to the prevailing ontology of security itself emerged. From their earliest origins, critical approaches to security studies have exhibited a shared concern with exposing the 'intellectual hegemony' of realism and challenging its attendant assumptions (Booth, 1991, p. 318). Indeed, in these anti- or counter-hegemonic aspirations, we can most readily discern the overt influence of critical theory more generally on security studies beginning in the 1980s, albeit with deeper roots (C.A.S.E. Collective, 2006).

In the quest to redefine security, the intellectual position articulated by Critical Security Studies (CSS) met significant resistance. This resistance was predicated on the presumption that increased elasticity in the definition of security portended a potentially dangerous loss of meaning (Deudney, 1990; Ayoob, 1997). Much of this opposition came from neo-realist scholars who sought to preserve a narrow, traditional reading of security in order to maintain the 'intellectual coherence' ostensibly provided by prevailing orthodoxies in the security studies field (Buzan, Wæver, & de Wilde, 1998).

The 'traditional' approach[2]

The introduction of the term 'new security environment' signaled an effort to refine, if not supplant, the traditional approach to security and its emphasis on nation-states, material interests, and coercive power (Krause and Williams, 1996; Wyn Jones, 1996). An accepted point of reference for over a generation in institutional contexts ranging from NATO (Vershbow, 2016) to the UNDP (UNDP, 1994), this term had the unintended effect of underscoring realism's role as the paradigmatic progenitor of the security studies field (Crawford, 1991).

Steeped in a Machiavellian appreciation for power, a Hobbesian pessimism regarding human nature, and a Clausewitzian belief in the notion of war as the paramount policy instrument, from its earliest discernible origins in the aftermath of World War II, the security studies field has long rested on a set of key propositions derived from realist thought. Indeed, under the guise of celebrating a 'renaissance' of the security studies field, Walt (1991) equated security studies with the study of

> [...] the conditions that make the use of force more likely, the ways that the use of force affects individuals, states, and societies, and the specific policies that states adopt in order to prepare for, prevent, or engage in war.
>
> (Walt, 1991, p. 212)

In doing so, the field was reduced to a single fundamental concern with "the *threat, use, and control of military force*" (Walt, 1991, p. 212; emphasis in original).

Following from this a priori proposition, the orthodox approach to security studies produced and reinforced several fundamental (and inter-related) bedrock concepts in the field – concepts that later became central objects for interrogation by those critical of prevailing orthodoxies in the security studies field. One such concept is that of **self-help anarchy**, and its proposition that the absence of a central governing authority necessarily produces an environment in which states exist in a self-help relationship with one another (Herz, 1950). From a security studies perspective, the chief implication of this assumption regarding the structure and animus of the international system is that anarchy provides the 'permissive conditions' for war; absent any global Leviathan, states can and will do whatever they must to survive and, further, to pursue their interests –frequently including the resort to armed conflict.[3]

Likewise, the emergence of the security studies field in the mid-twentieth century chiefly arose out of a concern with maintaining the **centrality of state sovereignty**. As Sheehan puts it,

> during the long domination of international relations by realism [approximately from the late 1930s to the late 1970s], the working definition of security was a strictly limited one, which saw its nature as being concerned with military power, and the subject of these concerns as being the state [...].
>
> (2005, p. 5)

The structuring of security thought and practice around the nation-state in turn rests on a particular conceptualization of the state articulated by the sociologist Max Weber in 'Politics as a Vocation' (1918, 2009). With the functionality of the state contingent on a shared social understanding that the state is the only actor with the legitimate right to employ organized violence, one can see (as Weber did) the construction of a mutually dependent relationship between violence and the state. Internally, such a monopoly underwrote the very authority of the state, as violence could be used to thwart potential internal challenges to ruling elites, leading to the consolidation of the modern state as a political unit (Mann, 1993). Externally, possessing such an unchallenged authority to utilize organized violence permits the state to employ violence to defend national interests and advance national objectives relative to other states, or even to divert attention from domestic problems by initiating armed conflict.

The notion of the ***balance of power*** is yet another central concept in traditional approaches to security studies. As articulated by Hans Morgenthau, the balance of power is a natural, even inexorable, mechanism akin to the laws of nature (1948, p. 173). Subsequent theoretical treatments of the balance of power only further reified its mechanistic effects, largely in service of explaining the structural constraints on state behavior imposed by anarchy (Waltz, 1979). Whereas classical realists such as Morgenthau contended that states consciously seek out partners to balance against adversaries and the threats they present, neo-realists argued that a balance of power arrangement is a structural artifact produced by the striving for dominance of states. The larger significance of the concept for the traditional approach to security studies stems from the animating role that the balance of power allegedly plays in shaping, and even dictating, the behavior of major powers. After all, the ultimate objective of balance of power or balance of threat arrangements is not peace, but maintenance of the status quo and prevention of the domination of the system by any one state or alliance (Walt, 1985, 1987).

The influence of prominent conceptual contributions such as these from the dominant strain in security studies is undeniable. However, the limits of their explanatory power are increasingly evident, largely due to their status as a by-product of specific temporal and contextual factors and conditions. Here it again bears mentioning that the earliest discernible origins of a distinct field of security studies are found in the beginning of the Cold War (Baldwin, 1995). Brought on by the perceived necessity of 'winning' the Cold War by imbuing strategy and policy with the contributions of leading intellectuals (such as Bernard Brodie, Herman Kahn, Thomas Schelling, and the like), the basic tenets of *realpolitik* were brought to bear on the pressing security threats of the time. However, many of those threats were spatially and temporally bound, and linked to the peculiar and unprecedented dynamic of a bipolar rivalry between two military and economic superpowers that produced them. Similarly restrictive was (and is) the unwavering emphasis placed on the state as the central security actor. Approaches to security thinking and practice calibrated in this way have proven incapable of accounting for or formulating an effective response to emerging security challenges which do not 'fit' with, or cannot be accommodated through, the state (Brown, 1998).

Critical reformulations

For the most part, the identification of those deficiencies was and remains the by-product of an intellectual movement for redefining security (Ullman, 1983). One can discern the origins of this redefinition even in the midst of the Cold War, as an expression of mounting disaffection with the facile yet insufficient prescriptions provided by realist-inflected thinking (Booth, 1997). Among the earliest examples of this disaffection was a shift in the central focus for security concerns evident in the evolution from 'strategic' to 'security' studies, as well as a migration of the referent point for security consideration from 'national' to 'international' security by the 1970s (Freedman, 1998). Such shifts betrayed dissatisfaction with the narrow conception of security prevalent at that time (UN, 1980; Ullman, 1983).

The fading of the Cold War military and ideological confrontation reaffirmed the ongoing efforts of CSS scholars to shift security thought and practice away from a singular emphasis on anarchy, sovereign states, and the balance of power. Such concepts were themselves indicative of a predominantly Eurocentric approach concerned with external threats to state security and a conceptualization of the international system that prioritized the experiences of Western countries (Acharya, 1997; Ayoob, 1997). The proliferation of ethnic conflict, humanitarian disaster, and general social disorder in Somalia, Rwanda, the former Yugoslavia, Liberia/Sierra Leone and elsewhere in the early to mid-1990s only helped further expose the inadequacy of the traditional approach for security thought and practice alike. Led by scholars such as Keith Krause, Michael Williams, Ken Booth and Richard Wyn Jones, the CSS approach drew from such diverse points of origin as Robert Cox's (1981) take on historical materialism, the post-positivism of Habermas and the Frankfurt School (Geuss, 1981), and the 'dissidence' of North American scholars such as R.B.J. Walker and Richard K. Ashley (1990) in service of exposing the limitations of traditional security studies.

In a general sense, many of the efforts toward reformulating security thinking and practice in that 'first generation' could be understood as motivated by a desire to 'broaden' and 'deepen' security as an analytical domain, as well as to provide a greater account for the coercive practices and logics of states as deployed against individuals. These concerns, advanced in turn by the Copenhagen, Aberystwyth, and Paris Schools, were each in their own way responses to the ontological and epistemological question of why some issues and actors receive priority treatment, while others with crucial security implications do not – the central question at the heart of the concept of securitization itself (Huysmans, 1998).[4]

The so-called Copenhagen School (McSweeney, 1996) sought to broaden the concept of security, introducing the sectoral approach and, by extension, a range of differing policy arenas in which securitization can and does occur. Initially laid out in *People, States, and Fear* (Buzan, 1991b), the sectoral approach moved security beyond the political-military sector. By "exploring threats to referent objects, and the securitization of those threats, that are non-military as well as military" in nature (Buzan et al., 1998, p. 4), the referent object for security studies and policy was no longer limited to states, and in light of the recognition of the socially constructed nature of security threats, the scope of securitizing actors and processes expanded significantly.

Scholars associated with the Aberystwyth School dedicated their labors toward 'deepening' the construct of security, advancing the fundamental argument that the only logical referent for security thought and practice was the human being. Building upon insights gleaned from the Frankfurt School and post-positivism, such arguments contended that security be defined as 'emancipation' from physical and human constraints, and only through emancipation can security be reached (Booth, 1997; Peoples & Vaughan-Williams, 2015). This view also necessarily imposes distance from a state-centric approach, arguing that states and their power are merely the means to emancipation and freedom for individuals (Booth, 1991. This central insight – sometimes characterized as 'emancipatory realism' – was oriented around the recasting of security studies and policies to emphasize the security of the individual (Booth, 1991, 2005; Krause & Williams, 1997; Wyn Jones, 1996, 2001).

One outcome of this recalibration was the concept of human security (Paris, 2001). This approach, which rose to prominence in the mid-1990s (though also with older antecedents), was borne of a concern with a fuller and more adequate accounting for human well-being and economic development concerns under the heading of security studies (Hettne & Söderbaum, 2005; Duffield, 1999). Advocates of a human security approach define economic well-being and inequality, public health, environmental quality, political empowerment, and a variety of other measures as primarily security concerns (Sheehan, 2005). The importance of these conditions is especially relevant for their impact on what Amartya Sen refers to as the "capabilities" and "functioning" (Sen, 2004) or Booth (1991) as the "emancipation" of the individual.

Another prominent 'school' within CSS is the 'Paris School,' drawing inspiration from Bourdieu on socialization and 'habitus' and Foucault on discipline, biopolitics, and technologies of security, and associated with scholars such as Didier Bigo (Bigo & Guild, 2005; Bigo, 2002, 2000, 1996) and Jef Huysmans (Huysmans, 2006, 2002, 2000). Triggered in part by *extant* changes within Europe – particularly concerning population movements and the fashioning of a 'justice and home affairs' pillar in the Treaty of Maastricht in 1992 – the Paris School forged insights from political sociology and critical social theory together in examining policing, coercion, and the securitization of migration (Bigo & Guild, 2005; Huysmans, 2000; Bonelli, 2005; Ceyhan & Tsoukala, 1997). Examining governmentality as a mechanism for imposing and maintaining a given social order provided a profoundly domestic, 'outside-in' orientation to the interrogations of the Paris School. This was a feature which not only distinguished it from the other prominent schools of CSS, but which positioned it in direct and profound opposition to the traditionalist approach to security studies, defined as it was by the unproblematic role of states and state coercion at its heart.

From the standpoint of CSS, perhaps the most problematic feature of the traditional assumptions undergirding the security studies field was that they directed scholarly attention to a particular and limited range of questions at the expense of a vast expanse of other security-related issues and concerns (Krause and Williams, 1996). Among other insights generated by the increasing infusion of critical theory into the security studies domain is the revelation of the profound impacts that idealized constructions of gender as well as ethnocentric worldviews have had on the security studies field and its dominant agenda. Though in some ways a microcosm of their impact on International Relations (IR) more generally, gendered and ethnocentric perspectives have had particularly pernicious implications for both security thought and practice, often shaping the 'securitization' process while also influencing the questions we ask and the issues we consider (Hudson, 2009; Hansen, 2013).

Thanks largely to the contributions of feminist IR, the pervasive influence of militarized masculinity and reified notions of the protective state were revealed as underpinnings of the dominant intellectual and ontological position in security studies (Detraz, 2012; Sjoberg, 2009). A chief consequence of this is the enduring and glaring omission of the role of gender and its impact on strategic and defense policy (Stiehm, 1996; Cohn, 1987), conflict behavior (Sjoberg, 2013), notions and relations of power (Shepherd, 2015), the appeal and use of violence (Carpenter, 2006; Caprioli, 2003), and the roles and contributions of women in the security arena more generally (Enloe, 2014; Ruane, 2011; Tickner, 2001).

Similarly, postcolonial and critical race theory has uncovered the extent to which IR in general, and security studies in particular, remains the by-product of assumptions unique to the 'West' and/or the 'Global North' as well as to a particular temporal and spatial context (Europe after the peace of Westphalia). As Acharya (2014) notes, this overwhelming Eurocentric orientation is directly responsible for a number of 'blind spots' in the field (most notably, the exclusion of non-military and intra-state/intra-societal considerations and phenomena), while at the same time over-determining the importance of the balance of power and state sovereignty. And while Ayoob's 'sub-altern realism' (2002) advances a more muted critique, it still demands acknowledgement and recognition of the contingency of the assumptions and concepts (such as the unitary, rational, Weberian state) which have long reigned supreme over both security studies and practice.

The 'constructivist turn' in security studies: key insights

The very existence of this project is a testimonial to a 'constructivist turn' in security studies which itself is a by-product of the emergence and evolution of critical security studies. Indeed, one result of the 'critical encounters' (C.A.S.E. Collective, 2006) described above has been the significant inroads in the security studies field made by constructivist thought. Prevailing insights gleaned from this 'constructivist turn' (Checkel, 1998) or research program (Farrell, 2002) undoubtedly speak to the importance of norms, ideas, and identity to the study and practice of security as well as to the practice(s) of security provision (Desch, 1998; Williams, 1998). Perhaps the most impactful results of the 'constructivist turn' in security studies have been those seeking to re-conceptualize the security referent, capture the inter-subjective dynamics of regional security, and expand the analytical scope of security studies itself.

Debating the referent

The encroachment of constructivist thought into the security studies arena helped reveal the limitations of equating security with material capabilities and empha-sizing the maintenance of order through the machinations of statecraft.[5] Accord-ingly, the most prominent point of demarcation among scholars of security studies today is the debate over the referent object; i.e., the unit or actor that is the centerpiece of one's concern when thinking about security. While largely a theoretical debate, differing views of the most appropriate referent object for security thinking and practices are important in practical terms. Who one chooses to prioritize plays an essential role in establishing how security is defined, what the chief threat(s) to security is (are), and how threats posed by conflict can be managed and contained (Walker, 1997).

Employing a *systemic* perspective requires adopting a holistic view based on the idea that security is an all-encompassing condition that applies, is provided, or is undermined in relation to the distribution of power prevailing within the international system at any given point in time. These perspectives come in more optimistic, neo-liberal (Keohane, 1989; Keohane & Nye, 2001) or more pessim-istic, neo-realist (Waltz, 2000) variants. Differences of theoretical orientation aside, constituent units are of secondary importance in comparison to the larger system in which they are embedded, and which operates according to its own dynamics. Therefore, those who consider the international system to be the ref-erence point for thinking about security tend to emphasize collective security threats and responses, and by extension the need to locate and marshal the appro-priate means for managing threats to the prevailing global or regional order.

Using the *state* as the referent necessarily directs one's analytical focus to the unique interests and imperatives that determine, and impinge upon, each state's own security. These interests and imperatives are assumed to be known to states and their leaders, who act rationally to process the information and assess the capabilities available to maximize that security (Katzenstein, 1996). Importantly, the security of the sovereign state is not bound up with or dependent upon the security of other states; security is a good that sovereign states can, do, and must provide for themselves. Likewise, threats are posed to (and by) states and their security interests in an independent fashion, irrespective of the threats or inter-ests concerning other states (Snow, 2015). For those who consider the state the primary security referent, the resulting conceptualization of security naturally leads to an emphasis on the security imperatives and threats of individual nation-states. This emphasis in turn places the unit of the state and the concept of state sovereignty at the forefront of the security agenda – with the security concerns of sub-state constituents, other states, or the international system are necessarily given short shrift (Masco, 2014).

Thinking of security as something derived from or resident in the system or state necessarily imposes a degree of intellectual and philosophical distance. As a result, those who advocate appreciation of security from the position of the *individual* contend that the security plight of human beings is often lost amidst the abstractions of systemic and state-level approaches to security. Threats to individual security fall into four main categories: physical, meaning threats leading to pain, injury, ailment, or death; economic, meaning threats to property, economic opportunity, or material resources; political, translated through a denial of civil rights, restriction on political participation or liberties; and status, understood as a threat to one's place within the social order (Hanlon and Christie, 2016). Generally speaking, threats to the security of the individual are of a social nature; the referent in this perspective on security is not viewed in isolation from the larger social and natural environment in which it exists (Adger et al., 2014). Consider, for example, that the factors that impact one individual's security usually impact the security of numerous others as well; an outbreak of disease, a proliferation of crime in one's neighborhood, or a policy of 'ethnic cleansing' declared by a government against a national group are all effective examples. Further, the diminution of one person's security will often diminish others' security as well. Finally, efforts to prioritize and adequately respond to threats to one's individual security are often beyond the means and capabilities of the individual affected. One is unlikely to be able to prevent or treat a disease, arrest criminals, or defend oneself against an ethnic cleansing campaign without some kind of institutional support (Black, 2016).

Regional security complexes

Another significant contribution resulting from the infusion of constructivist thought comes in the emphasis on regions as a distinct level of analysis as well as domain of operation. Regions emerged as a primary level of analysis between the state and the global system after the Cold War, in part because the collapse of the bipolar order paved the way for the entry of a wider scope of participation and, by extension, an opportunity for challenges to Eurocentrism in international security thinking and practice (Kelly, 2007). Regional sub-systems took on increasing importance in the 'new security environment,' independent of the states that comprised them or the global system in which they were embedded. Indeed, regions came to be seen as political-security units having "substantial autonomy from the system-level interactions of global powers" (Buzan & Wæver, 2003, p. 4; Acharya, 2007).

'Regional Security Complexes' (RSCs) were first conceptualized in relation to dynamics of intense rivalry and enmity between states (Buzan, 1991b). However, as discussed in Chapter 2, they are now understood to exist along a spectrum of amity and enmity, with conflict formation at one end and a pluralistic security community at the other (Buzan et al., 1998). Securitization is therefore an inherent part of RSCs, as securitization of external threats allows for understanding, inter-dependence, and coherence within a group of actors (Buzan et al., 1998; Peoples & Vaughan-Williams, 2015, p. 100). Many scholars continue to stress the import-ance of proximity and geographic ties, as well as "shared histories of interaction" in the creation and reinforcement of Regional Security Complexes (Buzan & Wæver, 2003; Katzenstein, 2005). Still others have highlighted the role of cultural, functional, and economic ties in creating distinct regions (Lake, 1997; Kelly, 2007). Ultimately, the socially constructed nature of RSCs is emphasized in works that examine the agency of weaker states and challenge traditional notions of power and control (Acharya, 2007). This expanded conceptualization of the scope of the security agendas associated with RSCs permit, and are permitted by, hetero-geneous formation in terms of participants and the ontology of the threats being securitized (Buzan et al., 1998). Still, the construction and nature of RSCs remains subject to various and contested interpretations (as discussed at length in Chapter 2).

The sectoral approach

An additional by-product of the constructivist turn in security studies is the intro-duction of the sectoral approach, as first articulated by Buzan (1991b). Buzan's menu allowed for thorough (re)appraisal of the effort to 'securitize' a wider range of phenomena in response to what he dubbed the "rising density" of glo-balization. Whether one's security referent is international, national, or indi-vidual, Buzan contends security concerns can be located in one (or sometimes more) of five sectors:

- **military security:** concerns produced by the reciprocal interaction of the armed offensive and defensive capabilities and/or perceptions of states and their leaders
- **political security:** concerns produced in relation to the organization stability (or instability) of states, governing systems, and ideologies
- **economic security:** concerns generated by limited or unequal access to eco-nomic resources (including financial capital and markets) needed to sustain an acceptable level of social welfare
- **societal security:** concerns triggered by either excessive adherence *or* real/perceived threats to traditional patterns of language, culture, religious and national identity, custom
- **environmental security:** concerns prompted by threats to the local, regional, or global ecosystem and the natural resource base on which human life depends

As this schema suggests, while military security is no longer equated with security per se, it retains a high degree of importance both in its own right, and in its interactions with other types of security threats and challenges. This latter point is especially crucial; one of the strengths of Buzan's multi-sectoral approach is the extent to which it not only illustrates distinct categories of security problems apart from military security, but also suggests a significant degree of overlap between and among sectors. In this way, we can see where, for example, an environmental security concern (e.g., a sudden decline in arable land) might trigger a military security concern (e.g., the outbreak of armed conflict over land rights and access), or vice versa (where, for instance, an ongoing civil war might reduce the availability of or access to arable land). While Buzan's schema is not all-encompassing, it does offer a basic conceptual roadmap for broadening the concept of security in the contemporary era by introducing a means of defining, analyzing, and responding to differing security threats (Buzan et al., 1998; Buzan & Wæver, 2003) as well as enhancing our recognition of interdependence and the non-military security threats it produces.

Operationalizing securitization

These and other key insights resulting from the 'constructivist turn' have significantly expanded the analytical scope of security studies, altering prevailing notions of security and recalibrating policy prescriptions and practices in the process. Yet at the heart of any effort to redefine the security referent, account for intersubjectivity within security complexes, or expand the landscape of security threats and challenges lies perhaps the singular insight of constructivist security studies: namely, the concept and process of securitization.

Securitization describes those highly politicized processes by which "the socially and politically successful speech act labels an issue a security issue, removing it from the realm of normal day-to-day politics, casting it as an existential threat calling for and justifying extreme measures" (Williams, 1998, p. 435). The concept itself both follows from, and folds back upon, the other leading insights of constructivist security studies. The securitization process can be applied to referent objects at the systemic, state/societal, or individual level, and moreover to issues or challenges across any or all of the 'sectors' advanced by Buzan, Wæver, and de Wilde (1998). As a fundamentally political process of meaning-making, it can and does unfold within (and shape) prevailing patterns of enmity or amity within regional security complexes, or any other political institution (domestic, regional, or global). This is, in fact, the point when it comes to securitization – anything, or anyone, can become securitized, and any and all audiences are subject to 'securitizing moves' (C.A.S.E. Collective, 2006).

The influence of the Copenhagen School on securitization is especially noteworthy in this regard, particularly in its conceptualization of a security issue as any issue posing (or thought to pose) an existential threat to the survival of a referent object (Peoples & Vaughan-Williams, 2015). The intersubjective nature of the securitization process therefore allows for the possible definition (or redefinition) of a wide range of normative concerns as 'security issues,' including (but not limited to) HIV/AIDS (Elbe, 2006), trafficking (Jackson, 2006), finance (Kessler, 2011), and cybersecurity (Hansen & Nissenbaum, 2009).

Following from this presumption, securitization is a formal process occurring in a defined context and framework (McDonald, 2008), one best understood as an extreme form of politicization through which security threats are viewed as existential issues and therefore fall outside of normal political rules. Threats are identified and created by securitizing actors (Buzan et al., 1998, p. 23). By distinguishing the securitizing actor from the referent object, securitization becomes a process that is highly dependent on the audience and their acceptance of a threat as existential and worthy of securitization, as well as their acceptance of the credibility of the securitizing actor or actors (Buzan et al., 1998, p. 41; Balzacq, 2005).

The contributions of constructivist thought to security studies (including and especially via securitization) are hardly unproblematic, particularly from the standpoint of critical theorists. In part, this line of critique rests on the notion that securitization advances an excessively narrow conceptualization of security and the actors within it. Whereas CSS embraces the concept of security as a socially constructed, 'derivative concept,' its continuing evolution has generated significant critiques directed at the efforts of Buzan and the Copenhagen School, contending that they do not go far enough in expanding the referent object away from a state-centered perspective (Peoples and Vaughan-Williams, 2015, p. 33). These theorists argue that security is defined by the relationship between the individual and security, which then determines security at an international level; security cannot be defined by states or governments (Rothschild, 1995; McSweeney, 1999, p. 16).

Such critiques are most applicable to the societal sector, where the intersection between identity and security are most vehemently contested. Although the sectoral approach allows for a wider interpretation of the referent object in international security, collective security is still privileged over individual security in the Copenhagen School. This creates and reinforces a dichotomy of individual security and the security of the state/nation (Hansen & Nissenbaum, 2009). The societal sector also draws critique for its assumption of a single, all-encompassing identity, discounting the socially constructed and fluid nature of identity (Peoples & Vaughan-Williams, 2015). Assuming and framing threats around a fixed identity encourages tribalism and delegitimizes identities apart from or outside of the referent object (McSweeney, 1999). Rather than thinking of securitization as a mechanism for mobilizing (some fixed and determinate) identity, it may instead be better understood as a mechanism which elicits and encourages identification with particular ideas, notions, or things being subjected to securitization; in other words, identity may be seen as an independent rather than dependent variable.

Critiques of securitization theory also emphasize the normative consequences of securitization (Eriksson, 1999; Hansen, 2000; Huysmans, 2006). Their criticism stems from the Copenhagen School's treatment of securitization as an objective process, without addressing the possibility of securitization increasing divides or allowing for oppressive, exclusionary, or violent policies (Williams, 2003, p. 522). In addition, applying securitization theory to societal issues such as poverty or disease may absolve states from moral responsibility and instead, view humanitarian issues solely in the language and framework of national security, discouraging long-term or compassionate responses (Elbe, 2006). This critique is partially addressed by the Copenhagen School, which states that securitization is not an "unambiguously positive value," and the ideal long-term outcome is a desecuritization process that moves threats out of the threat-defense sequence and into the ordinary public sphere (Williams, 2003 Buzan et al., 1998, p. 32).

Securitization theory is further critiqued by feminist theorists for excluding gender as an explicit concern. Feminist theorists view the societal sector approach as subsuming gendered security problems, because gender itself is rarely defined as a self-contained referent object, and gendered subjects are therefore subjugated to broader identities (Hansen, 2000). In addition, feminist scholars challenge the constitutive nature of speech-acts as exclusionary (Hansen, 2000). This speaks to the power dynamics of the securitizing actor and the agency of the audience, as insecurity may be "silent" because of a lack of agency or exclusion from the securitized audience (Hansen, 2000). This particular insight drawn from critical feminist scholarship raises a larger challenge for securitization; namely, the extent to which prevailing applications of securitization emphasize the influence of the "speech act."

Indeed, to this point, the speech-act was afforded unquestioned prominence by the originator of securitization, Ole Wæver: "security is not of interest as a sign that refers to something more real; the utterance *itself* is the act (Wæver, 1995, p. 55)." Traced to its logical conclusion, the utterance and definition of an existential threat by a securitizing actor was seen to signify security action or construct security conditions that must be met (Peoples and Vaughan-Williams, 2015, p. 95). At odds with this rarified status is the narrow understanding of what constituted a speech-act – i.e., a formal structure through which securitizing actors following the power threshold and processes can label and create an existential threat, and therefore treat it outside of the realm of normal politics (Buzan et al., 1998).

These tensions have led some scholars to contend that equating securitization with the speech-act without also addressing the context in which both are embedded is problematic. To this end, speech-acts would be better understood as a "strategic practice that occurs within, and as part of, a configuration of circumstances" (Balzacq, 2005, p. 172). The historical and cultural context must contribute to the audience's understanding and accepting of the speech-act as an existential threat (Williams, 2003; Balzacq, 2005; McDonald, 2008). In addition, scholars have expanded the medium through which the securitizing process can take place. The shift in the political "communicative environment" has led to greater emphasis on images and televisual media as well as other forms of non-discursive securitization moves (Williams, 2003, p. 523). These critiques in particular have informed a number of the contributions to the present volume.

Securitization revisited: a roadmap

Intellectual rationale

As the labors of a previous generation of scholars were oriented around a common proposition of challenging the prevailing orthodoxy in security studies, so too are the efforts of the authors contributing to this volume rooted in a shared interest in examining the prospects and problems of securitization in application (securitization as a process), as well as the implications of those applications for its explanatory power (securitization as a concept). This starts with the recognition that security is the epitome of what the prominent social theorist W.B. Gallie referred to as an 'essentially contested concept' (Gallie, 1956). Indeed, perhaps the main contribution of the 'constructivist turn' in security studies has been its reaffirmation and demonstration of this assertion, through systematic revelation of the intersubjective, contextually bound, and contingent nature of security. The contributors to this volume accept this premise, and take up the associated challenge of advancing our collective knowledge base relative to processes of securitization in specific domestic, regional, and global contexts and in conjunction with various security actors and issues – and beyond that, to consider the implications of those processes on both politics and policy.

In that spirit, this book was inspired by and is oriented around a single broad question: in light of the realization of securitization, what does and can it (securitization) tell us about contemporary security issues and practices? In turn, addressing this question required the contributors to this volume to conceptualize their inquiries with a set of related, if lower-order, questions in mind, in order to lend some consistency to their respective contributions to this collective enterprise in examining securitization:

*   relative to the security issue, topic, or context of concern, what is the prevailing definition and operationalization of security? What factors (material and non-material) inform and shape that definition and operationalization … and what factors are excluded?
*   how is the securitization process – and the attendant political endeavors at its heart – evident relative to the security issue, topic, or context of concern? Which actor(s) are essential to the process of securitization, and in what way(s)?
*   what are the major speech-acts and other securitizing and de-securitizing 'moves' employed in the construction of a given security issue, threat, and/ or response?
*   what is – or should be – the 'referent object' for security thinking and practice relative to a given issue, topic, or context?

Unsurprisingly, the responses to these questions from the contributors to this volume varied significantly, as is reflected in the chapters that follow. As the table of contents for this volume reflects, these issues, actors, and domains were themselves disparate. It is therefore also unsurprising that the 'answers' to these questions we have produced are at least in part a function of the particular security issues, actors, and domains of concern.

In taking up these questions, the process of collaborative and critical inquiry at the heart of this project inspired three shared analytical concerns that served as common points of orientation for all of the contributions to this volume, regardless of the policy issues, actors, or domains at play. The first of these concerns lies in identifying how each contribution to this volume might seek to *reveal deficiencies in and through the application of securitization*. Doing so is important, in that such deficiencies can and do obscure our understanding of the various security implications and practices considered in this book. Meeting this objective required that each author employ a critical bent in their application, as the selections included here undoubtedly reflect. The second concern shared by the contributing authors was a desire to *consider units of analysis other than speech-acts and discourse*. Here, we determined that going beyond the speech-act and including non-discursive phenomena and their role and impact as securitizing 'moves' would not only enhance our understanding of securitization, but would allow us to see securitization (and desecuritization) revealed in other areas of social, political, and cultural activity (McDonald, 2008), and through distinct actors and categories of actors often excluded from the official practice(s) and discourse(s) of security (C.A.S.E. Collective, 2006). Third, we collectively prioritized the need to *search for and expose any latent orthodoxies embedded in the conceptualization and underlying assumptions of securitization* – both our own, and those of other similarly engaged scholars. As critical theorists before us have revealed, constructivist security studies retain some vestiges of traditional thinking about security, and by extension we expect these may be evident in the development and application of securitization theory. For example, the persistent tendency to assume that securitization moves in one direction, thereby overlooking the mechanisms and 'moves' of desecuritization (a problem perhaps first identified by Knudsen, 2001). Thus, we share an interest in determining what, if any, 'latent orthodoxies' might be revealed, and how can they be controlled for in order to enhance the explanatory power of securitization as a concept.

Scope and contents

The present volume engages with a diverse set of securitized phenomena, including, in some instances, things such as memory, sexual violence, and climate change that have heretofore received scant attention in the securitization literature. Here too, we are concerned with chronicling not only the 'how' of securitization, but beyond that the 'what and to what effect.' The disciplinary, methodological, and especially geographic diversity of the contributors, drawn widely from across Europe and the U.S., is important in this regard. Indeed, if critical security studies – and by extension securitization – can be thought of as a 'European wave,' this volume stands as a testimony of it breaking on North

American shores, only to cycle back; representing, in the language of the C.A.S.E. Collective (2006, p. 446), another "encounter" of sorts.

As members of a second generation of scholars employing securitization, we consider engaging with the three concerns identified above to be vital, if we are to build on the insights of our predecessors. Those insights – particularly theoretical and conceptual – are the central focus of Part I. They are chronicled in detail in *Roxanna Sjöstedt*'s chapter contextualizing and critiquing securitization theory (Chapter 1). Sjöstedt devotes equal attention to identifying and evaluating both the ideational and empirical contributions of the first generation of securitization research, establishing an intellectual baseline for this book in its entirety. Following this, *Jarosław Jarząbek* (Chapter 2) takes up the task of critically appraising another crucial product of the 'constructivist turn' in security studies – namely, Regional Security Complexes (RSCs). As Jarząbek reveals, RSCs are a dynamic concept fundamentally informed by securitization theory, making it necessary – as he contends – for RSCs to be revisited and updated for the realities of the contemporary security landscape.

The remainder of the book turns more directly to the task of applying and interrogating securitization (Part II), and appraising mechanisms and processes of and for desecuritization (Part III). Part II features three chapters concerned with securitization as both concept and process in three distinct (and heretofore under-examined) security domains. *Blanca Camps-Febrer* (Chapter 3) takes up perhaps the most highly securitized issue of the twenty-first century – global terrorism – from a critical posture. Camps-Febrer explores both the means and the ends of the securitization process with respect to terrorism, examining how the 'technology' associated with a securitized terrorism is employed to reinforce prevailing power relations, especially in non-Western contexts (with an emphasis on the representative case of Morocco).

Subsequent chapters continue to extend securitization into diverse intellectual terrain where it has been less frequently utilized as a tool for structured analysis. To that end, *Natalie Hudson* and *Alexandra Budabin* (Chapter 4) unpack the gendered securitization of sexual- and gender-based violence (SGBV). They examine the ways in which the securitization process unfolds not only through official discourse, but also via prominent and critically-timed public advocacy efforts. In doing so, they identify and critically appraise the many and varied implications of securitizing SGBV for women and girls, both pro and con. *Mark Boyer* and *Neil Oculi* (Chapter 5) engage with perhaps *the* existential security challenge of our time – climate change. With a particular focus on the implications of climate change for small island states, Boyer and Oculi demonstrate the ways in which securitization 'moves' can be made through the strategic use of empirical data and scientific evidence. While scientific data and expertise can be potential catalysts for securitization, Boyer and Oculi also acknowledge the prospect that entrenched political opposition can override them in order to obstruct securitization.

Part III of the book turns the reader's attention to the important – and, again, under-specified – parallel process of desecuritization. Part III begins with *Siniša*

Vuković's (Chapter 6) exploration of the role that securitizing discourse plays in the intensification and entrenchment of armed conflicts, as a prelude to a more direct and thorough examination of the relationship between desecuritization and conflict management techniques (especially mediation). Vuković demonstrates the potential that strategic implementation of de-securitizing moves has for enhancing the success of conflict management. Another area of inquiry which securitization theory has the potential to illuminate, but which heretofore has been largely absent from, is that of conflict resolution and peacebuilding. *Katerina Antoniou* (Chapter 7) and *Valérie Rosoux* (Chapter 8) provide two examples of the explanatory power of securitization in this realm. Antoniou examines intergroup dynamics within the context of the protracted conflict in Cyprus. She explores the ways in which social psychological parameters such as contact between and among peacebuilders and other constituents to the peace process impact broader receptivity to speech-acts as well as various non-discursive methods of desecuritization. Rosoux follows with a nuanced consideration of the role and impact of memory both as a securitizing and de-securitizing agent, with a particular emphasis on inter-societal conflicts. She looks at the individual and collective psychological effects of constructed memories pertaining to mass atrocity events and wars and how these phenomena can be deployed both to sustain (securitize) and to de-escalate (de-securitize) conflictual relationships and attitudes.

Examining securitization within a variety of policy domains and across a range of issues, as we do here, affords us the opportunity not only to learn more about how disparate issues become securitized (or de-securitized), but beyond that, to use those insights to consciously and systematically reflect back on and critically interrogate how we think about securitization itself. This reflexivity is not only in the spirit of critical security studies, it is also crucial to the previously stated goal of a more robust understanding of securitization theory and practice, in that knowledge about security is best understood as a co-production between theorists, analysts, and policymakers (C.A.S.E. Collective, 2006). Highlighting latent orthodoxies and deficiencies in the conceptual formulation of securitization revealed in its application(s) can only enhance the future applicability of the concept and advance the larger enterprise of constructivist security studies more generally (McDonald, 2008). It is to that aim that we direct our collective efforts here.

Notes

1 The chapter following this one (Chapter 1) engages in a parallel, but more refined, endeavor – namely, providing a full and comprehensive assessment of securitization theory. For another in-depth treatment of the intellectual links between constructivism and securitization, see Balzacq (2009).
2 Here, the use of the adjective 'traditional' should not be taken as suggestive of being confined to the past; rather, what the term means to convey here is an orthodox position with long and deep roots in both security thought and practice which remains very much evident and prominent in both domains.

3 The relationship between states and the anarchical order in which they operate varies in accordance with variations on realist theory. Classical and neo-classical realists conceive of anarchy as an outward manifestation of state behavior and interaction (Mearsheimer, 2001; Rose, 1998). Structural realists invert the causal arrow, viewing anarchy as an independent condition that impinges upon and structures the behavior and interaction of states (Waltz, 2000). Despite these differences, the common thread is the crucial role that power, force, threat, and, by extension, armed conflict, plays in an international system without rules and institutions that can effectively govern the actions of states.

4 The relationship between and among the Copenhagen, Aberystwyth, and also Paris Schools and their positions relative to securitization will be considered in greater detail in Chapter 1.

5 At least two considerations are relevant on this front. First, the assertion that maintaining order and stability through material force is the primary imperative shaping the behavior of actors in the international system has proven problematic. This is especially true when seeking to examine the behavior of actors who may be threatened by or opposed to the prevailing status quo, or whose actions do not relate to or correspond in any way with the order it produces (Katzenstein, 1996). Second, whereas the current reassertion of the authority of the state in the form of the 'new authoritarianism' (Krastev, 2011) is undeniable, this seeming recalibration should be understood as a reaction to the broader, multi-sectoral, and transnational nature of security issues and concerns and the extent to which they challenge the state-centric paradigm both politically and intellectually.

Bibliography

Acharya, A. (1997). The periphery as the core: The Third World and security studies. In K. Krause & M. Williams (Eds.), *Critical security studies* (pp. 299–328). Minneapolis: University of Minnesota Press.

Acharya, A. (2007). The emerging regional architecture of world politics. *World Politics, 59*(4), 629–652.

Acharya, A. (2014). *Rethinking power, institutions and ideas in world politics: Whose IR?* New York: Routledge.

Adger, W. N., Pulhin, J. M., Barnett, J., Dabelko, G. D., Hovelsrud, G. K., Levy, M., Oswald Spring, Ú., & Vogel, C. H. (2014). Human security. In C. B. Field, V. R. Barros, D. J. Dokken, K. J. Mach, M. D. Mastrandrea, T. E. Bilir, M. Chatterjee, K. L. Ebi, Y. O. Estrada, R. C. Genova, B. Girma, E. S. Kissel, A. N. Levy, S. MacCracken, P. R. Mastrandrea, & L. L. White (Eds.), *Climate change 2014: Impacts, adaptation, and vulnerability. Part A: Global and sectoral aspects. Contribution of working group II to the fifth assessment report of the intergovernmental panel on climate change* (pp. 755–791). Cambridge & New York: Cambridge University Press.

Ashley, R. K., & Walker, R. B. J. (1990). Introduction: Speaking the language of exile: Dissident thought in international studies. *International Studies Quarterly, 34*(3), 259–268.

Ayoob, M. (1997). Defining security: A subaltern realist perspective. In K. Krause & M. Williams (Eds.), *Critical Security Studies* (pp. 121–146). Minneapolis: University of Minnesota Press.

Ayoob, M. (2002). Inequality and theorizing in international relations: The case for subaltern realism. *International Studies Review, 4*(3), 27–48.

Baldwin, D. A. (1980). Interdependence and power: A conceptual analysis. *International Organization, 34*(4), 471–506.

Baldwin, D. A. (1995). Security studies and the end of the Cold War. *World Politics,* *48*(1), 117–141.

Baldwin, D. A. (1997). The concept of security. *Review of International Studies,* *23*(1), 5–26.

Balzacq, T. (2005). Three faces of securitization: Political agency, audience and context. *European Journal of International Relations, 11*(2), 171–201.

Balzacq, T. (2009). Constructivism and securitization studies. *The Routledge handbook of security studies* (pp. 72–88). London & New York: Routledge.

Black, D. R. (2016). *A decade of human security: Global governance and new multilateralisms.* New York: Routledge.

Bigo, D. (1996). *Polices en réseaux. L'expérience européenne* [Police in networks: The European experience]. Paris: Presses de Sciences Po.

Bigo, D. (2000). When two become one: Internal and external securitisations in Europe. In M. Kelstrup & M. C. Williams (Eds.), *International relations theory and the politics of European integration, power, security, and community* (pp. 171–205). London: Routledge.

Bigo, D. (2002). Security and immigration: Toward a critique of the governmentality of unease. *Alternatives, 27*(1), 63–92.

Bigo, D., & Guild. E (Eds.). (2005). *Controlling frontiers: Free movement into and within Europe.* Aldershot: Ashgate.

Bonelli, L. (2005). Un ennemi anonyme et sans visage [An invisible, faceless enemy]. *Cultures & Conflits, 58,* 101–130.

Booth, K. (1991). *New thinking about strategy and international security.* London: HarperCollins.

Booth, K. (1997). Security and self: Reflections of a fallen realist. In K. Krause & M. Williams (Eds.), *Critical Security Studies.* Minneapolis: University of Minnesota Press.

Booth, K. (Ed.). (2005). *Critical security studies and world politics.* Boulder: Lynne Reinner Publishers.

Brown, S. (1998). World interests and the changing dimensions of security. In M. T. Klare & Y. Chandrani (Eds.), *World security: Challenges for a new century* (3rd ed.). New York: St. Martin's Press.

Buzan, B. (1991a). New patterns of global security in the twenty-first century. *International Affairs (Royal Institute of International Affairs 1944–),* 431–451.

Buzan, B. (1991b). *People, states, and fear: The national security problem in international relations* (2nd ed.). Boulder, CO: Lynne Rienner Publishers.

Buzan, B., & Wæver. O. (2003). *Regions and powers: The structure of international power.* Cambridge: Cambridge University Press.

Buzan, B., Wæver, O., & de Wilde, J. (1998). *Security: A new framework for analysis.* Boulder, CO: Lynne Rienner Publishers.

Caprioli, M. (2003). Gender equality and state aggression: The impact of domestic gender equality on state first use of force. *International Interactions, 29*(3), 195–214.

Carpenter, R. C. (2006). Recognizing gender-based violence against civilian men and boys in conflict situations. *Security Dialogue, 37*(1), 83–103.

C.A.S.E. Collective. (2006). Critical approaches to security in Europe: A networked manifesto. *Security Dialogue 37*(4), 443–487.

Ceyhan, A. & Tsoukala, A. (Eds.). (1997). Contrôles: Frontières-identités. Les enjeux autour de l'immigration et de l'asile [The control of immigration: Myths and reality]. *Cultures & Conflits, 26–27,* 7–14.

Checkel, J. T. (1998). The constructivist turn in international relations theory. *World Politics, 50*(2), 324–348.

Cohn, C. (1987). Sex and death in the rational world of defense intellectuals. *Signs: Journal of Women in Culture and Society, 12*(4).

Collier, P. (2003). *Breaking the conflict trap: Civil war and development policy*. Washington, D.C.: World Bank Publications.

Cox, R. W. (1981). Social forces, states and world orders: Beyond international relations theory. *Millennium: Journal of International Studies, 10*(2), 126–155.

Crawford, N. (1991). Once and future security studies. *Security Studies, 1*(2), 283–316.

Desch, M. C. (1998). Culture clash: Assessing the importance of ideas in security studies. *International Security 23*(1), 141–170.

Detraz, N. (2012). *International security and gender*. London: Polity.

Deudney, D. (1990). The case against linking environmental degradation and national security. *Millennium: Journal of International Studies, 19*(3), 461–476.

Duffield, M. (1999). Globalization and war economies: Promoting order or the return of history? *Fletcher Forum of World Affairs, 23*(2), 21–38.

Elbe, S. (2006). Should HIV/AIDS be securitized? The ethical dilemmas of linking HIV/AIDS and security. *International Studies Quarterly 50*(1), 119–144.

Enloe, C. (2014). *Bananas, beaches, and bases: Making feminist sense of international politics* (2nd ed.). Berkeley: University of California Press.

Eriksson, J. (1999). Observers or advocates? On the political role of security analysts. *Cooperation and Conflict, 34*(3), 311–330.

Farrell, T. (2002). Constructivist security studies: Portrait of a research program. *International Studies Review, 4*(1), 49–72.

Freedman, L. (1998). International security: Changing targets. *Foreign Policy, 110*, 48–63.

Friedman, T. L. (2007). *The world is flat: A brief history of the twenty-first century*. New York: Picador/Farrar, Straus and Giroux.

Gallie, W. B. (1956). Essentially contested concepts. *Proceedings of the Aristotelian Society, 56*(1), 167–198.

Geuss, R. (1981). *The idea of a critical theory: Habermas and the Frankfurt School*. Cambridge: Cambridge University Press.

Hanlon, R. J., & Christie, K. (2016). *Freedom from fear, freedom from want: An introduction to human security*. Toronto: University of Toronto Press.

Hansen, L. (2000). The Little Mermaid's silent security dilemma and the absence of gender in the Copenhagen School. *Millennium: Journal of International Studies, 29*(2), 285–306.

Hansen, L. (2013). *Security as practice: Discourse analysis and the Bosnian war*. New York: Routledge.

Hansen, L., & Nissenbaum, H. (2009). Digital disaster, cyber security, and the Copenhagen School. *International Studies Quarterly, 53*, 1155–1175.

Herz, J. H. (1950). Idealist internationalism and the security dilemma. *World Politics, 2*(2), 157–180.

Hettne, B., & Söderbaum, F. (2005). Intervening in complex humanitarian emergencies: The role of regional cooperation. *The European Journal of Development Research, 17*(3), 449–461.

Homer-Dixon, T. (1999). *Environment, scarcity, and violence*. Princeton: Princeton University Press.

Hudson, N. F. (2009). *Gender, human security and the United Nations: Security language as a political framework for women*. New York: Routledge.

Huysmans, J. (1998). Security! What do you mean? From concept to thick signifier. *European Journal of International Relations, 4*(2), 226–255.

Huysmans, J. (2000). Migration and the politics of security. In S. Body-Gendrot & M. Martinello (Eds.), *Minorities in European cities: The dynamics of social integration and social exclusion at the neighborhood level* (pp. 179–189). London: Palgrave Macmillan.

Huysmans, J. (2002). Defining social constructivism in security studies: The normative dilemma of writing security. *Alternatives, 27*, 41–62.

Huysmans, J. (2006). *The politics of insecurity: Fear, migration and asylum in the EU.* New York: Routledge.

Jackson, N. J. (2006). International organizations, security dichotomies and the trafficking of persons and narcotics in post-Soviet Central Asia: A critique of the securitization framework. *Security Dialogue, 37*(3), 299–317.

Kaplan, R. D. (1994). The coming anarchy. *Atlantic Monthly, 273*(2), 44–76.

Katzenstein, P. J. (1996). *The culture of national security: Norms and identity in world politics.* New York: Columbia University Press.

Katzenstein, P. J. (2005). *A world of regions.* Ithaca: Cornell University Press.

Kelly, R. E. (2007). Security theory in the 'new regionalism.' *International Studies Review, 9*(2), 197–229.

Keohane, R. (1989). *International Institutions and State Power.* Boulder, CO: Westview Press.

Keohane, R. & Nye, J. S. (2001). *Power and interdependence* (3rd ed.). Boston, MA: Addison, Wesley, Longman.

Kessler, O. (2011). Beyond sectors, before the world: Finance, security, and risk. *Security Dialogue, 42*(2), 197–215.

Knudsen, O. F. (2001). Post-Copenhagen security studies: Desecuritizing securitization. *Security Dialogue, 32*(3), 355–368.

Krahmann, E. (Ed.). (2005). *New threats and new actors in international security.* New York and Basingstoke: Palgrave Macmillan.

Krastev, I. (2011). The paradoxes of the new authoritarianism. *Journal of Democracy, 22*(2), 5–16.

Krause, K., & Williams, M. C. (1996). Broadening the agenda of security studies: Politics and methods. *Mershon International Studies Review, 40*(2), 229–254.

Krause, K., & Williams, M. C. (Eds.). (1997). *Critical security studies.* Minneapolis: University of Minnesota Press.

Lake, D. A. (1997). Regional security complexes: A systems approach. *Regional Orders: Building Security in a New World, 52.*

Mann, M. (1993). *The sources of social power: Volume 2: The rise of classes and nation states 1760–1914.* Cambridge: Cambridge University Press.

Masco, J. (2014). *The theater of operations: National security affect from the Cold War to the war on terror.* Durham, NC: Duke University Press.

Matthews, J. T. (1989). Redefining Security. *Foreign Affairs, 68*(2), 162–177.

McDonald, M. (2008). Securitization and the construction of security. *European Journal of International Relations, 14*(4), 563–587.

McSweeney, B. (1996). Identity and security: Buzan and the Copenhagen School. *Review of International Studies, 22*(1), 81–93.

McSweeney, B. (1999). *Security, identity, and interests: A sociology of international relations.* Cambridge: Cambridge University Press.

Mearsheimer, J. J. (2001). *The tragedy of great power politics.* New York: W. W. Norton.

Morgenthau, H. J. (1948). *Politics among nations: The struggle for power and peace.* New York: Alfred A. Knopf.

Paris, R. (2001). Human security: Paradigm shift or hot air? *International Security, 26*(2), 87–102.

Peoples, C., & Vaughan-Williams, N. (2015). *Critical security studies: An introduction.* New York: Routledge.

Rose, G. (1998). Neoclassical realism and theories of foreign policy. *World Politics, 51*(1), 144–172.

Rothschild, E. (1995). What is security? *Daedalus, 124*(3), 53–98.

Ruane, A. E. (2011). Pursuing inclusive interests, both deep and wide: Women's human rights and the United Nations. In L. Sjoberg & J. A. Tickner (Eds.), *Feminism and international relations* (pp. 48–67) (3rd ed.). New York: Routledge.

Sen, A. (2004). Capability and well-being. In M. Nussbaum & A. Sen (Eds.), *The quality of life* (pp. 30–53). New York: Routledge.

Sheehan, M. (2005). *International security: An analytical survey.* Boulder, CO: Lynne Rienner Publishers.

Shepherd, L. J. (2015). *Gender matters in global politics.* New York: Routledge.

Sjoberg, L. (2009). *Gender and international security: Feminist perspectives.* New York: Routledge.

Sjoberg, L. (2013). *Gendering global conflict: Toward a feminist theory of war.* New York: Columbia University Press.

Snow, D. M. (2015). *National security for a new era.* New York: Routledge.

Stiehm, J. H. (Ed.). (1996). *It's our military too: Women and the U.S Military.* Philadelphia: Temple University Press.

Tickner, J. A. (2001). *Gendering world politics: Issues and approaches in the post-Cold War era.* New York: Columbia University Press.

Ullman, R. (1983). Redefining security. *International Security, 8*(1), 129–153.

United Nations Development Programme. (1994). *Human development report 1994: New dimensions of human security.* New York: Oxford University Press.

United Nations Organization. (1980). *Report of the independent commission on international development issues, North-South: A programme for survival* (Brandt Commission). London: Pan Books.

Vershbow, A. (2016, June 23). *The Warsaw summit and the new security environment.* Keynote address delivered at the Assembleia da Republica, Lisbon, Portugal. Available online at: www.nato.int/cps/en/natohq/opinions_132747.htm. Last accessed May 17, 2017.

Wæver, O. (1995). Securitization and desecuritization. In R. D. Lipschutz (Ed.), *On security* (pp. 46–87). New York: Columbia University Press.

Walker, R. B. J. (1997). The subject of security. In K. Krause & M. Williams (Eds.), *Critical security studies* (pp. 61–81). Minneapolis: University of Minnesota Press.

Walt, S. (1985). Alliance formation and the balance of world power. *International Security, 9*(4), 3–43.

Walt, S. (1987). *The origins of alliances.* Ithaca: Cornell University Press.

Walt, S. (1991). The renaissance of security studies. *International Studies Quarterly, 35*(2), 211–239.

Waltz, K. N. (1979). *Theory of international politics.* Reading, MA: Addison-Wesley.

Waltz, K. N. (2000). Structural realism after the Cold War. *International Security, 25*(1), 5–41.

Weber, M. (1918/2009). Politics as a vocation. *From Max Weber: Essays in sociology.* London & New York: Routledge.

Williams, M. C. (1998). Modernity, identity and security: A comment on the 'Copenhagen controversy.' *Review of International Studies, 24*(3), 435–439.

Williams, M. C. (2003). Words, images, enemies: Securitization and international politics. *International Studies Quarterly, 47*(4), 511–531.

Wyn Jones, R. (1996). Travel without maps: Thinking about security after the Cold War. In J. M. Davis (Ed.), *Security issues in the post-Cold War world* (pp. 96–218). Cheltenham: Edward Elgar.

Wyn Jones, R. (2001). *Critical theory and world politics*. Boulder, CO: Lynne Rienner Publishers.

Zartman, I. W. (2008). Introduction: Toward the resolution of international conflicts. In W. I. Zartman (Ed.), *Peacemaking in international conflict: Methods & techniques* (pp. 3–22) (Rev. ed.). Washington, D.C.: U.S. Institute of Peace Press.

1   Assessing securitization theory

Theoretical discussions and empirical developments

Roxanna Sjöstedt

For the past two decades, securitization has become an established approach to the study of international security issues. The ideas launched by the so-called Copenhagen School during the 1990s, and encapsulated in the seminal book *Security: A Framework for Analysis*, have clearly influenced a number of scholars in their views on what constitutes threats and security. This chapter will provide a discussion on the core aspects of securitization theory, elaborating on both its strengths and weaknesses and on how its assumptions and arguments relate to other contemporaneous developments within the field of security studies. The chapter will thereafter move on to discuss the main theoretical critiques against and contributions to securitization for the past 20 years. Finally, the chapter will address the numerous empirical applications of the securitization framework, in which the theoretical assumptions have been employed to analyze threat constructions of areas such as terrorism, climate change, sexual violence, and intergroup conflict in various empirical settings. By way of conclusion, the chapter discusses how the aforementioned intellectual debates have resulted in theoretical refinement, but stresses nonetheless that the plasticity of the original securitization framework – often criticized for its imprecision – is actually its main asset.

As will be further demonstrated in the remaining chapters of this volume, it is precisely the malleability of what constitutes the securitizing agent and the audience, as well as the openness regarding the threat and the referent object, that makes the theory suitable for analyzing a broad range of issues, contexts, and actors. Moreover, and as demonstrated by the subsequent chapters, it is the various empirical applications that really move the boundaries of securitization theory, contributing to its development. The overall contribution of both this chapter and of the volume as a whole is to point out some of the deficiencies in the theory and its applications – for instance the predominant focus on speech acts; the under-specified relationship between securitization and power, and its Eurocentrism – as well as attempting to rectify this state of affairs.

Securitization as theoretical framework

Securitization theory moves beyond the traditional definition of security as being the absence of military coercion from antagonistic states, and argues that anyone or anything can be constructed as a threat. Thus, threats are not contextually given in the anarchic system but rather should be viewed as the by-product of the intersubjective constructions of actors. In the traditional interpretation of securitization, this construction occurs through different types of framing and speech (Wæver, 1995). These assumptions link securitization to the broader field of critical security studies as it shares the main ontological premise that security "is not objective or neutral, but predicated on normative choices with inherent political implications" (Browning & McDonald, 2011, p. 238). One can also see clear similarities between the key assumptions of securitization and other critical security claims regarding, for instance, the inextricable inter-relation between power and security, security as discourse, and how construc-tions of security shapes understandings and practices (cf. Campbell, 1998; Booth 2007).

In particular, one can detect two main intellectual antecedents of the assump-tions of securitization. As briefly introduced in the preceding chapter, the first is found in Buzan's reconceptualization of security and the groundbreaking notion of a deepening and a broadening of the security concept (1983, 1991). In essence, the deepening aspect concerns the inclusion of other levels of analysis than the state level. The broadening means that security can be divided into five sectors: military security; political security; economic security; societal security; and environmental security.[1]

Although these sectors overlap and are analytically related, the identification of five different areas in which threats to the individual, the group, or the nation can arise is an important move from a static and objectivist view of threats and security. Second, there is an obvious linkage between securitization and theories emphasizing the powers and constitutive qualities of discourses and speech acts. Building on language philosophy, and on Austin's (1976) speech act theory in particular, securitization theory has emphasized that speech has powers beyond being a mere communication tool. In terms of security matters, securitization theory (and applications thereof) have long considered speech essential in the construction of threat images and in the execution of security policy, even to the point of equivalence: "[t]he way to study securitization is to study discourse […]" (Buzan et al., 1998, p. 25). This means that the statements are to be viewed as "performatives as opposed to constatives" (Balzacq, 2011, p. 1) as they help to shape the contextual setting, and construct different threat images in that setting, rather than solely being reflections of an objective state of affairs.

Securitization theory is not a traditional theory in terms of causality mapping or hypothesizing on the explanatory powers of a particular variable. Rather, it is argued that it should either be viewed as a constitutive theory or, as suggested by Guzzini, should be viewed as a causal mechanism (Balzacq & Guzzini, 2015). Regardless of which epistemological standpoint one adopts, securitization is quintessentially an analytical framework that helps to pinpoint the different steps in a security process. In this process, issues are constructed as threats by actors, accepted by others, and moved onto the security agenda. It could thus be argued that the theory helps to answer 'how possible' questions by mapping out how speech acts as well as non-discursive practices can result in political agenda setting, ultimately leading to new security strategies.

Key elements

Four elements in particular are central to the securitization framework. First, the so-called securitizing actor is the entity who frames an issue as an existential threat. As argued by the Copenhagen School, and as shown below in the overview of the plentiful empirical applications of securitization theory, any actor can become a securitizer, but a securitizing agent is typically thought of as someone who represents a broader collective – political leaders and governments, international organizations, lobbyists, or the media. Also, in order to have any chance of success in instigating a securitization process, the securitizing actor needs to have the necessary platform and authority to be able to construct threat images. In addition, the actor must possess some degree of power (discursive or materialist) in order to convey the importance of threat construction. Determining who is the securitizing actor is mainly dependent on which issue is the focus of study. Sometimes several concurrent securitization processes regarding the same issue take place and the research focus is then normally delimited to one particular actor.

The second element in the securitization framework is the securitizing move, or when the securitizing agent constructs an issue as a threat. In line with the broadening of security into five sectors, issues that can be securitized by far extend the traditional linkage between military issues and security threats, and securitizing moves can concern, for instance, migration (societal sector); global warming (environmental sector); or stock market crashes (economic sector). Regardless of issue, a securitizing move commands action and obligates as well as enables the securitizing actor to a particular subsequent behavior: if you construct a threat image, you more or less have to act upon and handle this threat. Linked to this is the third element of securitization – the referent object. Also, with regard to this factor, there is a theoretical plasticity (or vagueness) with regard to what can be the object of security – in essence, being threatened – something which moves the notion of security away from the nation state as the obvious unit of analysis. Rather, the referent object depends on which threat image is constructed through the securitizing move and on who is doing the move.

The first round of securitization arguments and applications in the 1990s can be linked to other critical approaches by emphasizing that security concerns should be addressed at different levels of analysis (Wæver, Buzan, Kelstrup, & Lemaitre, 1993; Bilgin, Booth, & Wyn Jones, 1998). It is sometimes argued that one of the main contributions of the Copenhagen School has been the concept of societal security, and the placing of migration and minority rights in this sector. Societal security is claimed to hold "a middle position between traditionalist state-centrism on the one hand and [...] critical security studies' calls for 'individual' and 'global security' on the other" (Buzan & Hansen, 2010). When migration is securitized it is the identity (such as culture, language, religion, traditions, etc.) of a society that is claimed to be threatened. Conversely, the integration of minorities can be viewed as a threat to minority rights and independence (cf. Roe, 2004). However, this contribution of securitization, and the importance of opening up the traditional 'black-box' of the state as the unit of analysis, addressing societal security concerns, has paradoxically become the main point of criticism against the theory (cf. McSweeney, 1996, 1998). It has been argued that the focus on identity and societal security makes securitization contextually narrow and is mainly applicable to the issue of immigration in a European context (cf. Huysmans, 1998; Ilgit & Klotz, 2014). As discussed below, this state of affairs has been rectified over the years as various empirical applications of securitization have examined a number of different issues, concerning different sectors and contexts.

Lastly, the fourth element of the securitization framework concerns the so-called audience. One cannot view a threat image as securitized unless an audience accepts the securitizing move. The key interaction in a securitization process is thus between the actor that frames an issue as a threat, and the collective towards which the securitization move is directed. Who these actors are remains an under-specified – and often criticized – part of the theory but it is generally suggested that the conception of audience is related to the securitizing actor; if the latter is the head of government, the audience could be the broader political elite in the parliament; the general public; or both (cf. Roe, 2008). What is important is that securitization requires both the framing of an issue as an existential threat and the acceptance of this framing strategy. If these two steps in the securitization process are met, the issue is moved from the arena of ordinary politics to the field of security, or in other words, the securitizing actor is empowered to move the issue onto the security agenda and, in turn, designate resources and draft policies to handle the threat. The audience is often considered to constitute the main problematic aspect of securitization as it is difficult to determine who the audience actually is, and how to measure audience acceptance (McDonald, 2008).

Securitization as dynamic process

As further discussed in the following sections, the process of securitization and the entities that make up this process have been thoroughly examined, both theoretically and empirically. There are, however, two other aspects of securitization that until fairly recently have received less scholarly attention. The first, which can be viewed as the other side of the same coin as securitization, is the phenomenon of desecuritization, or when a securitized issue is moved down from the security sphere and back to so-called normal politics (Wæver, 1995). This is generally seen as an outcome of a democratic deliberation that shifts an issue or concern "out of the emergency mode and into the normal bargaining process of the political sphere" (Buzan et al., 1998, p. 4).

Although many claim that the concept of desecuritization is underdeveloped and underspecified (Aradau, 2004), there is a growing field of studies that try to probe the securitization – desecuritization dynamic. Hansen (2012) attempts to theorize the concept of desecuritization beyond the mere removal of an issue from the security agenda and argues that desecuritization can take different forms, such as replacement, re-articulation, fading, and silencing. In addition, desecuritization has been examined with regard to different empirical issue areas, for instance, traditional inter-state relations in the Middle East and in the Arctic region (Aras & Polat, 2008; Åtland 2008); societal security concerns and minority integration (Roe, 2004); and the gendered aspects of ex-combatants in post-civil war disarmament, demobilization, and reintegration (DDR) processes (MacKenzie, 2009).

Following desecuritization comes another even less investigated phase of securitization, namely re-securitization. Although underexamined, one can quite easily find examples where an issue is framed as a threat, only – due to various contextual reasons – to be moved down on, or even removed from, the security agenda, and then re-framed yet again as an existential security threat. The securitization of Russia in the political discourse of many Nordic and Western European countries constitutes one example of this, where the Soviet Union was securitized until the end of the Cold War, with the Russian Federation then being de-securitized and replaced by other issues on the security agenda, and eventually, in the last couple of years, having re-entered at the top of the agenda. Somewhat surprisingly, the re-securitization phase has not generated any larger scholarly interest, although one could argue that the processes of reinstating something onto the security agenda could be quite different from the process of constructing a politicized issue as a security threat. McDonald, however, is one exception who traces how asylum-seekers to Australia have been securitized, de-securitized, and then re-securitized by the Australian government (McDonald, 2011). This dynamic quality of the securitization process, and the related recognition that the very process that results in the securitization of an issue or phenomenon can be reversed (or re-doubled), is a recurring concern of several of the subsequent chapters in this volume.

Exploring the Copenhagen, Paris, and Aberystwyth Schools

Reviewing the landscape

Having had enormous impact on how security concerns can be addressed and analyzed, securitization theory has also been the subject of lively debates and extensive scrutiny – from those who work within the securitization paradigm and those who adhere to other types of critical security studies. Critique from this last cluster has often been formulated in terms of clashes or debates between different 'schools' of critical security studies. The first such school is the 'Copenhagen School'. Interestingly enough, this label was not invented by any of the assumed key affiliates of this very school, but coined by Bill McSweeney (1996) in a well-known critique, which later was to be known as the 'McSweeney debate' (C.A.S.E. Collective, 2006). In essence, McSweeney's criticism against the Copenhagen School concerns the above-discussed emphasis on identity as the referent object and the societal sector as the primary location for the securitization of migration. In contrast, McSweeney argues that identity is not a fixed entity but should be viewed as fluid processes of identification, and this identification is not the referent object being threatened but rather the result of securitization. However, and as pointed out by Balzacq, Léonard and Ruzicka (2016), this disagreement on identity can be boiled down to a question of research objective and whether one seeks to understand the construction of identity or whether one is more concerned with establishing the effect of an 'analytically' given identity on thought and behavior (Balzacq et al., 2016, p. 508).

Following the establishment of the idea of a Copenhagen School, Wæver and others have identified the parameters of an Aberystwyth (sometimes called Welsh) School, as well as a Paris School of critical security studies (Wæver 2004, p. 6). Scholars such as Ken Booth and Richard Wyn Jones are commonly believed to belong to the first as they share very similar ideas regarding the conception of security, and offer strong critique against traditional realist conceptions of power, security, and the state. Instead of viewing security as the absence of threats from antagonistic states it is argued that

> [s]ecurity and emancipation are two sides of the same coin. Emancipation, not power or order, produces true security. Emancipation, theoretically, is security.
>
> (Booth, 1991, p. 319)

In the view of adherents to the Welsh school, the concept of the sovereign state, and the security matters of that state, are the root causes of insecurity (cf. Wyn Jones, 2001). This clearly normative approach aims to uncover hierarchal structures, coercion, and tyranny. This critical disclosure has implications both academically – given the dominance of the realist view on the world order – and in an empirical sense, as it can help to reveal structures of oppression and violence. As argued by Booth (2004), by avoiding "the hegemonial agenda of mainstream Security Studies [...] human rights abuses, the oppression of minorities, the powerlessness of the poor, and violence against women, [issues that] have been all too 'traditional' to their victims" can finally become the core of the security agenda (Booth, 2004 pp. 5, 7–8). Emphasizing this view of security as emancipation, Booth sees problems not only with realist ontology, but with securitization theory as well, and argues that the existence of a security issue is not dependent on the success of a speech act – issues like the ones above exist and threaten people regardless of whether anyone talks about them (Booth, 2007, pp. 167–168). However, although the critique against both the realist and securitization's view on security makes valid points, the view of security as emancipation is complex and exhibits clear weaknesses with regard to empirical application. In addition, the Aberystwyth School has been criticized also on a theoretical note, for not fully exploring the relationship between emancipation, normality, and normativity (C.A.S.E. Collective, 2006; Floyd, 2007).

Unlike both the Copenhagen and Welsh Schools, the Paris School has its roots in political theory and sociology rather than international relations theory (C.A.S.E. Collective, 2006). Rather than stressing the exceptionality in securitization – in terms of speech acts stressing existential threats and extraordinary measure to handle these threats – the Paris School employs a practice-oriented approach, focusing on 'the ordinary,' or routine behavior. Inspired by Bourdieu, political practices and 'habitus' – i.e., the socialized norms that guide behavior – are important in shaping security and insecurity. Also, Foucault's notions of governmentality and 'dispotif' – or institutional or administrative mechanisms and knowledge structures – are central aspects that should be included in securitization processes (Balzacq, 2011). By stressing the routine work of, for instance, the bureaucracy or security professionals, processes of security and insecurity can be detected and mapped (Bigo & Guild, 2005; Bigo, 2014; Huysmans, 2006). Huysmans argues, for instance, that it is the "technologies of government," or the development of both techno-logical devices and technocratic routines that are the forces that make issues, for instance immigration, become securitized. According to Huysmans, the Copenhagen School's focus on the importance and constitutive nature of the political speech act on security

> mask[s] the technical nature of the implementation process and its constitu-tive importance. Taking the implementation process and the technological nature of the spill-over more seriously opens a second way of embedding the discursive processes of securitization.
>
> (Huysmans, 2004, pp. 301–302)

The importance of the theoretical contributions of the Copenhagen, Aberyst-wyth, and Paris Schools aside, the usefulness of separating different strands of research into 'schools' has been called into question. The C.A.S.E. Collective argues that it is difficult to draw "clear-cut dividing lines between the three schools" (C.A.S.E. Collective, 2006 p. 450). Balzacq et al., (2016) point out that there are several scholars who do critical or constructivist security studies that do not fit into any of the three constructs and that it might make more sense to talk about the linguistic and sociological approaches to securitization. Agreeing with this reasoning, this chapter believes that even though it sometimes is prac-tical to link a particular point to a particular school – as we know that the Welsh School stresses the linkage between individual insecurity and oppression and the Paris School highlights the importance of habitus and dispotif – it is not neces-sary to try to place every theoretical critique or development under these umbrellas. As the perspective of the various authors contributing to this volume suggests, it seems more important to examine what aspects of securitization and related concepts have been refined or developed in application, thereby showing the evolving and dynamic nature of the theory.

Main critiques of the securitization framework

Not surprisingly, the securitization framework in general, as well as its translation through the various 'schools' outlined here, have all faced sufficient critique. To try to provide a comprehensive overview of all criticisms and developments is, however, a difficult task as there are almost an endless number of articles – as well as entire special issues – that devote themselves to the probing of various theoretical and conceptual aspects of securitization. Some of these aspects concern the ontology and epistemology of the securitization framework; the theoretical nature(s) of securitization; the different entities of the framework; and the politics of securitization (see for example Balzacq, 2005, 2011; Balzacq et al., 2015, 2016; McDonald, 2008; Pram & Petersen, 2011; Stritzel, 2007; Williams, 2003). One key criticism, taken up by several contributors to this volume, concerns the role the speech act plays in the Copenhagen School, and the claim that "the way to study securitization is to study discourse" (Buzan et al., 1998, p. 25). Following the so-called 'sociological turn' proposed by Balzacq, which can be related to the everyday routines stressed by the Paris School, "practices, context, and power relations" should also take center stage in the analysis (Balzacq, 2011, p. 1).[2] There are also others who stress that context is particularly crucial, and that the lack of contextual sensitivity in the original take on securitization is problematic as

> the performative power of a speech act cannot be captured only in the abstract and in the form of a single linguistic act, but needs to be contextually located within broader structures.
>
> (Stritzel, 2014, p. 46)

Linked to this is the argument that an emphasis on the speech act restrains the application of the securitization framework to many settings due to a "silent security dilemma" (Hansen, 2000, p. 287). The idea of silencing indeed points to some of the assumptions of the Aberystwyth School in that there are oppressive structures that deem the use of a security speech act impossible. This means that in some contexts people, even those in leading positions, do not possess "the ability to express societal security concerns actively" (Wilkinson, 2007, p. 12). This restraint can be due to systematic oppression, discrimination on the basis of gender, sex, race, or the like, freedom of speech limitations, or fear of repercussion from adversaries (Sjöstedt, Söderberg, & Themnér, 2017). In other words, contextualization is needed in a securitization analysis as

> the semantic repertoire of security is a combination of textual meaning – knowledge of the concept acquired through language (written or spoken) – and cultural meaning – knowledge historically gained through previous interactions and current situations
>
> (Balzacq, 2011, p. 4)

The need to examine and contextualize both the roles and the discursive powers of the securitizing actors, as well as the formulation of the securitizing move, relates to a second area in which securitization has been criticized (Sjöstedt, 2017). The question of whether securitization "successfully travels" empirically (Ilgit & Klotz, 2014, p. 138), or whether it is stuck in a "Westphalian strait-jacket" (Wilkinson, 2007, p. 11) has been discussed and many – including some of the contributors to the present volume – argue that due to its European ethno-centrism, securitization theory has limited analytical powers in settings "that are characterized by different configurations of state-society dynamics" (Bilgin, 2011, p. 401). It can nevertheless be argued that it is not any inherent design problem of the securitization framework that prevents its application to non-European settings, but rather a lack of cross-disciplinary and cross-national interaction. For example, as also claimed by Bilgin, not only securitization, "but theory-informed studies in general [...] are in short supply in international relations studies outside the Western Europe and North American core" (Bilgin 2011, p. 400). This view is echoed by others who, when reviewing the field of security studies in Latin America, argue that

> even in those cases in which scholars explicitly set out to explore 'concepts' and 'theories' what emerges in their stead are descriptive reflections on Latin American security dynamics and prescriptive policy recommendations.
> (Tickner & Hertz in Bilgin, 2011, p. 401)

The apparent Eurocentrism of securitization might be due to academic practice rather than theoretical limitations and it could actually be argued that "due to its reflective nature securitization theory is better suited than many other theories to analyze a variety of threat constructions and policies in a broad range of settings" (Sjöstedt, 2017). As pointed out by Wæver, any presumed theoretical bias ultimately becomes "an empirical question – i.e., to study non-Western cases with particular attention to possible limitations stemming from Western assumptions" (Greenwood & Wæver, 2013, p. 486) – an admonition taken to heart by the contributors to this volume.

A third area of securitization that has spurred scholarly attention and debate concerns the phenomenon called the audience. As described above, the audience is addressee of the speech act (Floyd, 2015) and whose acceptance is required for an issue to be securitized. Critics stress that "the role played by the audience in securitization processes lacks precision and clarity" (Léonard & Kaunert, 2011, p. 58), and it has been suggested that the audience should rather be viewed as several different entities and these "depend on the function the securitization act is intended to serve" (Vuori, 2008, p. 72). A recent meta-study examining 32 articles on securitization that include the role of the audience focused on the identity(ies) and capacity(ies) of the audience(s) in order to assess how it is dealt with in securitization research generally (Côté, 2016). Some of the main conclusions drawn from this study – which in turn have informed some of the chapters which follow – are that the identity of the audience varies. A securitizing move can be directed towards the general public, different branches of government, elites, organizations, or sometimes even multiple audiences, although the choice of audience is somehow related to the issue being securitized. In other words, a securitizing act can be directed towards different audiences based on what the securitizing actor intends to achieve with the securitizing move, for instance, convincing the political elite; gain public support; or get attention from the broader international sphere (Roe, 2008; Salter, 2008).

Côté also found that in many studies the audience had a very active role in the securitization process and that there were repeated interactions between the securitizer and the audience that led to "modified securitizing moves designed to secure audience acceptance [...] [suggesting] that securitization proceeds in an iterative fashion, where previous actor–audience interactions affect future securitizing moves" (Côté, 2016, p. 546). This view on the audience as an active participant in a securitization process rather than a passive recipient can be related to whether one conceives threats as subjectively or intersubjectively constructed (Sjöstedt, 2017). In the Copenhagen School's original take on securitization, the illocutionary aspect is stressed – meaning that an actor subjectively constructs the threat image through the speech act. However, it is also stressed that the threat image is not securitized until it has been intersubjectively recognized as a threat, that is, until the audience has accepted it. This indicates that the perlocutionary aspect, or effects of the securitizing move, is central. Critics argue that this dynamic has not been fully addressed by the Copenhagen School, something that can be remedied by placing more attention to context and to securitizer – audience interaction and recognizing audience participation "in the intersubjective construction of security meaning" (Côté, 2016, p. 546).

An additional critique of securitization theory relates to the assumptions of the Welsh School and concerns the question of whether there are normative aspects embedded in securitization theory. Some argue that the securitization process is inherently a negative one as it bypasses normal democratic procedures and pushes issues into the covert and hostile security realm (Aradau, 2004; see also Camps Febrer, Chapter 4 in this volume). Others mean that the secrecy associated with securitization is exaggerated and that the outcome of a securitization process is not always inimical (Roe, 2012). Floyd argues in her work on the environmental sector that both referent objects and securitizing actors can benefit from securitization and that "not all securitizations are morally equal" (Floyd, 2010, p. 56). In other words, to lift an issue to the security agenda can thus, depending on context, have positive aspects. The securitization of, for instance, global warming can have positive effects for the broader public as it contributes to a healthier environment (see Boyer & Oculi, Chapter 5 in this volume).

This aspect of contextuality applies to other securitization issues as well (Sjöstedt, 2017). Epidemics such as HIV/AIDS are often constructed as security rather than health issues. This can result in the violation of human rights and civil liberties and it is the HIV infected who become securitized (Elbe, 2006). To the contrary, highlighting an epidemic can lead to state mobilization and increased resources. According to Elbe, the possibility of moral dilemmas can be amended by the careful consideration of both what is being securitized and the referent object of this securitization. Floyd moves the discussion on the moral implications of securitization even further and proposes three criteria that – if fulfilled at the same time – would render a securitization morally right. If there is an objective existential threat; if the referent object is morally legitimate; and if the security response is appropriate, one can actually argue that a securitization process is morally right, or just, something which makes possible the normative evaluation of securitization processes (Floyd, 2011).

Developing securitization theory through empirical applications

As noted in the preceding introductory chapter, the main concern of this volume lies in the extension of securitization theory through empirical application into new domains and in relation to new actors and dynamics, in part as a means of reflecting back on and refining the insights of the theory itself. Although, as discussed above, the debates between so-called schools have been lively and a great number of works have probed key aspects of the securitization framework, it can be argued that it is the empirical applications that have contributed most to its development (Sjöstedt, 2017). This chapter thus agrees with Balzacq et al., who mean that the "empirical enquires have played a decisive part in the development of studies of securitization [...] [and] are not merely limited to applying existing concepts" (Balzacq et al., 2016, pp. 14–15). It is therefore important to now highlight some empirical areas in which securitization has been a useful analytical framework and which have also contributed to the development of the theory – and, by extension, providing the impetus for the present book.

Prominent applications

The first research area concerns, as briefly discussed above, migration and integration in relation to identity and societal security. Already in the late 1980s migration became connected to securitization (Jahn, Lemaitre, & Wæver, 1987), and thereby set the path for the Copenhagen School's subsequent highlighting of the societal sector as a key unit of analysis. In his seminal article, Huysmans further problematized the securitization of migration by showing that this image is not one-dimensional but rather a multifaceted phenomenon containing a number of different types of threats. Which one is emphasized depends a great deal on which audience is being addressed. In his analysis on the securitization of migration in the European Union, Huysmans shows that although international crime and terrorism constitutes the key threat frames, these are in turn connected to a more general framing strategy that portrays immigrants as threatening national identity, the labor market, and welfare systems (Huysmans, 2000). Migration can thus be securitized as a threat, not only to the societal sector, but to economic security as well.

A number of studies have continued to investigate different aspects of the securitization–migration dynamic. Clearly linked to the ideas of the sociological turn in securitization Léonard argues that the security practices by FRONTEX, the EU's agency for external border control, contributes to the securitization of migration in the EU (Léonard, 2010). In a similar vein but more directly connected to the Paris School, Bigo argues that routines and everyday structures are more important than discourses when trying to understand the notions of borders and border control and their relation to practices of (in)securitization (Bigo, 2014). Although most studies on the securitization of migration focus on the EU, there are examples of applications to non-European contexts as well – examining the extent to which securitization can 'travel.' Curley and Wong examine securitization regarding unregulated and illegal migration in Asia, focusing on both sending, transit, and receiving countries (Curley & Wong, 2008). Ilgit and Klotz analyze the immigration policies of South Africa by testing four claims embedded in the securitization debate. These can be seen as being influenced by both the Copenhagen and Paris Schools, thus demonstrating the difficulty in separating these constructions, and examine if there are securitizing moves regarding immigration performed by securitizing actors; where these speech acts have become practices in bureaucratic procedures; whether these discourses are challenged by society and how these challenges are linked to identity-based contestation; and whether successful securitization expands societal identity constructions. A systematic empirical testing of these claims demonstrates that securitization can indeed travel beyond its customary context and that "the societal security concept merits greater integration into comparative studies of immigration policy and immigrant incorporation" (Ilgit & Klotz, 2014, p. 150).

Following the initial works from the late 1990s on societal securitization, some studies analyze how minority groups can be the subject of securitization. Some argue that the very issue of minority rights is "predicated on an inherent condition of securitization" (Roe, 2004, p. 280). This means, in other words, that minority groups are connected, both by themselves and by others, to a security discourse which actually serves to maintain group identity. This makes desecuritization of a minority issue impossible since that would end group cohesion and make identity redundant. Others take a different view on the possibilities of desecuritization and have examined how norm diffusion processes of organizations such as the European Union, the Council of Europe, and the Organization for Security and Cooperation in Europe, have tried to de-securitize the minority issue in order to transform inter-ethnic relations (Galbreath & McEvoy, 2012).

Public health emergencies and epidemics is another field in which different aspects of securitization theory have been employed. Although traditional security studies clearly refute disease as a topic of security (Walt, 1991, p. 213), both more constructivist inclined security studies and actual empirical practices have, since the turn of the millennium, started to consider health as a matter of both global and national security. In the year 2000, the Security Council passed Resolution 1308 which states that HIV/AIDS is an international security threat, which was the first time a non-military issue had been subjected to this degree of attention in this forum. Using this securitization of AIDS as a point of departure, a number of studies have investigated securitization processes in different contexts and security sectors and involving different actors. Some stress both at the international and national levels of analysis, arguing that the securitization of AIDS can be viewed as an international norm, diffused by a multitude of securitizing actors, such as states, organizations, and transnational advocacy networks. Once settled, this norm has influenced and shaped policy nationally and locally. (Viera, 2007).

However, other studies have found that audience acceptance of such international norm diffusion has varied greatly among national decision-makers. The initial refusal to securitize HIV/AIDS in Russia is a case in point of audience refusal of a securitizing move. Due to domestic and international identity constructions, Russian decision-makers proved resistant to the idea that HIV/AIDS constituted a threat to Russian national security – despite securitizing moves by the international community. Only after several years of facing one of the world's most rapid rates of infection did Russian President Vladimir Putin in 2006 acknowledge that the HIV/AIDS epidemic constituted a threat to Russian national security (Sjöstedt, 2008). Another study, analyzing the securitization process of HIV/AIDS in the U.S, shows the opposite process, namely that societal and political domestic actors were the important norm entrepreneurs, securitizing HIV/AIDS, and that this process led to the international recognition of HIV/AIDS as a security threat (Sjöstedt, 2011).

Problematizing securitization

These examples highlight four aspects that problematize securitization theory: First, the securitization of many threat images can be viewed as a form of two-level game, where securitization at one level can – but does not always – generate securitization at another. Second, it indicates that the roles of securitizing agent and audience fluctuates; a national decision-maker can be the audience of a securitizing move by an international actor, and then in turn, become the securitizer of that very issue vis-à-vis a domestic audience. Third, it brings up the question of what makes actors securitize things in the first place, in the sense that "although the world presents decision-makers with a range of complex situations that could be interpreted as threatening, only some of these issues generate socially constructed problem formulations" (Sjöstedt, 2008, p. 8). In other words, the logic behind securitizing moves needs to be problematized. Finally, it can be argued that securitization processes are not necessarily negative as the emergency measures in these examples were not expressions of power or repression, but rather allocated necessary institutional actions and resources. This focus on the important function of actors at different levels of analysis and in different contexts agrees with the idea that securitization should be viewed as intrinsically related multi-level, as also suggested by McInnes and Rushton (2012).

A more traditional area of security analysis concerns military threats and terrorism. Although these issues have been probed from a number of angles, a non-traditional security framework like securitization can help to discover power relations and processes that a traditional state-centric approach, focusing on antagonistic states, would not capture. Also, with regard to these types of issues, the subjective – or intersubjective – construction of threat images is central. There are some examples of studies on military securitization that have moved outside of the European setting. Haacke and Williams' analysis of how securitization can be employed in a traditional interstate or regional security setting examines how the African Union (AU) and the Association of Southeast Asian Nations (ASEAN) have securitized transnational threats and security challenges (Haacke & Williams, 2008). Studying post-conflict securitization and desecuritization of male and female ex-combatants in Sierra Leone, MacKenzie argues that the immediate post-conflict desecuritization of female combatants resulted in the exclusion of women in the disarmament, demobilization, and reintegration (DDR) programs (MacKenzie, 2009). This was clearly a case of gender inequality in the post-conflict reconstruction process and can be viewed as a form of silencing of women's experiences and grievances (cf. Hansen, 2000). In an analysis on how the Iranian nuclear program has been continuously securitized over time in the Israeli political discourse, with each successful securitization generating another one, Lupovici stresses the importance of viewing securitization as a process building on prior securitizing moves, eventually reaching a so-called "securitization climax" (Lupovici, 2016).

The securitization framework has also been employed in studies analyzing the process preceding armed conflict. A study analyzing British foreign policy vis-à-vis different African states, discerns a clear change over time as it has altered from "'development/humanitarianism' toward a category of 'risk/fear/threat' in the context of the 'war on terrorism,'" something which sets the path for subsequent military action (Abrahamsen, 2005, p. 56). Roe analyzes the securitization process that eventually resulted in the decision by the British government to join U.S. troops and invade Iraq in 2003, discovering that the British government faced two main audiences: the British public and Parliament. This duality in audience led to the result that the first securitizing move by the Blair government was not accepted by the public audience, while a second attempt of securitization eventually managed to convince Parliament. This study demonstrates that audiences can have different functions in a securitization process, and the importance of a particular audience is contingent on what type of support the securitizer needs (Roe, 2008). Studying the same case but employing a theoretical framework that draws both from securitization and social identity theory Hayes argues that a deeply rooted sense of democratic identity made it possible for the Blair government to construct Iraq as a threat, despite the fact that Iraq did not pose an obvious threat to Britain (Hayes, 2016). This shows that the securitizer's identity type can play an important part in explaining both why a securitizing move is made in the first place and whether the audience accepts the move (cf. Sjöstedt, 2007). A similar argument which focuses on the linkage between securitization, social identities, and the democratic peace theory, helps to explain why an audience completely rejects the move (Hayes, 2012). In this study it is the identity of being a democratic state that hinders military action against another democratic state.

Concluding remarks

This chapter has provided a brief outline of the central arguments of securitization theory, the main critiques against the original framework, and three empirical areas in which securitization has been employed. In doing so, it seems evident that 20 years on, securitization theory and its various dimensions and insights have provided a dynamic and fruitful approach to the study of international security affairs. It is equally clear that interest in applying and extending securitization theory does not appear to be in decline. As I argue here, although many of the theoretical criticisms have pointed out important weaknesses and areas for development in the securitization framework, it is in the empirical applications that we are really able to detect both its shortcomings and suggest further theoretical developments. It is this insight that provides both the impetus and the animus for the chapters that follow.

Notes

1 Gender security is notably missing, both in Buzan's (1983) original introduction of the broader agenda, and in the Copenhagen School's subsequent usage of it. For a critique, see Hansen (2000).
2 Even though Balzacq is often viewed as belonging to the Paris School, he, being a strong critic of labelling, argues that similarities and differences among scholars do not necessarily indicate some shared identity but "are formulated in terms of theoretical influences as researchers tend to draw upon the works that they deem most useful to specific cases that they are examining" (Balzacq et al., 2016, p. 499).

Bibliography

Abrahamsen, R. (2005). Blair's Africa: The politics of securitization and fear *Alternatives, 30*, 55–80.
Aradau, C. (2004). Security and the democratic scene: Desecuritization and emancipation. *Journal of International Relations and Development 7*(4), 388–413.
Aras, B., & Polat, R. K. (2008). From conflict to cooperation: Desecuritization of Turkey's relations with Syria and Iran. *Security Dialogue, 39*(5), 495–515.
Åtland, K. (2008). Mikhail Gorbachev, the Murmansk initiative, and the desecuritization of interstate relations in the Arctic. *Cooperation and Conflict 43*(3), 289–311.
Austin, J. L. (1976). *How to do things with words*. Oxford: Oxford University Press.
Balzacq, T. (2005). The three faces of securitization: Political agency, audience and context. *European Journal of International Relations 11*(2), 171–201.
Balzacq, T. (2011). A theory of securitization. Origins, core assumptions and variants. In T. Balzacq (Ed.), *Securitization theory. How security problems emerge and dissolve*. London & New York: Routledge.
Balzacq, T., & Guzzini, S. (2015). Introduction: 'What kind of theory – if any – is securitization?' *International Relations, 29*(1), 97–102.

Balzacq, T., Guzzini, S., Williams, M. C., Wæver, O., & Patomäki, H. (2015). Forum: What kind of theory – if any – is securitization? *International Relations, 29*(1), 96–136.

Balzacq T., Léonard S., & Ruzicka J. (2016). 'Securitization' revisited: Theory and cases. *International Relations 30*(4), 494–531.

Bigo, D. (2014). The (in)securitization practices of the three universes of EU border control: Military/Navy – Border Guards/Police – Database Analysts. *Security Dialogue, 45*(3), 209–225.

Bigo, D., & Guild, E. (Eds.). (2005). *Controlling frontiers: Free movement into and within Europe*. Aldershot: Ashgate.

Bilgin P. (2011). The politics of studying securitization? The Copenhagen School in Turkey. *Security Dialogue, 42*(4–5), 399–412.

Bilgin, P., Booth, K., & Wyn Jones, R. (1998). Security studies: The next stage? *Nac̦aoe Defesa, 84*, 137–157.

Booth, K. (1991). Security and emancipation. *Review of International Relations 17*(4), 313–326.

Booth, K. (2004). Realities of security: Editor's introduction. *International Relations 18*(1), 5–8.

Booth, K. (2007). *Theory of world security*. Cambridge: Cambridge University Press.

Browning, C. S., & McDonald, M. (2011). The future of critical security studies: Ethics and the politics of security. *European Journal of International Relations 19*(2), 235–255.

Buzan, B. (1983). *People, states, and fear: The national security problem in international relations*. Sussex: Wheatsheaf Books.

Buzan, B. (1991). *People, states, and fear: An agenda for international security studies in the post-Cold War era* (2nd ed.). Boulder, CO: Lynne Rienner Publishers.

Buzan, B., & Hansen, L. (2010). Defining–redefining security. *Oxford Research Encyclopedia of International Studies, Security Studies*. doi:10.1093/acrefore/9780190846626.013.382

Buzan B., Wæver, O., & de Wilde, J. (1998). *Security: A new framework for analysis*. Boulder, CO: Lynne Rienner Publishers.

Campbell, D. (1998). *Writing security: United States foreign policy and the politics of identity*. Minneapolis: University of Minnesota Press.

C.A.S.E. Collective. (2006). Critical approaches to security in Europe: A networked manifesto. *Security Dialogue, 37*(4), 443–487.

Côté, A. (2016). Agents without agency: Assessing the role of the audience in securitization theory. *Security Dialogue, 47*(6): 541–558.

Curley, M., & Wong, S.-L. (2008). *Security and migration in Asia. The dynamics of securitisation*. London: Routledge.

Elbe, S. (2006). Should HIV/AIDS be securitized? The ethical dilemmas of linking HIV/AIDS and security. *International Studies Quarterly, 50*(1), 119–144.

Eriksson, J., & Rhinard, M. (2009). The internal–external security nexus. Notes on an emerging research agenda. *Cooperation and Conflict, 44*(3), 243–267.

Floyd, R. (2007). Towards a consequentialist evaluation of security: Bringing together the Copenhagen and the Welsh Schools of security studies. *Review of International Studies, 33*, 327–350.

Floyd, R. (2010). *Securitization theory and the US environmental security policy*. Cambridge: Cambridge University Press.

Floyd, R. (2011). Can securitization theory be used in normative analysis? Towards a just securitization theory. *Security Dialogue, 42*(4–5), 427–439.

Floyd, R. (2015). Just and unjust desecuritization. *Contesting Security: Strategies and Logics*, 122–138.

Galbreath, D., & McEvoy, J. (2012). European organizations and minority rights in Europe: On transforming the securitization dynamic. *Security Dialogue, 43*(3), 267–284.

Greenwood, M. T., & Wæver, O. (2013). Copenhagen – Cairo on a roundtrip: A security theory meets the revolution. *Security Dialogue, 44*(5–6), 485–506.

Haacke, J., & Williams, P. D. (2008). Regional arrangements, securitization and transnational security challenges: The African Union and the Association of Southeast Asian Nations compared. *Security Studies, 17*, 775–809.

Hansen, L. (2000). The Little Mermaid's silent security dilemma and the absence of gender in the Copenhagen School. *Millennium: Journal of International Studies. 29*(2), 285–306.

Hansen, L. (2012). Reconstructing desecuritisation: The normative-political in the Copenhagen School and directions for how to apply it. *Review of International Studies, 38*, 525–546.

Hayes, J. (2012). Securitization, social identity, and democratic security: Nixon, India, and the ties that bind. *International Organization, 66*(1), 63–93.

Hayes, J. (2016). Identity, authority, and the British war in Iraq. *Foreign Policy Analysis, 12*(3), 334–353.

Huysmans, J. (1998). Revisiting Copenhagen: Or, on the creative development of a security studies agenda in Europe. *European Journal of International Relations, 4*(4), 479–505.

Huysmans, J. (2000). The European Union and the securitization of migration. *Journal of Common Market Studies, 38*(5), 751–77.

Huysmans, J. (2004). A Foucaultian view on spill-over: Freedom and security in the EU. *Journal of International Relations and Development, 7*(3), 294–318.

Huysmans, J. (2006). *The politics of insecurity*. London: Routledge.

Ilgit, A., & Klotz, A. (2014). How far does 'societal security' travel? Securitization in South African immigration policies. *Security Dialogue, 45*(2), 137–155.

Jahn, E., Lemaitre, P., & Wæver, O. (1987). *European security: Problems of research on non-military aspects* (Vol. 1). Centre of Peace and Conflict Research, University of Copenhagen.

Léonard, S. (2010). EU border security and migration into the European Union: FRONTEX and securitisation through practices. *European Security, 19*(2), 231–254.

Léonard, S., & Kaunert, C. (2011). Reconceptualizing the audience in securitization theory. In T. Balzacq (Ed.), *Securitization theory. How security problems emerge and dissolve.* London & New York: Routledge.

Lupovici, A. (2016). Securitization climax: Putting the Iranian nuclear project at the top of the Israeli public agenda (2009–2012). *Foreign Policy Analysis, 12*(3), 413–432.

McDonald, M. (2008). Securitization and the construction of security. *European Journal of International Relations, 14*(4), 563–87.

McDonald, M. (2011). Deliberation and resecuritization: Australia, asylum-seekers and the normative limits of the Copenhagen School. *Australian Journal of Political Science, 46*(2), 281–295.

McInnes, C., & Rushton, S. (2012). HIV/AIDS and securitization theory. *European Journal of International Relations, 19*(1), 115–138.

McSweeney, B. (1996). Identity and security: Buzan and the Copenhagen School. *Review of International Studies, 22*(1), 81–93.

McSweeney, B. (1998). Durkheim and the Copenhagen School: A response to Buzan and Wæver. *Review of International Studies, 24*(1), 137–140.

MacKenzie, M. (2009). Securitization and desecuritization: Female soldiers and the reconstruction of women in post-conflict Sierra Leone. *Security Studies, 18*, 241–261.

Pram, G. U., & Petersen K. L. (2011). Special issue on the politics of securitization. *Security Dialogue, 42*(4–5), 315–452.

Roe, P. (2004). Securitization and minority rights: Conditions of desecuritization. *Security Dialogue, 35*(3), 279–294.

Roe, P. (2008). Actor, audience(s) and emergency measures: Securitization and the UK's decision to invade Iraq. *Security Dialogue, 39*(6), 279–294.

Roe, P. (2012). Is securitization a 'negative' concept? Revisiting the normative debate over normal versus extraordinary politics. *Security Dialogue, 43*(3), 249–266.

Salter, M. B. (2008). Securitization and desecuritization: A dramaturgical analysis of the Canadian Air Transport Security Authority. *Journal of International Relations and Development, 11*, 321–349.

Sjöstedt, R. (2007). The discursive origins of a doctrine. Norms, identity, and securitization under Harry S. Truman and George W. Bush. *Foreign Policy Analysis, 3*(3), 233–254.

Sjöstedt, R. (2008). Exploring the construction of threats: The securitization of HIV/AIDS in Russia. *Security Dialogue, 39*(1), 7–29.

Sjöstedt, R. (2011). Health issues and securitization. The construction of HIV/AIDS as a US national security threat. In T. Balzacq (Ed.), *Securitization theory. How security problems emerge and dissolve.* London & New York: Routledge.

Sjöstedt, R. (2017). Securitization and foreign policy analysis. *Oxford Research Encyclopedia of Politics.* New York: Oxford University Press (published online before print. doi:10.1093/acrefore/9780190228637.013.479).

Sjöstedt, R., Söderberg Kovacs, M., & Themnér, A. (2017). Demagogues of hate or shepherds of peace? Examining the threat construction processes of warlord democrats in Sierra Leone and Liberia. *Journal of International Relations and Development* (published online before print. doi:10.1057/s41268-017-0111-3).

Stritzel, H. (2007). Towards a theory of securitization: Copenhagen and beyond. *European Journal of International Relations, 13*(3), 357–383.

Stritzel, H. (2014). *Security in translation: Securitization theory and the localization of threat.* Basingstoke: Palgrave Macmillan.

Viera, M. (2007). The securitization of the HIV/AIDS epidemic as a norm: A contribution to the constructivist scholarship on the emergence and diffusion of international norms. *Brazilian Political Science Review, 1*(2), 137–181.

Vuori, J. A. (2008). Illocutionary logic and strands of securitization: Applying the theory of securitization to the study of non-democratic political orders. *European Journal of International Relations, 14*(1), 65–99.

Walt, S. M. (1991). The renaissance of security studies. *International Studies Quarterly, 35*(2), 211–239.

Wæver, O. (1995). Securitization and desecuritization. In R. D. Lipschutz (Ed.), *On security* (pp. 46–86). New York: Columbia University Press.

Wæver, O. (2004, March 17–20). *Aberystwyth, Paris, Copenhagen: New 'schools' in security theory and their origins between core and periphery.* Paper presented at the 45th annual convention of the International Studies Association, Montreal, Canada.

Wæver, O., Buzan, B., Kelstrup, M., & Lemaitre, P. (1993). *Identity, migration and the new security agenda in Europe.* New York: St Martin's Press.

Watson, S. D. (2012). Framing the Copenhagen School: Integrating the literature on threat construction. *Millennium: Journal of International Studies, 40*(2), 279–301.

Wilkinson, C. (2007). The Copenhagen School on tour in Kyrgyzstan: Is securitization theory useable outside Europe? *Security Dialogue, 38*(1), 5–25.

Williams, M. C. (2003). Words, images, enemies: Securitization and international politics. *International Studies Quarterly, 47*(4), 511–31.

Wyn Jones, R. (2001). *Critical theory and world politics*. Boulder, CO: Lynne Rienner Publishers.

2 Regional security complex theory

Reflections and reformulations

Jarosław Jarząbek

Introduction

Regional Security Complex Theory (RSCT) emerged from the recognition that a fuller understanding of global security dynamics requires greater focus on the regional level of analysis (Williams, 2008, p. 68). The theory, together with securitization and sectoral security, is one of the three main elements constituting the so-called Copenhagen School. In many ways these three elements are inter-related; in seeking to create a framework for analysis of security at the domestic, regional, inter-regional and global level, RSCT is itself strongly based upon the assumptions underlying securitization and sectoral security. The common ideational underpinning of RSCT and securitization in particular allows for an in-depth study of security interactions within and outside of the regional security complexes, which are not treated as a set of states that threaten one another or mutually secure each other. Instead, by defining and redefining the referent object, securitizing actor and audience, the concept of securitization provides a useful analytical tool allowing for investigation of the processes of constructing and deconstructing security within and across regional security complexes.

Securitization is in many ways the animating mechanism for RSCT, explaining differences in the security environment within and across regions. It assumes that securitizing actors (governments, political leaders, lobbies, bureaucratic apparatus, etc.) start the process of securitization. They do that by declaring that the object of security (some particularly important and protected subject, feature or idea like the state, society, territory, ideology, culture, economy, identity, environment, etc.) is existentially threatened. This sanctions the use of exceptional measures, reaching beyond the scope of standard political procedures, to protect the object of security. The undertaken actions, or securitization moves, are addressed to the specific recipient (an audience). The audience needs to be convinced that the object of security is indeed existentially threatened and that the undertaken measures are reasonable, necessary and appropriate to avert the danger (Buzan, Wæver, & de Wilde, 1998, pp. 36–42).

The intersubjective character of securitization means that the reality and seriousness of the threat are of a lesser importance. What matters more is the linguistic dimension (speech act) and the social relations (position of the actor who 'speaks' security, mutual relation of actor and audience, common understanding of security, the context of the securitization move, etc.) (Balzacq, 2015, pp. 103–113; Guzzini, 2011, pp. 329–341). The securitizing move may also have a non-discursive character, but can take the form of undertaking specific actions (e.g., power projection, mass protests, boycott, etc.). It is a situation similar to what Lene Hansen described as "the silent security dilemma," which occurs "when the potential subject of (in)security has no, or limited, possibility of speaking its security problems" (Buzan & Hansen 2009, p. 216; Hansen, 2000).

Notwithstanding its general utility and its relationship to securitization as a concept and process, it is important to note that RSCT was constructed almost two decades ago. As such, the theory remains based on the geopolitical, political, social, economic, scientific and cultural realities prevailing at the turn of the twentieth and twenty-first centuries. The ongoing dynamic flux in the security arena, itself produced by the securitization process, stands in stark contrast to some of the more static assumptions and aspects of RSCT. This contrast requires us to reconsider RSCT in order to keep it relevant and adequate in changing circumstances. Accordingly, this chapter identifies and explores five areas in which RSCT can be revised in order to maintain its applicability and utility in a changing (and highly politicized) security environment.

First, the theory is strongly based on the concept of regional complexes where security dynamics depend on interactions and the balance of power between actors. As some states (and non-state actors) grow stronger or weaker and their activity in individual regions increases or decreases, it is extremely important to review and update those developments. Second, the emergence of non-state actors as increasingly important and independent subjects, challenging the position of states, must be taken into account. Doing so could potentially undermine one of the main assumptions of RSCT – namely, that states are the primary securitizing actors affecting the dynamics of security in the regional complexes. Third, the boundaries of regional complexes were drawn on the basis of the geopolitical realities of the second half of the 1990s – realities which have appreciably changed. As previously mentioned, changes to the global balance of power have caused said regional complex boundaries to shift slowly but constantly. This fundamental change to the structure of the international system cannot be omitted, if the theory is to retain its explanatory power. Fourth, there is a huge gap between the catalogue of primary security threats and challenges today and those that were identified and prioritized 20 years ago, when some of them (e.g., cyberthreats) did not exist at all, while others (e.g., religious radicalism) were very much underestimated. Fifth, there is a problem of variable patterns of amity and enmity that shape the dynamics of security within RSCs, and which heretofore have not been well accounted for within RSCT. Changes in these patterns over time within and across RSCs may greatly influence the balance of power and security dynamics within and across the regional complexes. Following a brief synopsis of the emergence and evolution of RSCT, the remainder of this chapter will explore these five aspects of the changing contemporary security landscape, and the ways in which securitization as a process necessitates a revision and updating of some of the core components of RSCT.

Origins and development of Regional Security Complex Theory (RSCT)

The security complex was originally defined by Buzan in 1983 as "a group of states whose primary security concerns link together sufficiently closely that their national securities cannot reasonably be considered apart from one another" (Buzan, 1983, p. 106). Since its initial introduction, what defines a 'security complex' has been a contest between neorealist and constructivist thought, with both structure and securitization as elements determining regional security (Basrur, 2006, p. 420). Upon subsequent reformulation 15 years later, regional security complexes were redefined as "a set of units whose major processes of securitization, desecuritization, or both are so interlinked that their security problems cannot reasonably be analysed or resolved apart from one another" (Buzan et al., 1998, p. 201; Buzan & Wæver 2003, p. 491). Tracking more closely to a constructivist approach, this second iteration aimed at encompassing various actors and sectors of security. It still underlined the main idea that "substantial parts of securitization and desecuritization processes in the international system will manifest themselves in regional clusters" which are "both durable and distinct from global level processes of (de)securitization" (Buzan & Wæver, 2003, p. 44).

RSCT: components and assumptions

The distinction introduced by securitization between referent object, securitizing actor, and audience allows for a more complex analysis of security interactions that, beside states, includes also sub-state actors (e.g., societal, ethnic or religious groups) and non-state actors (e.g., inter-governmental organizations, non-governmental organizations, transnational companies, terrorist groups). Thus, "RSCs are ultimately defined by the interaction among their units – the causes behind their action might be bottom-up (and thus internal to the region) or top-down (and thus external/global) [...]" (Buzan & Wæver, 2003, p. 72). Securitization also implies that the actors may differ in their perception of threats. So, in accordance with the assumptions of constructivism, it is actually the subjective perception of threat(s) that drive the dynamics of RSCs. However, because RSCT utilizes such concepts as the balance of power, anarchic structure or the security dilemma, and states remain primary actors and objects of security, some still place it "within general constraints of neo-realism" (McSweeney, 1999, pp. 54–55). This intellectual tension lies at the heart of the necessary revisions to RSCT discussed later in this chapter.

From the outset, RSCT included three key elements: arrangements of units and the differentiation among them, patterns of amity and enmity, and the distribution of power among major units (Buzan et al., 1998, p. 13). Its architects argued that security issues could grouped by geographically separated regional complexes and "Anarchy plus the distance effect plus geographical diversity yields a pattern of regionally based clusters, where security interdependence is markedly more intense between the states inside such complexes than between states inside the complex and those outside it" (Buzan & Wæver, 2003, p. 46). The regional security complex is arrayed around a group of states with a certain degree of security interdependence, which both links them internally and differentiates them from surrounding regions. The boundaries of RSCs do not have to correspond to the boundaries of traditional geographical or geopolitical regions. Buzan and Wæver note that "[…] RSCs define themselves as substructures of the international system by the relative intensity of security interdependence among a group of units, and security indifference between that set and surrounding units" (Buzan & Wæver, 2003, p. 48). However, despite the authors' claims that not only states, but also various non-state actors are subjects and objects of securitization in the RSCs, the sets of units they mention here consist entirely of states – a flaw in RSCT revisited later in this chapter.

RSCT assumes that geographical proximity plays a major role in defining boundaries of a security complex, as security issues rarely affect more distant regions and security interactions are considered strongest between adjacent states. The interdependence and intensity of security interactions between states within one security complex are most visible in the military, political, societal and environmental sectors, and to a lesser extent in the economic one (because of the prevalence of globalizing trends in the security dynamics in the economic sector [Buzan et al., 1998, pp. 109–115]). Likewise, the similar dangers and security threats occur mostly in specific regions and rarely translate across large distances. Of course, "[…] all the states in the system are to some extent enmeshed in a global web of security interdependence" (Buzan & Wæver, 2003, p. 46), but still interdependence between actors in the same region is much stronger than between actors from the different regions or between the whole regions. This important assumption is in fact the foundation of the whole theory. For such an important statement, the authors devote relatively little attention to its justification, stating only (after Walt, 1987, pp. 267–268) that "adjacency tends to generate more security interactions among neighbors than among states locked in different areas" and that "Adjacency is potent for security because many threats travel more easily over short distances than over long ones" (Buzan & Wæver, 2003, p. 46).

RSCs can be seen by existing patterns of amity and enmity "taking the form of subglobal, geographically coherent patterns of security interdependence" (Buzan & Wæver, 2003, p. 45). These patterns may take a form of long-standing enmity or cultural/civilizational proximity and as such may significantly affect the local complex. Depending on the prevalence of amity/enmity patterns, their dynamics, and prevailing levels of interdependence, security complexes have been identified as one of three types, where actors perceive each other respectively as enemies, rivals, and friends. This corresponds to Wendt's "idea of social structures of anarchy (Hobbesian, Lockean, Kantian) based on what kind of roles – enemy, rival, friend – dominate the system [...] and how deeply inter-nalized these roles are – by coercion, by interest, and by belief in legitimacy" (Buzan & Wæver, 2003, p. 50). In conflict formations, interdependence is mainly related to fear, rivalry, and mutual distrust. In security regimes, states still per-ceive one another as potential threats but have undertaken some steps (e.g., reas-surance arrangements) to reduce the security dilemma and mitigate the tensions among them. In so-called pluralistic security communities, states do not expect or plan to take up military actions against each other[1] (Buzan et al., 1998, p. 12).

Another typology, based on polarity as the main variable, categorizes RSCs into various types. A standard RSC is one in which polarity is determined by regional powers and none of those powers is a global level one (e.g., the Middle East, South America, Southeast Asia, the Horn of Africa, Southern Africa). Cen-tered RSCs may take one of four forms. The first three types are centered on a superpower, a great power or a regional power that dominate the region and do not allow for the rise of any potential regional power. Those types are exempli-fied by the case of the U.S. as a superpower in a North American RSC and Russia as a great power dominating the post-Soviet areas. An RSC centered on regional power in South Asia has not been present; however, it could potentially emerge with India as the regional power. The last sub-type of centered RSC is an institutional one, where the integration processes transform the region into a security community or a single actor in its own right (e.g., the European Union). Two special cases are the complexes with more than one global level power within the system. They may take a form of a great power RSC (like East Asia with China and Japan as regional poles) or a super-complex, which arises when strong, inter-regional security dynamics bind together separate complexes (a potential super-complex is the one including East and South Asia) (Buzan & Wæver, 2003, pp. 53–62). Moreover, across the typology of security complexes, the security dynamic within the complex itself can and does vary, taking one of four forms: maintenance of status quo (changes support the structure of local complex or do not damage it seriously so it remains mostly intact), internal transformation (when the structure changes within the context of existing outer boundary of complex), external transformation (expansion or contraction of region's boundaries results in an essential change to the structure of complex), overlay (when influence of some external power(s) in the region results in sup-pressing indigenous security dynamics) (Buzan et al., 1998, pp. 13–14).

RSCT in Application

RSCT is supposed to allow for an understanding of a new structure of security system, as well as evaluation of relative balance of power and interdependence between regionalizing and globalizing trends. To qualify a group of states as a security complex, one has to indicate a certain level of their interdependence, sufficient to present them as interlinked in terms of security challenges, but at the same time providing the basis for their distinction from surrounding states that make up the other security complexes. Key elements that define dynamics inside and outside the regions are: mutually exclusive regional security complexes with their historically conditioned relations and persistent patterns of amity and enmity, global powers (superpowers and great powers) that penetrate and influence the complexes, and insulators and buffers that separate security complexes and rival powers[2] (Buzan & Wæver, 2003, pp. 40–49).

RSCT differentiates four levels of analysis with implications for assessing regional security: domestic, regional, inter-regional, and global. The domestic level covers the issues of internal security and stability as well as security threats and vulnerabilities generated by the sub-state actors and their interrelations. On the regional, or state-to-state level, are the security interactions between states within one security complex. This level plays a major role in defining security and here most interactions take place. The inter-regional level is less important, because the theory assumes that the nature of the system makes interactions between states belonging to different regional complexes relatively limited. The global level resembles the influence of global and great powers on a given region and their interplay with regional security structures (Buzan & Wæver, 2003, p. 51). The theory's overriding focus on the regional level means that the other levels of analysis are marginalized. This applies both to the global level, where security issues are not limited only to the interactions of superpowers and great powers, and the domestic level which is a much more serious source of security threats and challenges than suggested by RSCT. These deficiencies will be considered in further detail below.

RSCT defines criteria for a three-tiered scheme of international system that includes superpowers, great powers, and regional powers. Only superpowers influence the system globally, being active in all or almost all regions of the world. They are required to possess the greatest military capabilities and powerful economies to support their global interest, a recognition of themselves as a superpower as well as acceptance as such by other actors, embrace of an active role in processes of securitization and desecuritization, and last, they must serve as a source of universal values and ideas that spread out on a global scale (Buzan & Wæver, 2003, pp. 34–35). The great powers are states that also operate on a global scale and are able to affect a few selected regions. They do not possess first-class capabilities in all sectors, although they are usually characterized by a high and balanced level of development of different sectors or unbalanced development of capabilities, with some sectors developed extremely well and some rather poorly. A great power must also be recognized as such by other actors and think of itself as more than regional power or a potential superpower.

For their part, regional powers operate at the regional level and possess limited capabilities. They are usually able to affect and define polarity of only one (their own) regional security complex, where they play a crucial role in securitization and desecuritization processes, but are excluded from decision-making processes referring to the other regions (even though some of them may think or wish otherwise) (Buzan & Wæver, 2003, pp. 35–39). This power schema clearly reflects the Cold War's perception of the international system, where hierarchically structured powers determined the security environment. Again, this schema does not take into account fundamental changes in the contemporary international system, such as the decentralization of the international system or the growing number of threats generated by non-state actors – a topic to which I will return later in this chapter.

One attempt to bridge the gap between the middle and system levels of world politics was introduced later by Buzan and Wæver as the concept of "macrosecuritization." Macrosecuritization as a concept was intended

> [...] to cover securitizations that speak to referent objects higher than those at the middle level (for example, 'universal' religions or political ideologies; one or more of the primary institutions of international society) and which aim to incorporate and coordinate multiple lower level securitizations.
>
> (Buzan & Wæver, 2009, p. 257)

As an "overarching securitisation that relates, organises and possibly subsumes a host of other middle-level securitizations" macrosecuritization could possibly explain some of the security interactions on the global level. But the authors themselves admit that macrosecuritizations are rare phenomena in history. They identify the Cold War as one example, adding that securitization of other cases such as the Global War on Terrorism, the anti-nuclear movement, global warming, or the war on drugs, cannot yet be defined as macrosecuritizations.

The post-Cold War era has been characterized by changes and an evolution of the global security system. To date, the primary architects of the RSCT have focused on the transition from a $2+3$ system, with two superpowers (U.S. and the Soviet Union) and three great powers (China, Europe, and Japan) to a $1+4$ system, with the U.S. as the only remaining superpower, and a group of four great powers, which consist of China, the European Union, Japan, and Russia (Buzan & Wæver, 2003, pp. 445–446). Proponents of the RCST as currently formulated believe that during the next decades this structure will not change. In their opinion, there is a small probability that the U.S. would be deprived of their status of superpower and an even smaller probability that China or the European Union would rise to the role of global superpower (Buzan & Wæver, 2003, pp. 446–447). The RSCT structured the world around four geopolitical units (Asia, the Middle East and Africa, the Americas, the Europes), each of them consisting of a few regional security complexes. When comparing the maps, one can find out that, according to the RSCT, the post-Cold War transformation has significantly changed the structure of the system in Europe and Asia, to a lesser extent in Africa and almost not at all in the Americas (Buzan & Wæver, 2003, pp. xxv–xxvi, 98–99, 189, 230–231, 266, 278, 306, 349–350). However, the suggested changes do not correspond to the security dynamic and the most recent developments in the international system that will be discussed later in this chapter. In this way, attempts at (literally) mapping RSCT onto the ever-changing global and regional security landscape reveal the need for revision of some of the core aspects of RSCT if it is to retain relevance and explanatory power.

Revising RSCT for the 'new security environment'

Since its introduction, RSCT has inspired numerous scholars, whose efforts resulted in significant development of the theory and its creative application. Interestingly, only a very limited number have tried to challenge the theoretical assumptions of RSCT as well as deepen or broaden its frameworks. Beside reconsiderations by Buzan himself, other prominent critiques have been advanced by Acharya, Adib-Moghaddam and Oskanian (Buzan, 2011a, 2011b; Acharya, 2007; Adib-Moghaddam, 2006; Oskanian, 2013). Attempts to apply and utilize the theory to explain the security dynamics of particular regions, and to critically test the theory in selected case studies and comparative studies, as well as empirical studies on RSCT application to analyze regional, inter-regional, and global levels of security, are far more numerous.[3] However, this imbalance between critique and application has hindered the continued evolution of RSCT, and threaten its continued applicability to a changing security land-scape. In light of the recent development of security studies and trends of globalization and regionalization, a few issues emerge as central challenges to the continued relevance of RSCT.

Power transitions

The shifting balance of power on the global, interregional and regional level is one of the main features of RSCT. This raises two problems that the theory must face. First is the question of how a changing balance of power between super-powers, great powers, and regional powers can be tracked and incorporated into theoretical assumptions in order to keep RSCT and its explanations up-to-date. Second is the problem of the theory's overreliance on the concept of polarity. This problem becomes more and more apparent in the face of the growing role of non-state actors in the constructing of security and the growing role of non-territorially bound threats. To date, the first problem has only been partially addressed, as various authors (including Buzan himself) describe the changing position of individual powers, while a more comprehensive approach has yet to be introduced. This section unveils the main variables regarding the position of super, great, and regional powers, while the issues of non-state actors and terri-toriality will be considered in the following sections.

A key assumption of RSCT is that the U.S. has maintained and will maintain its position as a sole superpower but, as Buzan notes, current changes are heading towards a more balanced, multi-polar system. American supremacy is eroding for various reasons that include the widespread global modernization and industrialization that closes the gap between the U.S. and the rest of the world, declining support for American values previously used to legitimize U.S. leadership, decreasing resources available to underwrite this leadership, and erratic and tumultuous shifts in U.S. foreign policy behavior in recent years. Also, the steady rise of new great and regional powers makes it increasingly difficult and expensive for the U.S. to maintain its superiority (Buzan, 2011a).

The very existence of a global system dominated by a superpower(s) is "an abnormal, exceptional condition, not a normal one" and it arose "from particular historical circumstances that are now receding into the past" (Buzan, 2011b, p. 15). The shift towards a more balanced global system with a more even distribution of power can be thus seen as a return to normalcy, rather than a new quality in international relations.

Simultaneously, other states are increasing their power and capabilities, rising to the status of regional and great powers, and in the process extending their influence and challenging the prevailing balance of power. This raises a question of how peaceful or violent this process can be, especially in the case of China. Despite its rhetoric of peaceful development, Chinese activities in the South China Sea and elsewhere are increasingly audacious and defiant. Despite its fast development, it is still not plausible that China (or any other state) will rise to the position of the superpower in the near term. There is, however, a growing consensus that the development and rising importance of India, not just regionally but interregionally and globally, justify classifying it as the next great power (Buzan, 2011b; Han & Saez, 2015). The position of Japan, both as a great power as well as within the East-Asian RSC, remains relatively stable. However, the North Korean threat, the rising power of China, and unresolved territorial disputes with Russia force Japan to build up its military capabilities and reconsider priorities of its politics of security (Wirth, 2015; Rinna, 2016; Japanese Ministry of Defense, 2016).

Meanwhile, the question of the future of another great power, the European Union, remains open. So far, the tightening integration and Europeanization of further policies has not resulted in the emergence of the European Union as a single, independent actor. On numerous occasions, individual interest and actions of the member states still prevail over the European perspective (Kostecki, 2016; Park & Ree, 2014). Currently, the transformation of the EU from institutional centered security complex into the pluralistic security community acting on its own rights (Buzan & Wæver, 2003, pp. 352–376) seems to be more doubtful than ever. Numerous internal and external problems (the Eurozone crisis, economic hardships, ideological differences, migration crisis, terrorism, etc.) have stopped the further transformation of the complex. The recent decision of the UK to leave the EU shows that the process is not irreversible both in terms of the depth and width of integration. Therefore, under certain circumstances, Europe may still re-emerge as a security complex, albeit of a different type. Brexit itself may have a twofold consequence. It may accelerate the erosion of the EU and its institutions as the next states try to leave it or at least renegotiate their membership conditions. On the other hand, it may also speed up the integration, as the UK has often been the state that delayed and obstructed attempts for further integration.

Since the breakup of the Soviet Union, the Russian Federation strove first to stop further erosion of its capabilities and then to regain, at least partially, the position and influence Moscow once had. Aggressive actions against Georgia and the Ukraine and military engagement in Syria, as well as active involvement in adjacent regions and subregions (Eastern Europe, the Balkans, the Middle East, the Caucasus, Central Asia, East Asia) indicate that Russia is back on the road to becoming a great power actively engaged in as many regions as possible (Nygren, 2008, 2010). While Russia strives to return to its former position in the global system, numerous regional powers try to strengthen and improve their own positions in their respective regional complexes (Brazil, Iran, Saudi Arabia, and Turkey, to name just a few). Their interrelations and impact on local security vary, depending on the region and circumstances; the details of those dynamics have been described and analyzed at length in numerous applications of the theory mentioned above.

It therefore seems that the question of the balance of power remains open – an observation which in turn illustrates that as presently constituted, the RSCT is too static and thus unable to follow the dynamics of relationships between and among great and regional powers. In this way, RSCT appears to be another remnant of Cold War and early post-Cold War logic, where the dynamics of changes in the structure of the international system were low. Improving RSCT in this vein requires a new (and perhaps perpetual) mapping of the international system, taking into account the changes in the status of the countries included in the categories of great and regional powers.

Similarly, RSCT's treatment of global level security considerations – restricting them largely to the interplay of superpowers and great powers only – is outdated and misleading in an era of global communication, extensive and intensive global economic integration, and the proliferation of transnational social and environmental problems. Likewise, the domestic level appears to be a more serious source of security threats and challenges than suggested by RSCT. For example, this is reflected in numerous data sets and studies demonstrating that domestic conflicts constitute a vast majority of all the armed conflicts in the modern world, while interpersonal violence and gang violence is responsible for much more death than political violence (Dupuy et al., 2016; Marc, 2016; Davis, 2016; Global Conflict Tracker, 2017).

Rising importance of non-state actors

Another of the more obvious areas of omission in RSCT concerns the rising importance of non-state actors and their increasingly powerful impact on security at the state, regional, interregional, and global level. In a large group of non-state actors there are, among others, sub-state/domestic actors (trade unions, religious associations, lobby and interest groups etc.), multinational corporations (MNCs), non-governmental organizations (NGOs), political groups advocating violence (militant national liberation movements, guerrilla groups, terrorist organizations), and international criminal groups. All of these non-state actors play an increasingly important role in the process of securitization and their involvement is visible on all levels of analysis. Non-state actors have increasingly come to challenge the dominant position of states, by extension threatening them indirectly and, in some cases, directly. By opposing or supporting state's politics of security they contribute to the change in the regional balance of power (Barthwal-Datta, 2012).

In the economic sector of security, the growing power of multinational corporations is reflected in the yearly revenue streams of hundreds of the world's largest companies, income flows that far exceed the national income of many small and mid-size states (Global 500, 2017; GDP ranking, 2017). New challenges posed by multinational corporations also manifest themselves in a growing number of cases: when MNCs sue national governments, when states become dependent on MNCs (their investment decisions, financial support, loans etc.), and numerous cases when states use public money to save MNCs and private enterprises (banks, hedge funds, automotive companies, airlines etc.) from bankruptcy (Gomes, 2009; Hamby, 2016; Wettstein, 2009).

The same is true of numerous other non-state actors like international lobbies and interest groups, transnational crime groups, and terrorist networks, whose strength grows noticeably in relation to the power of states (Josselin & Wallace, 2001; Arts, Noortmann, & Reinalda, 2001). In various contemporary armed conflicts, Private Military Companies (PMCs) support and sometimes replace the regular armed forces of some states. This leads to increasingly frequent situations wherein armed forces that are not formally an army of any state face each other on the battlefield. The Middle East provides numerous examples, e.g., Academi mercenaries fighting Houthi rebels in Yemen, or Wagner Group mercenaries fighting Kurdish-led Syrian Democratic Forces in Syria (Yaffa, 2018; Hager & Mazzetti, 2015). The development of this sector since the end of the Cold War challenges the very idea of the Weberian modern rational corporate state (*rationaler Anstaltsstaat*) as the sole actor that possesses a monopoly on legitimate violence. The functioning of PMCs in various sectors of security on the domestic, regional, and global level cause numerous threats and problems, including their unclear legal status, responsibility for actions taken, or regulation and supervision of their activities to name just a few (Chesterman & Lehnardt, 2007; Liu, 2010).

Changing boundaries

To date, RSCT has been somewhat inconsistent in terms of defining the boundaries of the regional security complexes. While some RSCs were sufficiently detailed, others (e.g., Africa [Buzan & Wæver, 2003, p. 232]) were much less structured. At the same time, since the end of the Cold War, the borders of RSCs in all parts of the world have changed. This has occurred for various reasons including: the intensification of security interactions with actors from other RSCs by some states, strengthening or weakened internal integration within some particular complexes, and the emergence of power vacuums and contested territories as the result of failing and collapsed states. Following and updating the changes to the structure of RSCs is crucial for the proper functioning of the theory, as it is the interactions between actors at different levels of the structure that determine the security dynamics.

The redefinition of the RSCT landscape requires a detailed look at all regional complexes and subcomplexes in order to verify their current status. This task goes beyond the scope of this chapter and should be undertaken in a separate study. This paragraph only briefly mentions the most obvious changes and developments. One such example is the potential emergence of an Asian supercomplex, arising from the further integration of Asian RSCs and comprising all the states of South, Southeast, and Northeast Asia (Buzan, 2011b). Another would be the emergence of Central Asia, originally classified as a subcomplex of the post-Soviet great power RSC, as a separate standard RSC (Musioł, 2015, pp. 197–214; Tadjbakhsh, 2012). High security dynamics and numerous violent conflicts in the Middle East (Syria, Iraq, Yemen, Libya) as well as growing ambitions and changing priorities in Turkey's policy force us to rethink and reformulate the structure of Middle Eastern RSC (Diez, 2005; Barrinha, 2014; Dilek, Iseri, & Nihat, 2015). Multiple security challenges and a rising number of security interactions between the states of the region led to consolidation of the outlined RSCs in Africa (Southern African, West African, Central African, and the Horn) (Hammerstad, 2005; Bah, 2005; Franke, 2008). The South American security complex may be slowly drifting from a standard one toward one centered around Brazil (Fuccille & Rezende, 2013). In Europe, the Baltic States (Lithuania, Latvia, and Estonia) integrated with the Western European structures (NATO and the European Union) and should be reclassified as part of the EU-Europe RSC (Buzan & Hansen, 2009, p. 180).[4] The increasingly aggressive politics of Russia towards Eastern and Central-Eastern Europe provides an opportunity for the emergence of a new subcomplex within the EU-Europe, consisting of the states of NATO/EU, the "Eastern flank" (Pop, 2016).

The increasing number of failed states and contested territories that become long-term or permanent war zones pose a different conceptual problem; namely, how do the security threats and challenges produced by sub-state as well as non-state actors and forces fit into RSCT? In 2017, South Sudan, Sudan, Somalia, Yemen, Syria, the Democratic Republic of Congo, and the Central African Republic were classified as failed states (Fragile States Index, 2017). In addition, there are a number of certain territories of other states that are actual war zones or, for various reasons, are not under the control of state's authorities.[5] They usually do not act as a single actor, but they still influence state, regional, interregional, and sometimes even global security because of their own internal security dynamics. As many of them are located on the frontiers of actual complexes, should they be treated as part of the complexes, or do they constitute some kind of subregional insulators?

This raises the question of whether, instead of the borders/boundaries, RSCT should utilize to a greater extent the concept of 'frontiers.' The latter delineates the level of political influence and is able to show how an actor extends its influences in a given region and transforms it (Prescott & Triggs, 2008; Prescott, 2015). The power vacuum created after the collapse of state authority is usually very quickly filled in by non-state actors, be they warlords, armed groups, tribal militias, terrorist organizations or quasi state structures. As soon as they start to serve as norm makers on a given territory, they become securitizing actors and project normative influence there, regardless of the formal borders of the states. RCST has to recognize this fact. The territories of failed states cannot be treated as black holes into which something falls, but from which nothing can emerge; an approach wherein securitization processes are thought to affect them, but they do not affect securitization, is problematic.

Emerging threats and challenges

One of the issues to which the RSCT needs to pay more attention is the emergence of new types of threats and challenges on the global and interregional level, including not only their changing character, but also their growing impact on security on the regional and domestic level. Among them are problems and challenges posed by a higher level of integration of the global economy than ever before. Of course, worldwide economic crises (most recently in 2007–2008) have threatened the stability of different regions of the world in the past. But the modern world economy, with its level of integration and interdependence is incomparable to anything we have seen before. Economic problems like governmental insolvency, market volatility, and rapid changes in prices of raw materials and products occur more often than ever and affect countries regardless of regions and continents (e.g., the financial crisis of 2008, the Greek debt crisis, or a sharp fall in oil prices in 2014).

Another emerging problem is the rising importance of non-territorial threats like transnational terrorism, organized crime, and issues related to cyberspace and cybersecurity. These are threats that were completely new, or perhaps more accurately unknown or little known, when RSCT was defined. In all three cases, the scale of these threats has increased significantly in recent years. In the sector of military security, non-state actors pose a direct threat as terrorist and militant groups declare wars against states (Al-Qaeda, ISIS) and carry out attacks on a global scale. New organizational forms, new attack methods, religious inspiration, and extensive use of new media have made terrorism a threat more global and omnipresent than it has ever been before (Hoffman, 2006). Similarly, organized crime networks have evolved on a global scale as the transnational crime groups have significantly expanded their business (financial crime, drug trafficking, human trafficking, arms smuggling, cybercrime, political corruption etc.) and now pose a threat to virtually every country in the world, regardless of distance (Mallory, 2007; Abadinsky, 2009). In this context, it is also worth noting the changing nature of armed conflicts. Development of improved air strike capabilities, ballistic missiles, cruise missiles, and unmanned aerial vehicles (UAVs) make it possible for the states to engage in armed conflicts far away from their own soil and to wage wars with their air, naval, and missile forces only, without engaging their ground troops at all (Bergen & Rothenberg, 2014; Hayward, 2016). This change increases the likelihood of the superpower's and great powers' military intervention in distant parts of the world and makes the conflicts between states from different RSCs more plausible (e.g. U.S. and Russian engagement in the civil war in Syria).

In addition to non-territorial threats, there are also a growing number of threats and challenges on the intra-state (domestic) level that plague various states in the world, regardless of the RSC they belong to. Among them are environmental degradation, drug addiction, the spread of chronic diseases, ethnic and religious conflicts, poverty, social exclusion, discrimination, and others. Some of them, in turn, trigger the emergence of threats on an inter-regional scale, such as the problem of refugees and economic migration (the recent migrant crisis in Europe caused by political turmoil and poverty in South Asia, Africa and the Middle East), large-scale man-made environmental catastrophes and pollution (e.g., the explosion at the Chernobyl nuclear power station), or the spread of dangerous infectious diseases (bird flu, swine flu, Ebola, etc.).

These developments urge us to reconsider one of the main assumptions of RSCT – that adjacency increases security interactions and that security interdependence is more intense between states inside the complex (Buzan & Wæver, 2003, p. 46). The consequence of a gradual increase in the importance of intra-state, interregional, and global threats in the military, political, economic, societal, and environmental sectors may be the reduction of the degree of interdependence of states within particular RSCs.

Variable patterns of amity and enmity

Patterns of amity and enmity characterize security actors as enemies, rivals, or friends and "... are influenced by various background factors such as history, culture, religion, and geography, but to a large extent they are path-dependent and thus become their own best explanation" (Buzan & Wæver, 2003, p. 50). They definitely affect actual politics and only a combination of patterns of amity and enmity with the distribution of power as well as threat perception, shape the dynamics of security within RSCs. Though discernable and coherent, patterns of amity and enmity are nevertheless variables that may occasionally shift. This, in turn, requires considering whether some external factors (e.g., state policies, deliberate actions of securitizing actors, the concerted spread of ideologies) may influence those patterns. In other words, should these relationships be treated as dependent or independent variables? It would seem that on most occasions they act as the latter, causing specific changes in other factors (variables). In some cases, however, the traditional patterns of amity and enmity are themselves influenced by other independent variables.

For example, the traditional Arab–Persian enmity seems to have faded away over the last few decades, giving way to a Sunni–Shiite enmity. This one is also traditional, but was much less important in the twentieth century, mainly due to the predominance of national and nation-building agendas over religious ones at that period of time in the Middle East. As religious issues re-emerged as the main source of conflicts at the end of the twentieth century, so did the Sunni-Shiite cleavage. By way of example, the Iraqi Shiite–Arab majority remained generally loyal to Saddam Hussein's regime during the Iraq–Iran War of 1980–1988, while today they predominantly support Iran. In this case, changing identity and predominant ideology (the decline of Pan-Arabism and the renaissance of a religious factor) influenced the mutual perception (from distrust to friendship), which in turn paved the way for the political turn in Iraqi-Iranian relations from enemies to rivals, and possibly to friends (Ricks, 2016).

This raises the question of other possible changes in patterns of amity and enmity. For example, Saudi Arabia has recently pursued a more cooperative tack with Israel, leading it to assume a neutral position in the disputes regarding Israel, despite the fact that it does not recognize the Jewish state and the two hold no diplomatic relations (Munayyer, 2016). So far, Saudi society is mostly unfriendly to Israel, but is it possible that changing state politics will influence and mitigate Arab–Israeli hostility? The close political, military, and economic collaboration between Israel and Turkey did not significantly change the patterns of amity and enmity from a longer perspective. After a series of political crises, the two countries remain regional rivals (Kosebalaban, 2010; Stern & Ross, 2013). On the other hand, the case of mutual perception of Germans and Poles shows that a deep and persistent change in the pattern is possible (Polish–German Barometer, 2017). Nevertheless, these examples show that patterns of amity and enmity are characterized by both internal and external dynamics filtered through the mechanism of securitization. Besides being an important factor in balancing powers and shaping security, they themselves are also subject to change.

An important role here is played by the processes of securitization and desecuritization that influence the threat perception of the regional actors, be they states, substate actors (political parties, ethnic and religious groups, state industries, labor unions, local governments, etc.) or non-state ones (MNCs, media organizations, liberation movements, lobby groups, violent armed groups etc.). In this way, a successful securitization or desecuritization of certain issues will result in a change of perception of a referent object by audience, which, in turn, may influence the patterns of amity and enmity over time.

Conclusions

Since the time of its ultimate conceptualization in *Regions and Powers* in 2003, Regional Security Complex Theory has confirmed its usefulness in studying different levels of security. Over the years, it encouraged numerous scholars to creatively use it in their research, contributing to the emergence of a vast literature in the field of regional security complexes. Interestingly, the practical applications of the RSCT to investigate specific case studies far outnumbered the attempts to critically assess and update the theory itself. That observation aside, the preceding confirms that RSCT remains an insightful, well-structured, and nuanced theoretical device. Its explanatory power, as well as many of its sustaining assumptions, remain intact. However, as the RSCT is so strongly related to the security dynamics on the regional and global level, it is also naturally susceptible to both structural changes in the distribution of power in the international system, as well as ideational changes produced by securitization processes.

On the former score, the balance of powers and security arrangements on the regional and interregional level have undeniably changed over the past two decades. Within RSCT, the U.S. continues to be conceived of as the sole super-power, but this assumed supremacy has been and continues to be challenged. At the same time some great powers, most notably China and Russia, increase their influences in some regional security complexes (South Asia, Africa, the Middle East). On the latter, the failure of RSCT to adequately account for changes such as the rising importance of non-state and substate actors reveals a more funda-mental inadequacy in accounting for the impact of securitization and desecuriti-zation processes. An analysis of regional security that focuses mainly on the interactions between state actors and marginalizes the role of the others does not fully explain it. And, on both a structural and ideational level, the concept of boundaries of regional complexes within RSCT also requires re-thinking, both in the context of their updates and in relation to numerous areas that cannot easily be classified into any RSC (failed states, contested territories). The replacement of boundaries by frontiers that focus on political influence and normative power instead of the formal affiliation of a given territory could introduce more clarity and flexibility to the theory. Similarly, RSCT's limited responsiveness to the variable nature of security threats and their perceptions that are particularly visible in relation to the new, emerging threats and challenges like cyber security, global health problems, financial crises and the like is problematic, as are the theory's inability to account for changes and fluctuations in patterns of amity and enmity.

In sum, in order for RSCT to retain its relevance moving forward, it must be revised in order to provide a fuller account for the pressing security problems and questions of the twenty-first century. To that end, it would seem that those working with RSCT should pay greater heed to the debt the theory owes to securitization as an underpinning and driving mechanism of the theory. This is particularly (but not only) true with respect to the variability of securitizing actors (i.e., the need for wider inclusion of non-state and substate actors), referent objects (i.e., the need to acknowledge the multiplicity of referent objects on different levels) and audiences (i.e., cross-country audiences, like tribes or diasporas, that are relevant for the whole regional security complex). The application of a revamped RSCT informed by a fuller appreciation for securitization as a process would represent a significant contribution to security studies going forward.

Notes

1 Extensive regional cooperation and integration may lead to an ultimate elimination of security complexes by transformation of the anarchic subsystem of states to a single actor within the system. (Buzan et al., 1998, p. 12).

2 A buffer is "a state or mini-complex *within* a security complex and standing at the center of a strong pattern of securitization, whose role is to separate rival powers". An insulator is "a state or mini-complex standing *between* regional security complexes and defining a location where larger regional security dynamics stand back to back". (Buzan & Wæver, 2003, pp. 489–490).

3 This includes hundreds of books, articles, papers, and book chapters. Their (incomplete) collection may be found i.a. on Academia.edu: www.academia.edu/Documents/in/Regional_Security_Complex_Theory, (June 2, 2017) and on Google Scholar: https://scholar.google.pl/scholar?hl=pl&q=regional+security+complex+theory&lr=&oq=regional+secu, (June 2, 2017).

4 Although some authors suggest that as Russia remains the main security concern for the Baltic states, there are no persuasive arguments for such a transition (Andžns, 2014).

5 Among them are large parts of North Western Frontier Province in Pakistan, territories of Afghanistan controlled by Taliban movement, parts of Libya, and some territories of Sub-Saharan African states (Mali, Mauritania, Niger, Nigeria, Chad).

Bibliography

Abadinsky, H. (2009). *Organized crime* (9th ed.). Belmont: Thomson Wadsworth.

Acharya, A. (2007). The emerging regional architecture of world politics. *World Politics, 59*(4), 629–652.

Adib-Moghaddam, A. (2006). Regional Security Complex theory: A critical examination. *International Studies Journal, 3*(1), 25–40.

Andžns, M. (2014, June). Transition of the Baltic States sub-region: From the "post-Soviet" to the "EU-Europe" Regional Security Complex? *Proceedings of the 55th International Scientific Conference of Daugavpils University.* Retrieved from www.academia.edu/32035993/Transition_of_the_Baltic_States_Sub-region_from_the_post-Soviet_to_the_EU-Europe_Regional_Security_Complex_2014_

Arts, B., Noortmann, M., & Reinalda, B. (Eds.). (2001). *Non-state actors in international relations.* Aldershot: Ashgate.

Bah, A. (2005). West Africa. From a security complex to a security community. *African Security Review, 14*(2), 77–83.

Balzacq, T. (2015). The 'essence' of securitization – theory, ideal type, and a sociological science of security. *International Relations, 29*(1), 103–113.

Barrinha, A. (2014). The ambitious insulator: Revisiting Turkey's position in regional security complex theory. *Mediterranean Politics, 19*(2).

Barthwal-Datta, M. (2012). *Understanding security practices in South Asia: Securitization theory and the role of non-state actors.* London: Routledge.

Basrur, R. M. (2006). Decentralizing theory: Regional international politics. *International Studies, 42*(4), 103–113.

Bergen, P. L., & Rothenberg, D. (Eds.). (2014). *Drone Wars.* Cambridge: Cambridge University Press.

Buzan, B. (1983). *People, states and fear: The national security problem in international relations* (1st ed.). Broughton: Wheatsheaf Books.

Buzan, B. (2011a). A world order without superpowers: Decentered globalism. *International Relations, 25*(1), 1–23.

Buzan, B. (2011b). The South Asian security complex in a decentring world order: Reconsidering regions and powers ten years on. *International Studies, 48*(1), 1–19.

Buzan, B., & Hansen, L. (2009). *The evolution of international security studies.* Cambridge: Cambridge University Press.

Buzan, B., & Wæver, O. (2003). *Regions and powers. The structure of regional security.* Cambridge: Cambridge University Press.

Buzan, B., & Wæver, O. (2009). Macrosecuritization and security constellations: Reconsidering scale in securitization theory. *Review of International Studies, 35*(2), 253–276.

Buzan, B., Wæver, O., & de Wilde, J. (1998). *Security: A new framework for analysis.* Boulder, CO: Lynne Rienner Publishers.

Chesterman, S., & Lehnardt, C. (Eds.). (2007). *From mercenaries to market. The rise and regulation of private military companies.* Oxford: Oxford University Press.

Davis, I. (2016). 6. Armed conflict data trends. *In SIPRI, SIPRI Yearbook 2016: Armaments, disarmament and international security.* Oxford: Oxford University Press. Retrieved May 26 2019 from www.sipriyearbook.org/view/9780198787280/sipri-9780198787280-chapter-006.xml

Diez, T. (2005). Turkey, the European Union and security complexes revisited. *Mediterranean Politics, 10*(2).

Dilek, O., Iseri, E., & Nihat, C. (2015). Turkey's regional powerhood within regional (in)security complex: Transformation from a conflict-ridden environment into a security community. *Journal of Regional Security, 10*(2), 155–176.

Dupuy, K., Gates, S., Nygård, H. M., Rudolfsen, I., Rustad, S. A., Strand, H., & Urdal, H. (2016). *Trends in armed conflict, 1946–2015.* Oslo: Peace Research Institute.

Fragile States Index (2017). The fund for peace. Available at http://fundforpeace.org/fsi/. Last accessed June 9, 2017.

Franke, B. (2008). Africa's evolving security architecture and the concept of multilayered security communities. *Cooperation and Conflict, 43*(3), 313–340.

Fuccille, A., & Rezende, L. P. (2013). South American regional security complex: A new perspective. *Contexto int.* [online], *35*(1), 77–104. doi:10.1590/S0102-85292013000100003. Last accessed June 9, 2017.

GDP ranking, World Bank. Available at http://data.worldbank.org/data-catalog/GDP-ranking-table. Last accessed June 7, 2017.

Global 500. 'Fortune.' Available at http://fortune.com/global500/. Last accessed June 7, 2017.

Global Conflict Tracker, CFR. Available at www.cfr.org/interactives/global-conflict-tracker#!/global-conflict-tracker. Last accessed August 14, 2017.

Gomes, L. (2009). *International economic problems.* London, Palgrave.

Guzzini, S. (2011). Securitization as a causal mechanism. *Security Dialogue, 42*(4–5), 329–341.

Hager, E. B., & Mazzetti, M. (2015, November 25). Emirates secretly sends Colombian mercenaries to Yemen fight. *New York Times.* Retrieved from www.nytimes.com/2015/11/26/world/middleeast/emirates-secretly-sends-colombian-mercenaries-to-fight-in-yemen.html.

Hamby, C. (2016, June). The billion-dollar ultimatum. *Buzzfeed.* Retrieved from www.buzzfeed.com/chrishamby/the-billion-dollar-ultimatum?

Hammerstad, A. (2005). Domestic threats, regional solutions? The challenge of security integration in Southern Africa. *Review of International Studies, 31*(1), 69–87.

Han, E., & Saez, L. (2015). China as "offshore balancer" and South Asia's regional security complex. *Routledge handbook of Chinese security.* London: Routledge.

Hansen, L. (2000). The Little Mermaid's silent security dilemma and the absence of gender in the Copenhagen School. *Millennium: Journal of International Studies, 29*(2), 285–306.

Hayward, J. (2016). Air power: The quest to remove battle from war. In J. Buckley & G. Kassimeris (Eds.), *The Ashgate research companion to modern warfare* (pp. 49–72). London: Routledge.

Hoffman, B. (2006). *Inside terrorism.* New York: Columbia University Press.

Josselin, D., & Wallace, W. (Eds.). (2001). *Non-state actors in world politics.* New York: Palgrave.

Kilroy, R. J., Sumano, A. R., & Hataley, T. S. (2013). *North American regional security: A trilateral framework?* Boulder, CO: Lynne Rienner Publishers.

Kosebalaban, H. (2010). The crisis in Turkish–Israeli relations: What is its strategic significance? *Middle East Policy, 17*(3), 36–50.

Kostecki, W. (2016). Transformacja Europejskiego systemu bezpieczeństwa [Transformation of the European Security Complex]. *Przegląd Strategiczny, 9*/2016, 17–29.

Liu, H.-Y. (2010). Leashing the corporate dogs of war: The legal implications of the modern private military company. *Journal of Conflict and Security Law 15*(1), 141–168.

Mallory, S. (2007). *Understanding organized crime.* Sudbury: Jones and Bartlett.

Marc, A. (2016). Conflict and violence in the 21st century: Current trends as observed in empirical research and statistics. Washington, D.C.: World Bank Group

McSweeney, B. (1999). *Security, identity and interests: A sociology of international relations.* Cambridge: Cambridge University Press.

Ministry of Defense, Government of Japan. 2016. Defense of Japan. Available online at www.mod.go.jp/e/publ/w_paper/2016.html. Last accessed June 5, 2017.

Munayyer, Y. (2016, June 13). Saudi-Israel: Mistaken hopes for an alliance. *MEI.* Retrieved from www.mei.edu/content/article/saudi-israel-mistaken-hopes-alliance. Last accessed November 14, 2017.

Musioł, M. (2015). *Kompleks bezpieczeństwa w regionie Azji środkowej po 1991 roku. [Security complex in Central Asia after 1991].* Warszawa: Dom Wydawniczy Elipsa.

Nygren, B. (2008). *The rebuilding of Greater Russia: Putin's foreign policy towards the CIS countries.* London: Routledge.

Nygren, B. (2010). Russia and the CIS region: The Russian regional security complex. In R. Freire Maria & R. E. Kanet (Eds.), *Key players and regional dynamics in Eurasia. The return of the 'great game.'* (pp. 13–28). London: Palgrave Macmillan.

Oskanian, K. K. (2013). Amity and enmity in its regional context. In K. K. Oskanian (Ed.), *Fear, weakness and power in the post-Soviet South Caucasus.* London: Palgrave Macmillan.

Park, W., & Ree, G. W. (2014). *Rethinking security in post-Cold War Europe.* London: Routledge.

Polish–German Barometer. (2017). (Available in Polish and German). Konrad Adenauer Foundation. Available at: www.kas.de/polen/pl/publications/48898// Last accessed June 12, 2017.

Pop, A. (2016). From cooperation to confrontation: The impact of bilateral perceptions and interactions on the EU–Russia relations in the context of shared neighbourhood. *Eastern Journal of European Studies, 7*(2), 47–70.

Prescott, J. R. V. (2015). *Political frontiers and boundaries.* London: Routledge.

Prescott, J. R. V., & Triggs G. D. (2008). *International frontiers and boundaries: Law, politics and geography.* Boston: Martinus Nijhoff.

Regional Security Complex Theory. Academia.edu. Retrieved from www.academia.edu/Documents/in/Regional_Security_Complex_Theory. Last accessed June 2, 2017.

Regional Security Complex Theory. Google Scholar. Retrieved from https://scholar.google.pl/scholar?hl=pl&q=regional+security+complex+theory&lr=&oq=regional+secu. Last accessed June 2, 2017.

Ricks, T. E. (2016). What Iranian and Iraqi Shiites think: A new survey of thousands of pilgrims. *Foreign Policy.* Retrieved from http://foreignpolicy.com/2016/10/21/what-iranian-and-iraqi-shiites-think-a-new-survey-of-thousands-of-pilgrims/ Last accessed November 14, 2017.

Rinna, A. V. (2016). The Northeast Asian regional security complex: Japan-Russia defense relations. *International Journal of East Asian Studies, 5*(1), 42–53.

Stern, M., & Ross, D. (2013). The role of Syria in Israeli–Turkish relations. *Georgetown Journal of International Affairs, 14*(2), 115–128.

Tadjbakhsh, S. (2012). Central Asia and Afghanistan: Insulation on the Silk Road, between Eurasia and the heart of Asia. *Paper 3 of the PRIO Project: Afghanistan in a Neighbourhood Perspective.* Oslo: Peace Research Institute.

Walt, S. (1987). The origins of alliances. Ithaca: Cornell University Press.

Wettstein, F. (2009). *Multinational corporations and global justice: Human rights obligations of a quasi-governmental institution.* Stanford: Stanford University Press.

Williams, P. D. (2008). *Security studies. An introduction.* London: Routledge.

Wirth, C. (2015). "Power" and "stability" in the China–Japan–South Korea regional security complex. *The Pacific Review, 28*(4), 553–575.

Yaffa, J. (2018, February 16). Putin's shadow army suffers a setback in Syria. *The New Yorker.* Retrieved from www.newyorker.com/news/news-desk/putins-shadow-army-suffers-a-setback-in-syria.

Part II

Securitization in application

3 Counter-terrorism as a technology of securitization

Approaching the Moroccan case

Blanca Camps-Febrer

From security to managing (in)securities

The Global War on Terror (GWoT)[1] as we know it emerged in the U.S. during the George W. Bush administration. Its Western ontology is evident and its narrative is mostly dominated by Western(ized) actors and experts (Bigo, 2005; Barkawi & Laffey, 2006; Buzan, 2006; Jackson, Gunning, & Smith, 2007; Buzan & Wæver, 2009). However, the GWoT narrative and the practices of counter-terrorism it has produced, encouraged, and sustained are pervasive all around the globe. Given its geo-cultural origins as a framing narrative, the global dimension of the GWoT has been under-researched even from the currents of critical security studies, and the theoretical toolboxes available at present are mainly developed within a Western ontology. The question that arises is if the current critical theories that engage with terrorism can be used to understand and analyze the phenomenon in the Global South. Studying cases in the Global South with a critical approach is especially beneficial in that it allows us to interrogate existing theory and concepts – such as securitization – and reflect on their resilience when confronted with other political and cultural contexts.

This objective is well-served with respect to an investigation of counter-terrorism in the Moroccan case. As an example of a neo-patrimonial monarchical state, Morocco can be regarded as a rather extreme departure from the European or 'Western' context. While it can be numbered among many illiberal regimes, the importance of the figure of the King, as well as the sacredness, infallibility and untouchability of the monarchy render the case particularly difficult to approach using ontologies developed in and specific to contemporary Europe. Nevertheless, I have found some of the analytical and conceptual tools provided by the proponents of International Political Sociology (IPS) a useful aid in overcoming some of the more Westphalian- and Weberian-oriented ideas arising from Securitization Theory (ST) and other schools[2] in critical security studies.

Linguistic analyses are central to understanding how counter-terrorism emerges discursively and is added to the policy agenda, but they fail to adequately address how the narrative acts as a technology in power relations, in the implementation of said policy or policies that are framed within the management of (in)security in a said context. Analyzing text and discourse provides only partial evidence of the process and strategies of power relations employed through the counter-terrorist narrative. Indeed, "[w]hile securitization theory is well equipped to deal with the official or formal level [...] this focus on state-level politics means that the analysis is in danger of obscuring informal politics and their dynamics" (Wilkinson, 2007, p. 13). It is in this sense that I see the use of the term 'technology' as a clarifying notion. I use the word technology informed by one of Foucault's main significations of the term. According to Michael C. Behrent, despite Foucault's ambivalence on the use of the term, he uses it as "[i]t refers to the ways in which modern social and political systems control, supervise, and manipulate populations as well as individuals" (2013, p. 55). Technology is thus used in this chapter to refer to a specialized know-ledge, and a set of processes, practices, and instruments, that are implemented in order to promote a specific social and political order.

In this way, the present chapter seeks to draw IPS, or what Didier Bigo (2011a) considers both 'frame and method,' out of its European natural habitat in order to test its ability to advance our understanding of the process of the securitization of terrorism and counter-terrorism and to identify its deficiencies as an analytical device. I do this first by turning to consideration of the orthodox-constructivist divide in security studies, and specifically of how the issue of 'global terrorism' has been approached by scholars concerned with examining it. In doing so, I outline some of the elements and insights of IPS and the ways in which they are particularly useful for the study of this issue in non-European contexts. Following this, the remainder of the chapter explores the case study of Morocco, as one such non-European context where terrorism and counter-terrorism have been at the forefront of the security agenda. I describe the process of the reinforcement of domination by the existing regime in Morocco through a concentrated and dif-fused model of security that permeates everyday lives. This analysis uncovers a narrative that includes discursive and non-discursive mechanisms, and is in essence ambiguous and contradictory. I conclude by drawing conclusions about the utility of introducing sociological tools for conceptualizing and analyzing power relations, and how these tools help us understand the embedded nature of the anti-terrorist narrative as a technology for authoritarianism within a longer historical process of managing (in)securities.

The global war on terror as a 'new' macro-securitization

Locating 'terrorism' within security studies

Growth in the amount of scholarly research on terrorism has been exponential since the end of the Cold War, and especially in the last two decades (Silke & Schmidt-Petersen, 2017). But is there anything new about twenty-first century terrorism? From state-terrorism to non-state terrorism, the significance of 'ter-rorism' within global, national, and local security contexts and agendas has been incorporated differently and been accorded variable importance throughout history. The novelties of what has been dubbed global terrorism (GT) might come from the evidence that this transboundary phenomenon of political violence now effectively dominates modern technologies (Johan Eriksson & Rhinard, 2009, p. 247). Alternatively, GT could also be the result of a post-bipolar world searching for a global structuring narrative. Barkawi and Laffey (2006), for example, described the Al-Qaeda attacks on U.S. soil as a new form of North–South confrontation, not in interstate terms, but as a globalized product of what was formerly called asymmetric wars or small wars. Although perceived terrorist threats have been highly prioritized on the political and security agendas in the last two decades, researchers must be ready to see through the political act and engage with the deeper socio-political and economic structures the GWoT is affecting.

In order to do this, looking beyond the label of 'terrorism' into political violence and its relation to existing power regimes becomes essential. Indeed, the task of defining terrorism has been largely reserved to legal scholars, proponents of traditional approaches to security studies, and realists. Conversely, alternative approaches emanating from scholars such as the sociologist Charles Tilly (2004) have attempted to separate the actor from the act, characterizing terrorism as a strategy at hand for certain actors or political situations. Feminist scholars (see, for example, Sjoberg, 2009) have questioned prevailing definitions of terrorism by comparing it to domestic violence, wartime rape or even by questioning the protector role of the state. The label 'terrorism' carries with it an instant moral judgment and a pejorative and negative weight (Hermann & Chomsky, 1988; Charbonneau & Jourde, 2016), in part due to the fact that the behaviors and actions associated with it have been disproportionately attributed to non-state actors (Ramsay, 2015) – especially non-white, non-Christian actors.

Scholarship of a more critical bent concerning terrorism has tended to focus especially on the narratives around terrorism and counter-terrorism. Such work sees terrorism as a socially constructed phenomenon that accords a distinct meaning to certain actions and actors enacting political violence (Jackson, 2011); in other words, a highly securitized phenomenon. To constructivist scholars, "[d]iscourses are seen as ways of reproducing or challenging relations of power and dominance in society" (Bartolucci & Gallo, 2013). Labeling an act as 'terrorism' becomes thus constitutive, productive and instrumental. How and which terrorism is identified and labeled thus depends more on who is identifying it and for what purposes.

This question becomes particularly interesting in the case of Morocco, when it is not the West that identifies the non-civilized, non-Western terrorist, but rather the Moroccan state itself. Examining the discursive construction of terrorism by and among non-Western actors – such as the Moroccan political elite – can help to clarify and reveal more nuanced underlying aspects of the terrorism narrative. To that end, the hegemonic implications of employing '9/11' as a starting and defining point for even critical terrorism studies has been criticized, and the importance of alternative chronologies emphasized (Tsui, 2014, 2015; Toros, 2017). It would indeed be misleading to think of the Global Terrorist narrative as something that sprung out of nowhere in September 2001, and its enhanced importance as a global legitimized framing of threats must be carefully contextualized. The narrative of GT after 9/11 has been defined as a macro-securitization (Buzan, 2006) or as a framing of the current globalization of (in)security (Bigo, 2008a), but beyond these attempts at providing a global understanding, the concrete functions of these framings in the local context must also be approached.

Understanding terrorism and counter-terrorism as a performative process provides not only an understanding of the signification of identified terrorist acts, individuals, groups, or communities. It is fundamentally about the power relations and the regime of truth that is reinforced by this technology. As we will see in the case study of Morocco below, the governmentality that arises from discourse and practices around counter-terrorism must be embedded within the power structure of various agents, elites, and populations of concern.

Beyond the speech-act: examining everyday practices of securitization

In 2006, a group of 25 scholars gathered around the name of C.A.S.E. Collective,[3] the acronym taken from the title of the workshop 'Critical Approaches to Security in Europe' that took place in Paris in June 2005. They published the Networked Manifesto where they criticized the development of critical security studies and the different 'Schools' and proposed some of the ideas that they considered pressing for an advancement of the field (C.A.S.E. Collective, 2006). The most interesting and complete proposal that arose from that discussion was that of 2010, by authors Thierry Balzacq, Tugba Basaran, Didier Bigo, Emmanuel-Pierre Guittet and Christian Olsson (Balzacq et al., 2010). To them, critical studies had excessively focused on linguistics and agenda-setting. Securitization Theory so far had mainly approached the issue using constructivist tools such as Critical Discourse Analysis[4] and had focused on the discursive speech-act that framed certain acts or issues within the security agenda.

Building on the constructivist approach, the proponents of International Political Sociology argue that security is a result of a process of (in)securitization and that as such, the research agenda should focus on the process and practices that engender it through historical and collective acts (Balzacq et al., 2010). It is security practices that include discursive and non-discursive practices that should be investigated. This could only be done through a transdisciplinary approach, especially by including sociological tools to IR. A sociological framework allows us to look at the conditions that make discursive practices possible. The proposed alternative analytical framework is International Political Sociology (Bigo, 2008c) where the focus is not so much about states and their relations to other states, but more about government and society (Bigo, 2011b).

IPS considers it paramount to focus the research agenda on the mechanisms that ensure the emergence of certain practices of security and insecurity while other voices and definitions remain unheard and violently countered by elite-constructed norms and technologies. In a post-structuralist effort, security is examined through the looking-glass of power relations in the world-system and in societies. As a result, understanding how a social and international order emerges requires the analysis of the construction of norms that constrain actors and shape them. Ultimately, the construction of norms and narratives takes a very materialist shape that conforms subjects, their experiences and everyday practices.

Clearly, IPS concedes a two-fold reality of things; i.e., a material and an ideational existence. The focus of the effort, however, is rather on what mechanisms are used to reinforce or advance certain power relations, and how they are employed to that end. The ideological hegemony of Gramsci can help as a conceptual tool to understand certain dynamics in which the diffusion of norms is used as a tool for certain elites' goals (Izquierdo Brichs, 2016). In this sense, it is fundamental to analyze power relations in connection with the development of a certain security narrative that can act as a systemic logic imposed by the most powerful elites. It is with this aim that IPS borrows from Foucault's epistemology and conceptual tools – tools that also inform my analysis of counter-terrorism as a technology of power and securitization in the Moroccan case.

One important insight derived from the IPS approach relative to security studies is that the narrative is not always rooted in emergency and exceptionalism, as Securitization Theory suggests, but also rooted in the "naturalness of a certain order" and in the "routinized practices of everyday politics" (Balzacq et al., 2010). As a result, the accepted efficacy of military security, the logic of the State, is the one that imposes the sense into the act. Indeed, discourse must be analyzed as a constitutive element inserted in a dynamic context of power relations whereby discourse is a result of power struggles between different actors and a resource of those able to master it. However, while Izquierdo Brichs (2016) sees a rationalist calculation that drives actors to attempt to dominate and produce a certain narrative, other scholars avoid or deny the task of understanding the intentions behind the (in)securitization practices, and rather prioritize the need to understand the mechanisms and how this process works (Balzacq et al., 2010).

The reification of terrorism as the main threat to collective security can be seen as a setback from liberal peace and the 'softer approach' to international relations after the end of the Cold War, representing in turn a move towards renewed 'hard' security practices (Toros, 2017). The illiberal practices that confront security with freedom, that militarize and securitize other policies, have a profound effect on the nature of politics and entail fundamental changes in the nature of the State. It is Foucault's biopolitics by other means. In Huysmans' words, we see a spill-over of the nature and modes of approaching security policies towards other domains: a modulation of the domains of (in)security (Huysmans, 2006).

As a result, policies that can be framed in very different logics are gradually or suddenly traversed by a security rationale. This process either elevates certain issues on the agenda or modulates the strategies to manage them. I use here Huysmans' concept of 'modulating (in)security domains' as it adequately captures the mechanisms of transversal securitization of policies and practices. Huysmans exemplifies this idea through migration and asylum policies in Europe (Huysmans, 2006). While these issues could be seen as a humanitarian or economic problem – leading them to be framed in very different ways – the inclusion of a security logic will bring more budgetary resources and will help prioritize the issue in the political, media, and social agenda, while configuring a different institutional response to the issue. State policies that were traditionally not about (in)security become traversed by a logic of (in)security, which attaches priority, urgency, exceptionalism, and executive processes that obscure the decision-process.

The securitization moves or processes of modulating (in)security domains described by scholars of critical security studies (Buzan, Wæver, & de Wilde, 1998; Huysmans, 1998) are obviously not a new thing. These illiberal practices are embedded in a genealogy of ancient technologies of domination. However, the perceived shift from interstate threats to non-state terrorism as the main (in)security challenge carries with it implications that go beyond a mere change of discourse. It is in this sense that the development of an analytical framework that looks at the counter-terrorist narrative as a technology of securitization will help grasp the social and ethical implications of the issue. At the global level, those implications are manifest in the employment of this counter-terrorist narrative as a means for a totalization of security, or what Buzan calls a macro-securitization (i.e., security in all aspects of life, like a rationalist utopia where everything is controlled and follows a protocol).

In fact, the dominant discursive interpretations of security are fed by the permanent risk of a terrorist attack. Here, the idea of exceptionalism becomes a thing of the past; a terrorist attack is always imminent and extraordinary security measures become permanent, routinized, and pervasive in all policy domains. Especially affecting the Global South, we find the new security-development nexus and the state-building and liberal peace-building narrative in the development of new wars and the making of the global order (Chandler, 2010; Duffield, 2005; Richmond & Tellidis, 2012). It is "[...] the interaction of liberal peace-building and orthodox terrorism approaches [that] has tended to reinforce securitised states" (Richmond & Tellidis, 2012, p. 121). Duffield, for example, looks at the importance of development policies in imperialist biopolitics and regards those policies as aimed at "[...] reconnect[ing] and rejuvenat[ing] earlier colonial modes of governing the world of peoples." In fact, "[...] the security function of such a biopolitics is that of bettering self-reliance as a means of defending international society against its enemies: it is the art of getting savages to fight barbarians" (Duffield, 2005, p. 141).

International political sociology goes south

The bulk of the scholarly research dealing with terrorism and non-western countries comes from orthodox terrorism/security studies, as is evident in the case of Morocco.[5] The Global South is commonly analyzed as the source and/or the victim of terrorism. As a result, protracted-civil-asymmetrical wars, radicalized ideologies in marginalized communities, and rogue or failed states are central to the development of security theories (Howard, 2010; Stewart, 2004). Most Western and westernized scholars look at terrorism as a consequence of a dys-functionality or inability to adequately implement state-building according to the liberal model. The degree of achievement of a Westphalian state, a centrally con-trolled territorial sovereignty, is the baseline against which terrorism is analyzed. It is the 'Westphalian straitjacket' identified by Barry Buzan and Richard Little (2001, p. 24).

In a way, constructivist approaches to terrorism might seem to start from a more context-nuanced framework. But constructivist approaches and most crit-ical security scholars also have trouble engaging with or from the Global South. The reasons for that, as discussed previously in this book (see especially Chapter 1) are that most critical security scholars have mainly engaged with the West, and specifically with the European process of securitization, and thus developed analytical tools that suited their object of study. The basic conceptual tools developed are thus based on the legal-rational bureaucratic state as the main *arrière pensée*. In Securitization Theory, for instance, Claire Wilkinson points out the centrality of the speech-act and of the western understanding of state, society, identity, and even communication (2007, para. 5).

When focusing on other types of regimes besides liberal ones, be they military dictatorships or illiberal monarchical states such as the Moroccan state, it is misleading to ignore the background pillars of power and state and how these will influence the framing of security and, ultimately, the understanding of government and how it relates to power structures. A debate on the issue would require a contextually embedded emic approach into the historical and political structures of power regimes, the contextualized genealogy of power, govern-ment, violence, and deviation. This is not to say that the goal of the constructiv-ist endeavor should be to determine the meaning of those significants in a non-western society. The danger of Orientalism would be lurking closely at that task. The goal, on the contrary, would be to assess the mechanisms of govern-ment and power without necessarily confronting them with the Weberian model of the state. Without this detachment from naturalized ideas of order and state, the analysis of a centralized power in a nation-state-like regime like Morocco will fall into the discourse of permanent transitology that places the country on an evolutionary path towards western modeling.

These different concerns raise the question as to how analytical and theoret-ical tools developed in the West can be suitable for understanding security prac-tices in the world, outside the small western fortress of government dynamics and power knowledge. As we will see in the following section, IPS in this sense offers not only the sociological tools but also the epistemological framework to approach the technology of securitization ingrained within everyday politics, and in the study of practices and meanings that go beyond the communicative act and agenda-setting of the counter-terrorist discourse analysis.

Concentrated and diffused: the securitization of terrorism and the production and reproduction of order in Morocco

The Kingdom of Morocco traces its origin to the Cherifien dynasty that has lasted for centuries. The King is the Prince of Believers, the Supreme Commander and the General Chief of Staff of the Royal Armed Forces – charges that are not just symbolic, but come with an important role as the protector of Islamic values and a tight grip and prerogatives over the management of the security sector. The evolution towards the hegemonic role of the King in the Moroccan regime of power has meant a process of power-accumulation through repression, co-opting, and a pactist strategy that has reinforced his primary role (Parejo Fernández, 2009; Feliu & Izquierdo Brichs, 2016). This power structure is obvious in the formal political structure of the State, and it is also replicated in other dimensions such as the control of economy and of natural resources, the religious sphere, etc. The diversity of resources of power, in contrast with other authoritarian regimes like rentier states where staying in power depends mainly on the control of one major resource, allows the elites space for bargaining and flexibility to cede to certain demands in order to stay in power (Feliu & Parejo, 2012).

The analysis of the evolution of power and domination in Morocco is essential if we are to break away from the limited self-reproducing image of the GWoT. As Moroccan historian Mohamed Tozy states, the "reception of ideas from hegemonic cultures (democracy, human rights) is not done without an alteration of the original sense" and in Morocco's case "the mechanisms of domination include a wordplay that equates an archaic reality with its modern institutional expression (Makhzen/institutional monarchy, subject/citizen)"[6] (Tozy, 1999, pp. 17–18). Indeed, the new dynamics emerging from the counter-terrorist narrative cannot be understood in a void and must be regarded as embedded within a longer cycle of power-relations and their discursive and non-discursive underpinnings.

In the case of Morocco, the concept of security is tightly linked to the monarchy. This nested conception of security onto the King's survival is a historical one, and becomes even more ambiguous through the 'modernization cover,' partly promoted by French royalist Lyautey's reforms during the French Protectorate in the early twentieth century. As Foucault sees for the early absolutist kings in Europe, the body of the King becomes the object of protection and security, to be protected and secured in order to preserve peace, unity, and security of Morocco.[7] Since the accession to the throne of King Mohamed VI in 1999, the monarchy has been able to effectively increase the blurring between nation, territorial integrity, and the monarchical system:

> Morocco has a monarchical conception of security, i.e. the primary raison d'être of the security sector is the protection of the monarchical institution. The sector remains a sovereign field in the hands of the King.
>
> Like in most Arab countries, it protects the regime, the leaders, their properties and their privileges. Politics follows security rather than the other

way round. The security sector defines itself as "protector of the nation" but the concept is very vague. [...S]ecurity as a public good and the security sector as an institution [...] are amalgamated.

(ARI, 2009)

A process of official democratization and human rights policies can in fact be traced back to the 1990s as an effort of international legitimacy and the appropriation of a human rights narrative by the late Hassan II, father of the current king (Feliu, 1994). The rebranding of the regime becomes especially successful inside and outside Morocco with a change of face, after the death of King Hassan II and the incumbency of Mohamed VI, presented as a new modern open-minded King committed to a limited process of transitional justice,[8] developing an active economic and development agenda, and later a new constitution to appease social unrest triggered by 2011 regional upheavals. Parallel to this top-down practice of controlled political liberalization, Morocco has often been labeled 'the good student' in a number of issues ranging from environmental policies, to IMF dictates, food security, tourism, the fight against clandestine migrations, or security.[9] In July 2016, the leading African magazine *Jeune Afrique* ran an article entitled "Security: How Morocco has become a reference in counterterrorism matters" (Iraqi, 2016). The article echoed a long worked-for narrative that located Morocco's regime at the spotlight of the global partnership in the GWoT.

The modulation of (in)security domains: a multifaceted approach to counter-terrorism

In the Moroccan context, we find no orthodox process of securitization in the terms explained by ST; as it does not happen outside ordinary politics, it is not triggered by exceptionality. The process is embedded within the meta-narrative of modernization and democratization. The ambiguity between democratization processes, reforms, reinforcement of domination, and an ever-growing process of symbolical symbiosis between the King and its people does not start in 2001, but it is reinforced by the anti-terrorist narrative as exemplified by the monarch's speech a few days after the attacks in Casablanca on May 16, 2003:

My dear people, firmly attached to the constants of their civilization, their sacred institutions and values, and their democratic achievements, I say: terrorism will not pass. Morocco will remain faithful to its international commitments and will continue, under Our leadership, with conviction, assurance and tenacity, the march undertaken to concretize our democratic and modernist societal project.

(Speech of the King Mohammed VI on May 29, 2003)

The security approach has been enhanced in Morocco since the beginning of the twenty-first century by aligning with the global counter-terrorism agenda, especially through four key elements. These elements illustrate the ideational and material interlock that performs the Moroccan reality of (in)securitization:

a   exceptionalism: Morocco as a space of relatively free terrorist attacks
b   the importance of suspected jihadist actors of Moroccan origin operating in Europe and in the Middle East
c   the efficiency and multifaceted approach of counter-terrorism policies; and
d   the cultural and religious background of Morocco

After the Civil War in Algeria, Morocco was presented as an exception, an oasis preserved by the role of the King as commander of the believers. This exceptionalism came to a halt with the events of May 16, 2003. On May 29, 2003, two weeks after the attacks in Casablanca, the King announced the end of laxness. In December 2003, Morocco's most prominent historian proclaimed that "Morocco [was] no longer the Arab exception, no longer protected by the political singularity behind the commander of the believers"[10] (Tozy, 2003). In 2011, a bomb in Argana Restaurant in Marrakech killed 17 people. Official and para-official media, however, as well as government staff keep using the 'Moroccan example of exceptionalism,' especially in regards to the European context, and to the so-called 2nd Front of the War on Terror in the Sahel-Saharan Region (Arieff, 2011). According to the organization Arab Reform Initiative (ARI), this is explained in the official narrative "[…] due to some objective reasons such as its power structure and the existence of moderate religious movements".[11] Alternatively, the attacks in Morocco were possible because "[… the country] was relatively open and had a wider range of personal freedoms than its peer states" (Kalpakian, 2011, p. 9).

The exceptionalism of Morocco's 'peace' is regarded as a product of its stern policies against 'terrorist cells.'[12] These measures effectively draw from a surveillance and intelligence system already in place through peripheral political actors, or even through the social-control mechanisms exerted over individuals by neighbors, co-workers and other fellow citizens in order to prevent moral deviation, a sort of Moroccan version of Foucault's interpretation of Bentham's panopticon (Bouchareb, 2016). The biopolitics of security can be seen in the suspicion raised by certain kinds of beards, or the 2017 prohibition of selling and manufacturing full-body veils (burqa) in Morocco. Islamic deviance represents a crisis of the monopoly of the State/the King's role as the only legitimate source of symbolic and religious values. Aesthetic elements representing *salafiya jihadiya* threaten the values of Moroccan Islam; they threaten 'spiritual security' in the country, as we will later see.

On the other hand, high-tech computer surveillance and big data management overlap in Morocco with the renewed importance of social surveillance and intelligence-gathering within the society. Traditional social control is positively reinforced, not only as a tool for regime domination but as a prevention against terrorism, while it is modernized through new specialized intelligence units such as the newly created *Bureau Central d'Intelligence Judiciaire* (BCIJ). The BCIJ, the most prominent counter-terrorist police unit, has become in fact a high-profile unit, closely followed by media coverage. Its director Abdelhaq Khiame is interviewed frequently in European media and his visibility presents a stark contrast, if only superficial, from the traditional obscurity of security forces.

This official exceptionalism has its counterpart in the high number of Moroccans joining jihadist groups, especially in the Middle East. Official figures counted more than 1,600 Moroccans in armed conflicts in the region by 2016. The enrollment of Moroccans in the Islamic State organization is significant; it is the second largest nationality of origin after the Tunisians. An article on *Foreign Policy* situated Morocco, and more precisely, its Rif Mountains in the North Mediterranean Front, as the "heart of terrorist strikes across the world" (Jacinto, 2016). The Madrid attacks in 2004 were perpetrated by Moroccans, most of them from the Rif.[13] Morocco is one of the main sources of jihadists to conflict zones. This picture has been framed by Morocco not as a weakness but as an actual tool for negotiation and international recognition. In competition with Algeria's information and intelligence capacity on Sahelo-Saharan armed groups – some of which have Algerian leaders – Morocco is also regarded as an intelligence source and is reported to have provided vital information to prevent attacks in different European countries.[14]

The Moroccan approach is however not only developed through hard security. The terrorist threat is explicitly tackled through a comprehensive global approach that includes legal and justice reforms, education, the religious field as well as socio-economic development policies, and the active participation and cooperation at the multilateral level in the 'fight against terrorism.' The approach taken by most Moroccan official discourses internationally and locally is imbued from a security-development nexus. It implies an amalgam of hard security policies and state-building policies and thus encompasses most issues on the Kingdom's agenda on different levels (domestic and regional as well as international). The comprehensive approach is best represented by the view of the Moroccan scholar Moha Ennaji:

> Appropriate laws should be enacted as soon as possible and policies must be implemented to ensure border control, the closure of financing ports, propaganda platforms, anti-addiction, etc. Civil society has to be proactive in countering Daesh and its allies. Counter terrorism should emanate from the inside, in coordination with the outside world, through sensitizing youth, reforming education and media, regional and international cooperation and coordination, and through awareness-raising in families, schools, universities and civil society organizations.
>
> (Ennaji, 2016, p. 9)

This rationale of the counter-terrorist technology encompasses all domains of policy; it modulates all domains of (in)security through the creation of regulatory and capacity instruments. As Bogaert (2018) shows in the case of slums and urban transformation, the danger of conflating terrorism with development is particularly worrying when counter-terrorism becomes the main technology in governing (in)security practices. This security-development nexus has indeed been common practice when security experts or well-intentioned politicians have focused on the origins of violent actors, coming from marginalized ghettos, seeking a way out of poverty and marginalization through radicalized ideologies and "irrational" and "barbaric" violence (Ennaji, 2016). The fight against terrorism, with its core military and police rationale, becomes entangled with development policies and social and economic programs as part of the justification for the government of (in)securities, and is thus managed in a securitized logic[15] (Piazza, 2006; Bogaert 2018). Counter- terrorism thus means upgrading state institutions and policies, as well as mobilizing private and transnational agents, in order to provide a human security that will make sure citizens (only citizens) do not fall into the luring trap of terrorism. The idea of sacrifice that Bigo raises is ever present, against the claim for the need of "[...] a balanced approach that guarantees security without sacrificing basic human rights and freedoms, one that restores confidence in the political process and integrates all groups that renounce violence" (Masbah, 2014).

The fourth feature, indeed a background element for the development of this technology, is that of Morocco's culture of tolerance, protected by the King. The concept of 'aman rouhi' or spiritual security is developed and exported. The so-called wasatiya, the middle way, promotes an open and tolerant Islam that, inscribed in the malikite school, nevertheless accepts and integrates the historical soufi tariqas as part of the 'normal' societal picture. It is in this sense that violent salafism is regarded as a foreign Islam, a 'foreign' but vague characteristic that does not however explicitly point at any national origin, but is not Moroccan, nor African:

> A destabilizing struggle, an undermining work, a work promoted from outside of Africa" [...] "we must revive the original immunity of African Islam. And this through a quality scientific training, as well as by the vulgarization of key notions that make the difference between what is right and what is misguidance.[16]
>
> (Ahmed Taoufiq, former Moroccan Minister of Islamic Affairs and Habous in Dakar, July 29, 2015)

Indeed, the government of the religious field in Morocco entails a more nuanced approach to religious political violence than that of most western regimes. The xenophobic or Islamophobic discourse on the rise in some western societies, alienating citizens with Muslim values, is not plausible in the same way in a Muslim-majority society where the King is the commander of the believers and a descendant of the Prophet Mohammed. The threat comes not from individuals that are alien to the nation, but from alien ideas that make their way onto weak, fragile, frustrated 'children' of the country.

As alluded to earlier, the management of religion by the State has been framed in the last decades through the essential and locally-grown concept of 'spiritual security' (*aman rouhi*). A Turkish term, it was appropriated first by the King in 2009 as it helped define the threat of Shi'ism to the tolerant values of moderate Sunni Islam in Morocco.[17] As a result, Shia conversions were severely punished, and bookstores and schools closed for their Shia tendencies. In the last few years, however, spiritual security has come to signify the goal that moves the regime to counter extremism and terrorism. The 'spiritual security' is promoted through the training of religious guides or spiritual guides (*morcheedat*), imams and other (Harrington, 2013). The statement of a *morcheeda* student for foreign media encapsulated the embodiment of her individual duty vis à vis the GWoT:

> This training doesn't just serve my nation, it has international importance. The West has a bad image of Islam and we have a role in changing that. I swear I am losing sleep when I hear a professor say we are the guardians of this religion.
>
> (Morcheeda student, Meriem Ouardi, to an international reporter,
> (PBS, May 20, 2015)

At the regional level, in 2015 the Institute Mohamed VI started training imams from other African countries in the values and creed of the Moroccan Maliki Islam. Since then, the Institute has trained almost 1,000 students, with 777 scholarships for imams from Mali, Guinea-Conakry, the Ivory Coast, Tunisia, and France via the Union of France's Mosques (UMF).[18] The King also established the Foundation Mohammed VI of African Oulemas in June 2015, in the sacred city of Fez, in order "to serve security, stability and development in Africa," as the Foundation "will work alongside all the religious bodies concerned to fulfill its role of spreading enlightened religious thought and facing the theses of extremism, isolationism and terrorism that some pseudo preachers peddled in the name of Islam, when it has nothing to do with it".[19]

As we can see, 'security' in Morocco is linked not only to the territory, but also to the King and the religious and cultural values he embodies. The concentrated absolutism of (in)security issues in the King is also understood in the mindset of the King being the father and provider of the sense of unity for the territory. The King, through the State and the paternal solace that it provides, is a protector against insecurity and instability. As a result, the King is at once a securitizing actor with a capacity to produce significations and the incarnation of the main referent object or signifier that must be protected. The entrenchment of the King with people's own security has so far prevented demands and social protests such as the 20th February Movement or the Hirak Movement[20] from openly pointing at the removal of the King. At the same time, the hard security approach is very tangible, and counter-terrorist measures are being used to muzzle free media and repress civil society organizations and activists. The repression of civil society as part of routinized domination strategies of the regime is enhanced by the new anti-terrorism technology, be it through the use of new units or intelligence-gathering methods, new legislation, and detention procedures as well as a legitimacy cloak that covers the practices.

A good student is a good teacher

These elements of the technology developed by the Moroccan regime and its elites explained above have obvious implications at the domestic level, in terms of the degree of *extant* governmentality. Nevertheless, the new institutions and the new knowledge that become pervasive and engulf the governing of conduct and minds in Morocco should also be regarded as a contribution to a globalized narrative. In fact, the Moroccan regime uses this anti-terrorism technology in order to push forward its diplomatic agenda. The Moroccan agenda, however, is not necessarily only about (in)securitization but about the accumulation of power of Moroccan elites in the international and transnational arena. It is thus here more about the knowledge power than about the technology as a whole, despite the entanglement of both phenomena.

As we have seen in the previous sections, counter-terrorism configures a narrative in which actions, knowledge, and instruments are built. Counter-terrorism acts as a technology, a catalyzer of discursive and non-discursive acts that configure and reconfigure a certain order of the world and society. It is in this sense that counter-terrorism has also been a technology through which the Moroccan elite has improved its stance at the international and transnational level. The security sector in Morocco has in fact reinforced its police and intelligence collaboration with Spain, Belgium, and France. It has co-chaired the Global Counter Terrorism Forum, has an active participation at the UN Counterterrorism Joint Committee and is a member of the UN Committee on the Counter Terrorism Advisory Board. Morocco, at the promotion of its King, has become the teacher of moderate Islam, and a source of original African and Islamic values.

A specific and relevant case to trace the workings of the counter-terrorist narrative is its embedding in the Western Sahara issue. The Western Sahara (WS) conflict is often portrayed as Morocco's most fundamental and existential issue. It is indeed described in official language as simply the 'national issue' and also seen as an 'inseparable part of the identity of Morocco,' in the King's own words. The area left by Spain in 1975 through the internationally unrecognized Madrid Accords[21] is regarded by Morocco as an integral part of its homeland and its occupation has been a priority since 1975. The de facto annexation is in full speed and currently supported by most U.S. and EU policies, but the recognition of the *marocanité* of the 'southern provinces' by the international community is still unmet. This recognition is indeed one of the main goals in Morocco's diplomatic agenda.[22]

The emergence of the GWoT at first comparatively weakened Morocco's diplomatic relations with the U.S. in particular, as Algeria's alignment gained strategic importance, especially during the Bush administration (2001–2009). The GWoT, however, provided new narrative resources for the Moroccan diplomatic agenda. Morocco has attempted to localize the GWoT narrative by repackaging it for the international community.[23] The failure to do this, directly labeling the Polisario as a terrorist organization, a textual practice that started long before (Solà-Martín, 2006), helps us understand the importance of a broader narrative of state-capacity and resilience. Indeed, the good student can show a record of step-by-step process, a permanent transition towards a modern liberal state that provides stability and national security and that is capable of engaging and becoming a reliable partner in the GWoT. As we see in the case of the Western Sahara issue, the counter-terrorist technology does not stand alone as a macro-securitization strategy. On the contrary, it reinforces and is reinforced by the hegemonic idea that only strong and stable state structures can preserve social order.

The regime is thus a good student as well as a teacher to other African countries, a domestic success story that is ready to be replicated outside, through active cooperation and aid programs in the continent. The export of Morocco's securitization practices and security model in the international arena must be seen also as an increased accumulation of power with consequences at the domestic level. This transfer of power is bidirectional in the sense that a stronger stance in international and regional security networks grants a stronger legitimacy of the (in)securitization practices at the national level.

Conclusions

The preceding demonstrates that the tools and insights revealed by IPS are especially applicable to unpacking the impact of the GWoT in Morocco – its people, its regime, and its position in the international and regional arena – and, potentially, on other non-western states and societies. As such, a Foucauldian-informed sociology and its development for IR through International Political Sociology has proven a useful complement to approach the mechanisms of the counter-terrorist technology. Although some of the concerns raised by scholars in reference to ST's applicability to non-Western societies may also be raised in the case of International Political Sociology and the Paris School, the sociological framework has proven better equipped to comprehend and adequately include other notions of State, identity, and in fact of power-relations and their workings.

The importance of taking into account government-society relations through a sociological framework when tackling counter-terrorism has been illustrated in Morocco's case. A genealogy of power-relations that takes into account a longer cycle than the western-imposed 9/11 narrative helps us better grasp the local effects and impacts of this GWoT narrative in contexts where unaccountable and exceptional practices are routinized historical features of power. In fact, in the case of Morocco, we found that the hegemonic anti-terrorist narrative exacerbates authoritarian measures by providing an internationally-sanctioned technology of securitization. The investment in developing anti-terrorism as a technology of securitization also configures the position and acts of bodies and individuals within a given power-relation.

In this sense, the anti-terrorist technology of securitization shapes not only security institutions and their policy implementation, but also the representations of the King himself and of Moroccans and their peers. The dominant security narrative in Morocco is constructed by discursive elements and non-discursive elements that go beyond the political elite and that are diffused in societal power relations. (In)security practices are reproduced and diffused even without a direct speech-act but nevertheless reinforcing the securitization and authoritarianism of the Moroccan state. Practices are not only derived from a controlled, centrally-designed narrative, and while most could be seen as the promotion of a certain hegemonic take on reality that helps the State justify securitization moves, the top-down securitization by political mechanisms does not explain all micro-securitizations of social relations. The development of certain security technologies in Morocco arise from an intersubjective construction of the terrorist threat.

Moving beyond the socio-linguistic approach of securitization studies can be useful to academics willing to approach security in the Global South without a fixed set of models and ontological underpinnings. The sociological lens enables the study of the historical continuities of political violence and repression, and will help us improve the understanding of how (in)security technologies work in a more nuanced understanding of the world. The task is challenging and demands an important level of societal and area expertise with no warranted ready-made answers (maybe not even questions). It is however essential that we undertake this task as a means of obtaining a deeper and more nuanced understanding of terrorism and counter-terrorism as mechanisms for securitization.

Notes

1 I will use the acronym GWoT to refer to the global narrative and practices that construe the current hegemonic technologies of (in)security in reference to terrorism. Although the expression Global War on Terrorism or on Terror has been disputed, rejected, or redefined as a fight or a struggle instead of a war, I choose to stick to the most common label of the ongoing phenomenon notwithstanding specific modifications of its linguistic formulation.

2 The Copenhagen School, the Welsh or Aberystwyth School, and the Paris School are among the commonly cited approaches that argue for critical security studies. Didier Bigo, one of the authors of the Paris School, has lately denied this division in different schools, suggesting that IPS as proposed by the Paris School is simply complementary and building up on other academic developments, especially from the Copenhagen School. See Bigo and McCluskey, 2018.

3 The collective included: Claudia Aradau, Thierry Balzacq, Tugba Basaran, Didier Bigo, Philippe Bonditti, Christian Büger, Stephan Davidshofer, Xavier Guillaume, Emmanuel-Pierre Guittet, Jef Huysmans, Julien Jeandesboz, Matti Jutila, Luis Lobo-Guerrero, Tara McCormack, Maria Mälksoo, Andrew Neal, Christian Olsson, Karen Lund Petersen, Francesco Ragazzi, Yelda S' ahin Akilli, Holger Stritzel, Rens van Munster, Trine Villumsen, Ole Wæver, and Michael C. Williams.

4 See on the use of CDA on terrorism for example (Atkinson, 2015; Baker-Beall, 2009; Bartolucci, 2014; Bartolucci & Gallo, n.d.; Jackson, 2007, 2011a; Tsui, 2014).

5 Some exceptions for Morocco are the works developed by Valentina Bartolucci or Konrad Bogaert.

6 Translated by the author from the Spanish version: "*recepción de ideas procedentes de culturas hegemónicas (democracia, derechos humanos) no se hace sin una alteración del sentido original*" "*los mecanismos de dominación incluyen un juego de*

palabras que establece equivalencias entre una realidad arcaica y su expresión institucional moderna (Majzen/monarquía constitucional, súbdito/ciudadano)."

 7 In 1970 the new constitution incorporates the conception that the King is "the supreme representative of the Nation," a linkage that according to Claisse, does not come from Islamic tradition nor from European constitutional law, but rather from 18th century monarchical theories in Europe (1987, p. 39).

 8 The creation of the Equity and Reconciliation Commission (E&R) in 2004 brought the opportunity to shed light on the abuses and human rights violations of the past decades committed by the regime, albeit with no victimizers brought to justice and thousands of potential individuals being excluded for administrative reasons. The Commission had the explicit "prohibition of 'invoking individual responsibility'," and it was made clear that it "should play no role in criminal prosecutions" (Hayner, 2011, p. 43).

 9 For examples of this see www.courrierinternational.com/grand-format/infographie-le-maroc-hote-bon-eleve-de-la-cop22; http://telquel.ma/2017/02/21/liberte-economique-le-maroc-bon-eleve-malgre-les-faiblesse-de-sa-justice_1536311; http://aujourdhui.ma/economie/securite-alimentaire-le-maroc-bon-eleve; http://aujourdhui.ma/economie/tourisme-en-afrique-le-maroc-bon-eleve-123039; www.leseco.ma/business/4992-infrastructures-le-maroc-bon-eleve.html; www.leseco.ma/economie/4490-le-maroc-en-bon-eleve-du-fmi.html; https://ledesk.ma/encontinu/le-maroc-bon-eleve-dans-la-lutte-contre-limmigration-clandestine/).

10 Translated by the author from French: "*Le Maroc ne constitue plus l'exception arabe, il n'est plus protégé par singularité politique derrière un commandeur des croyants.*"

11 On the conference about SSR held in Rabat in 2009. Retrieved from http://ari-3.eweev.com/en/node/959.

12 In February 2017, Mohamed Moufakir, General Director of International Cooperation at the Interior Ministry, announced that there had been 169 terrorist cells dismantled in Morocco since 2001, 2,963 individuals detained and more than 341 criminal plots aborted. *Le360* (avec MAP). (2017, February 10). Démantèlement de 168 cellules terroristes au Maroc depuis septembre 2001.. Retrieved from: http://fr.le360.ma/politique/demantelement-de-168-cellules-terroristes-au-maroc-depuis-septembre-2001-107325.

13 The Rif is a predominantly amazic-speaking region in the North of Morocco. Home of nationalist Abdelkrim Khattabi, it has traditionally been regarded as a rebel region and has suffered a long history of repression, upheavals, isolation, and discrimination.

14 It is the case for the capture of Abdelhamid Abaaoud, suspected leader of the Paris attacks of November 13, 2015. *France24*. (2015, November 20). Attentats de Paris: le rôle du Maroc dans la localisation d'Abdelhamid Abaaoud. Retrieved from www.france24.com/fr/20151120-attaques-paris-role-maroc-abdelhamid-abaaoud-renseignements-france-paris-raba (Accessed September 3, 2018).

15 This process is taking place within a phase of roll-out neoliberalism (Bogaert, 2018) whereby the state acts as a media for private agents who effectively benefit from this modulation of (in)security domains, among them the royal family.

16 Translated by the author from French: "*[...] déséquilibre, destabilisateur, un travail du sape, un travail animé de l'étranger de l'afrique*" il faut reanimer l'immunité orginal de l'islam africain. Et ce par une formation scientifique de qualité, ainsi que par la vulgarisation de notions clés qui Font la différence entre ce qui est juste et ce qui est égarement.*"

17 This was the time that Hizbollah was becoming extremely popular for its sole opposition to the State of Israel and the rise in sympathy for the Shiite movement was at its highest in Morocco and throughout the region. See Yahyaoui, Y. (2013, May 7). On the thesis of spiritual security in Morocco (*'an 'utruhat al'amn alruwhii bialmaghrib*). *Al Jazeera Arabic*. Retrieved from www.aljazeera.net/knowledgegate/opinions/2013/5/7/%D8%B9%D9%86-%D8%A3%D8%B7%D8%B1%D9%88%D8%AD%

D8%A9-%D8%A7%D9%84%D8%A3%D9%85%D9%86-%D8%A7%D9%84%D8%
B1%D9%88%D8%AD%D9%8A-%D8%A8%D8%A7%D9%84%D9%85%D8%BA%
D8%B1%D8%A8.

18 Website of the Ministry of the Habous and Islamic Affairs. Available at www.habous.
gov.ma/fr/institut-mohammed-vi-pour-la-formation-des-imams,-morchidines-et-
morchidatesi.html. Last accessed May 3, 2017.

19 The translation was made by the author from the official French version of the Speech
by the King Mohammed VI at the occasion of the Ceremonial Establishment of the
Higher Council of the Mohammed VI Foundation of the African Oulémas (Published
on Wednesday June 15, 2016). Last accessed May 25, 2017. www.habous.gov.ma/fr/
fondation-mohammed-vi-des-oul%C3%A9ma-africains/579-articles-fr/3475-sm-le-
roi-prononce-un-discours-%C3%A0-l-occasion-de-la-c%C3%A9r%C3%A9monie-
d%E2%80%99installation-du-conseil-sup%C3%A9rieur-de-la-fondation-mohammed-
vi-des-oul%C3%A9mas-africains.html. The French excerpt reads:

> Nous estimons que la Fondation Mohammed VI des Oulémas africains est un
> cadre pour la coopération et l'échange des expériences et la coordination des
> efforts entre les Oulémas pour qu'ils puissent remplir le devoir qui leur incombe
> de faire connaître l'image réelle de la religion tolérante de l'Islam et de promou-
> voir ses valeurs que sont la modération, la tolérance et la volonté de coexistence,
> et afin que la Fondation soit au service de la sécurité, de la stabilité et du dévelop-
> pement en Afrique. // Nous sommes convaincu que cette Fondation, à travers ses
> différentes filiales dans les pays africains, œuvrera aux côtés de toutes les
> instances religieuses concernées, à remplir le rôle qui lui revient de répandre la
> pensée religieuse éclairée et de faire face aux thèses d'extrémisme, de repli sur soi
> et de terrorisme que certains pseudo-prédicateurs colportent au nom de l'Islam,
> alors que celui-ci n'a rien à voir avec elles.

20 The 20th February Movement is the name given to the social movement that organized
the demonstrations and protests that took to the streets in 2011 in Morocco. The Hirak is
the movement that took to the streets in Alhuceimas and other towns of the Northern Rif
region, especially during 2017, and that was met with violent repression and resulted in
hundreds of activists being imprisoned with harsh judicial sentences. El Malki, F. Z.
(June 2, 2017). Morocco's Hirak movement: The people versus the Makhzen. *Jadaliyya.*
Retrieved from www.jadaliyya.com/Details/34330/Morocco%60s-Hirak-Movement-
The-People-Versus-the-Makhzen. Last accessed September 3, 2018.

21 The Madrid Accords negotiated the end of the Spanish presence in the territory and
divided the former Spanish Sahara between Morocco and Mauritania. The Accords
are not recognized by international law and so has the United Nations expressed it.
The Western Sahara continues to be regarded as a non-sovereign territory, awaiting
formal decolonization, with its de facto administering power being Morocco.

22 On this issue see for example Feliu, 2016; Fernández-Molina, 2016; Zunes &
Mundy, 2010.

23 See Acharya for a discussion on the localization of international norms in Asia
(2004).

Bibliography

Acharya, A. (1997). The periphery as the core: The Third World and security studies. In
K. Krause & M. C. Williams (Eds.), *Critical security studies* (pp. 299–328). London:
UCL Press.

Acharya, A. (2004). How ideas spread: Whose norms matter? Norm localization and
institutional change in Asian regionalism. *International Organization, 58*(2), 239–275.
doi:10.1017/S0020818304582024

Arab Reform Initiative (ARI). (2009). ARI working group report. Published September 21, 2009. Available at: www.arab-reform.net/event/ari-working-group-report/

Arieff, A. (2011, July). Morocco: Current issues. Washington, D.C.: U.S. Library of Congress, Congressional Research Service.

Atkinson, C. (2015). *Tracing the discourses of terrorism: Identity, genealogy and the state*, by Ondrej Ditrych. *Critical Studies on Terrorism, 8*(2), 332–335. doi:10.1080/17 539153.2015.1049462

Ayoob, M. (1991). The security problematic of the Third World. *World Politics, 43*(2), 257–283. doi:10.2307/2010473

Ayoob, M. (1997). Defining security: A subaltern realist perspective. In K. Krause & M. C. Williams (Eds.), *Critical Security Studies* (pp. 121–146). London: UCL Press.

Ayoob, M. (2002). Inequality and theorizing in international relations: The case for subaltern realism. *International Studies Review, 4*(3), 27–48.

Ayoob, M. (2010). Making sense of global tensions: Dominant and subaltern conceptions of order and justice. *International Studies Review, 47*(2–4), 129–141. doi:10.1177/002088171104700405

Baker-Beall, C. (2009). The discursive construction of EU counter-terrorism policy: Writing the "migrant other", securitisation and control. *Journal of Contemporary European Research, 5*(2), 188–206. Retrieved from www.jcer.net/index.php/jcer/article/view/161

Balzacq, T., Basaran, T., Bigo, D., Guittet, E.-P., & Olson, C. (2010, January). Security practices. *International Studies Encyclopedia Online.* doi:10.1111/b.9781444336597.2010.x

Barkawi, T., & Laffey, M. (2006, May). The postcolonial moment in security studies. *Review of International Studies, 32*, 329–352. doi:10.1017/S0260210506007054

Bartolucci, V. (2010). Analysing elite discourse on terrorism and its implications: The case of Morocco. *Critical Studies on Terrorism, 3*(1), 119–135. doi:10.1080/17539151003594269

Bartolucci, V. (2014). Security vs. liberty: The discourse on terrorism in the United States and Morocco and its societal effects. *Democracy and Security, 10*(1), 1–21. doi.org/10.1080/17419166.2013.819782

Bartolucci, V., & Gallo, G. (2013). Terrorism, system thinking and critical discourse analysis. *Systems Research and Behavioral Science, 32*(1), 15–27. doi:10.1002/sres.2206

Behrent, M. C. (2013). Foucault and technology. *History and Technology, 29*(1), 54–104. doi:10.1080/07341512.2013.780351

Berling, T. V. (2012). Bourdieu, international relations, and European security. *Theory and Society, 41*(5), 451–478. doi:10.1007/s11186-012-9175-7

Bigo, D. (2005). La mondialisation de l'(in)securité? *Cultures & Conflits, 58.* doi:10.3917/lig.712.0071.

Bigo, D. (2008a). Globalized (in)security: The field and the ban-opticon. *Terror, Insecurity and Liberty. Illiberal Practices of Liberal Regimes after 9/11,* 10–48. doi:10.4324/9780203926765

Bigo, D. (2008b). International political sociology. In P. D. Williams (Ed.), *Security studies: An introduction* (pp. 116–130). London & New York: Routledge.

Bigo, D. (2008c). Sociologie politique de l'international: Une alternative (French). *Cultures & Conflits, Articles i.*

Bigo, D. (2011a). Pierre Bourdieu and international relations: Power of practices, practices of power. *International Political Sociology, 5*(3), 225–258. doi:10.1111/j.1749-5687.2011.00132.x

Bigo, D. (2011b). Le "nexus" sécurité, frontière, immigration: Programme et diagramme. *Cultures & Conflits, 84,* 7–12.

Bigo, D. (2016). International political sociology: Rethinking the international through dynamics of power. In T. Basaran, D. Bigo, E.-P. Guittet & R. B. J. Walker (Eds.). *Transversal Lines*. International Political Sociology series. London & New York: Routledge.

Bigo, D., & McCluskey, E. (2018). Chapter 9: What is a Paris approach to (in)securitization? Political anthropological research for international sociology. In A. Gheciu & W. C. Wohlforth (Eds.), *The Oxford Handbook of International Security*. Oxford: Oxford University Press.

Bogaert, K. (2018). *Globalized authoritarianism: Megaprojects, slums, and class relations in urban Morocco*. Globalization and Community series. Vol. 27. Minneapolis/London: University of Minnesota Press.

Bouchareb, H. (2016, May 24). L'article 222, Foucault et le Maréchal Lyautey. *Huffpost*. Retrieved from www.huffpostmaghreb.com/hatim-bouchareb/larticle-222-foucault-et-le-marechal-lyautey_b_10654304.html

Buzan, B. (2006). Will the "Global War on Terrorism" be the new Cold War? *International Affairs, 82*(6), 1101–1118.

Buzan, B., & Little, R. (2001). Why international relations has failed as an intellectual project and what to do about it. *Millennium: Journal of International Studies, 30*(1), 19–39. doi:10.1177/03058298010300010401

Buzan, B., & Wæver, O. (2009). Macrosecuritisation and security constellations: Reconsidering scale in securitization theory. *Review of International Studies, 35*, 253–276. doi:10.1017/S0260210509008511

Buzan, B., Wæver, O., & de Wilde, J. (1998). *Security: A new framework for analysis*. Boulder, CO: Lynne Rienner Publishers.

C.A.S.E. Collective. (2006). Critical approaches to security in Europe: A networked manifesto. *Security Dialogue, 37*(4), 443–487. doi:10.1177/0967010606073085

Claisse, A. (1987). Chapter 2: Makhzen traditions and administrative channels. In W. I. Zartman (Ed.), *The political economy of Morocco* (pp. 34–58). New York, Westport, London: Paeger Publishers.

Chandler, D. (2008). Review essay: Human security: The dog that didn't bark. *Security Dialogue, 39*(4), 427–438. doi:10.1177/0967010608094037

Chandler, D. (2010). *International statebuilding: The rise of post-liberal governance*. London & New York: Routledge. Retrieved from http://samples.sainsburysebooks.co.uk/9781136940491_sample_864464.pdf

Charbonneau, B., & Jourde, C. (2016). *Les dilemmes de la résolution des conflits face aux défis de la "guerre au terrorisme."* Montréal: Chaire Raoul-Dandurand en études stratégiques et diplomatiques | UQAM.

Duffield, M. (2005). Getting savages to fight barbarians: Development, security and the colonial present. *Conflict, Security & Development, 5*(2), 141–159. doi:10.1080/14678800500170068

Ennaji, M. (2016). Recruitment of foreign male and female fighters to Jihad: Morocco's multifaceted counter-terror strategy. *International Review of Sociology, 26*(3), 546–557. doi:10.1080/03906701.2016.1244954

Eriksson, J., & Rhinard, M. (2009). The internal–external security nexus: Notes on an emerging research agenda. *Cooperation and Conflict, 44*(3), 243–267. doi:10.1177/0010836709106215

Feliu, L. (1994). *Els drets humans al Marroc. Un instrument polític més enllà de tota ètica*. Barcelona: Universitat Autònoma de Barcelona.

Feliu, L. (2016). Estados Unidos y la cuestión del Sahara Occidental. In I. Barreñada & R. Ojeda García (Eds.), Sahara Occidental, 40 años después (pp. 205–220). Madrid: Catarata.

Feliu, L., & Izquierdo Brichs, F. (2016). Estructura de poder y desafíos populares. La respuesta del régimen marroquí al movimiento 20 de febrero. *Revista de Estudios Políticos, 174*, 195–223.

Feliu, L., & Parejo, M. Á. (2012). Morocco: The reinvention of a totalitarian system. In F. Izquierdo Brichs (Ed.), *Power and regimes in the contemporary Arab world*. London: Routledge.

Feliu Martínez, L. (2017). El concepto de terrorismo en España y la Unión Europea. Implicaciones para el derecho. In *España y la Unión Europea en el orden internacional: XXVI Jornadas ordinarias de la Asociación Española de Profesores de Derecho internacional y Relaciones internacionales, Universidad de Sevilla, 15 y 16 de octubre de 2015* (pp. 499–522). Valencia: Tirant lo Blanch.

Fernández-Molina, I. (2016). *Moroccan foreign policy under Mohammed VI, 1999–2014*. Oxon & New York: Routledge.

Harrington, S. (2013, December 12). Women provide 'spiritual security' in Morocco. *Reuters*. Retrieved from http://news.trust.org//item/20131212010325-jkva6/

Hayner, P. B. (2011). *Unspeakable truths: Transitional justice and the challenge of truth commissions*. London & New York: Routledge.

Hermann, E. S. & Chomsky, N. (1988). *Manufacturing consent: The political economy of mass media*. New York: Pantheon Books.

Howard, T. (2010). Failed states and the spread of terrorism in sub-Saharan Africa. *Studies in Conflict & Terrorism, 33*(11), 960–988. doi:10.1080/1057610X.2010.514696

Huysmans, J. (1998). Security! What do you mean? *European Journal of International Relations, 4*(2), 226–255.

Huysmans, J. (2006). *The politics of insecurity: Fear, migration, and asylum in the EU*. London: Routledge.

Iraqi, F. (2016, July 7). Sécurité: comment le Maroc est devenu une référence en matière d'antiterrorisme. *Jeune Afrique*. Retrieved from www.jeuneafrique.com/mag/336594/politique/securite-maroc-devenu-reference-matiere-dantiterrorisme/

Izquierdo Brichs, F. (2012). Political regimes in the Arab world: Society and the exercise of power, *317*. doi:10.4324/9780203102626

Izquierdo Brichs, F. (2016). *Poder global y teoria de RRII*. Barcelona: Bellaterra.

Jacinto, L. (2016, April 7). Morocco's outlaw country is the heartland of global terrorism. *Foreign Policy*. Retrieved from https://foreignpolicy.com/2016/04/07/the-rif-connection-belgium-brussels-morocco-abdeslam/

Jackson, R. (2005). *Writing the war on terrorism: Language, politics and counter-terrorism*. Manchester: Manchester University Press.

Jackson, R. (2007). An analysis of EU counterterrorism discourse post-September 11. *Cambridge Review of International Affairs, 20*(2), 233–247. doi:10.1080/09557570701414617

Jackson, R. (2011). Culture, identity and hegemony: Continuity and (the lack of) change in US counterterrorism policy from Bush to Obama. *International Politics, 48*(2–3), 390–411. doi:10.1057/ip. 2011.5

Jackson, R., Gunning, J., & Smith, M. B. (2007, August 30–September 2). The case for critical terrorism studies. *Annual Meeting of the American Political Science Association*. Copyright by the American Political Science Association.

Kalpakian, J. (2011, May 13). *Current Moroccan anti-terrorism policy*. Real Instituto Elcano, 89. Available online at www.files.ethz.ch/isn/142915/E_ARI_89-2011_Kalpakian_Morrocan_anti-Terrorism_Policy.pdf. Last accessed June 4, 2019.

Masbah, M. (2014, April 10). Moroccan fighters in Syria. *The Carnegie Middle East Center*. Retrieved from http://carnegie-mec.org/sada/55313?lang=en

Meli, M. C. (2014). El Derecho Penal Antiterrorista Español Y La Armonización Penal. *Revista Justiça E Sistema Criminal, 6*(10), 45–72.

Parejo Fernández, M. A. (2009). *Viejos y nuevos defensores del trono. La metamorfosis del autoritarismo marroquí.* Asociación Española de Ciencia Politica y de la Administración. Available online at: https://aecpa.es/files/congress/9/actas/grupos-trabajo/area07/GT02/11.pdf. Last accessed June 4, 2019.

PBS NewsHour. (2015, May 20). Morocco trains female spiritual guides to fight extremism and empower women [video and transcript]. *PBS News Hour.* Retrieved from www.pbs.org/newshour/bb/morocco-trains-female-spiritual-guides-fight-extremism-empower-women/#transcript.

Piazza, J. A. (2006). Rooted in poverty? Terrorism, poor economic development, and social cleavages. *Terrorism and Political Violence, 18*(1), 159–177. doi:10.1080/095465590944578

Ramsay, G. (2015). Why terrorism can, but should not be defined. *Critical Studies on Terrorism, 9153* [July], 1–18. doi:10.1080/17539153.2014.988452

Richmond, O. P., & Tellidis, I. (2012). The complex relationship between peacebuilding and terrorism approaches: Towards post-terrorism and a post-liberal peace? *Terrorism and Political Violence, 24*(1), 120–143. doi:10.1080/09546553.2011.628720

Silke, A., & Schmidt-Petersen, J. (2017). The Golden Age? What the 100 most cited articles in terrorism studies tell us. *Terrorism and Political Violence, 29*(4), 692–712. doi:10.1080/09546553.2015.1064397.

Sjoberg, L. (2009). Feminist interrogations of terrorism/terrorism studies. *International Relations, 23*(1), 69–74. doi:10.1177/0047117808100611

Solà-Martín, A. (2006). *United Nations mission for the referendum in Western Sahara.* New York & Wales: Edwin Mellen Press.

Stewart, F. (2004). Development and security. *Conflict, Security & Development, 4*(3), 261–288.

Tilly, C. (2004). Terror, terrorism, terrorists. *Sociological Theory. 22*(1), 5–13. doi:10.1111/j.1467-9558.2004.00200.x

Toros, H. (2017). "9/11 is alive and well" or how critical terrorism studies has sustained the 9/11 narrative. *Critical Studies on Terrorism, 10*(2), 1–17. doi:10.1080/17539153.2017.1337326

Tozy, M. (1999). *Monarquía e Islam Político en Marruecos* (Biblioteca). Barcelona: Bellaterra.

Tozy, M. (2003). La fin de l'exception Marocaine L'Islamisme Marocain face au défi du salafisme. *Idées, Afkar, 1,* 63–67. Retrieved from www.iemed.org/observatori/arees-danalisi/arxius-adjunts/afkar/afkar-ideas-1/TOZY frcorr.pdf

Tsui, C-K. (2014). *Tracing the discursive origins of the war on terror: President Clinton and the construction of new terrorism in the post-Cold War era.* Retrieved from https://ourarchive.otago.ac.nz/handle/10523/4771

Tsui, C-K. (2015). Framing the threat of catastrophic terrorism: Genealogy, discourse and President Clinton's counterterrorism approach. *International Politics, 52*(1), 66–88.

Walter, C. (2003). Defining terrorism in national and international law. In C. Walter, S. Vöneky, V. Röben, & F. Schorkopf (Eds.), *Terrorism as a challenge for national and international law: Security versus liberty?* Berlin/Heidelberg: Springer.

Wilkinson, C. (2007). The Copenhagen School on tour in Kyrgyzstan: Is securitization theory useable outside Europe? *Security Dialogue, 38*(1), 5–25. doi:10.1177/0967010607075964

Zunes, S., & Mundy, J. (2010). *Western Sahara.* Syracuse: Syracuse University Press.

4 When advocacy securitizes

Non-state actors and the circulation of narratives around sexualized violence in conflict

Natalie Florea Hudson and
Alexandra Cosima Budabin

Introduction

Despite the passing of UNSCR 1325 by the UN Security Council, the scourge of sexual and gender based violence (SGBV) was neglected in major episodes of violence and conflict in the early 2000s. UNSCR 1325 culminated in a decade of international efforts to put women's rights and gender equality on the international peace and security agenda, and represented a significant securitizing move for women's experiences in armed conflict (Hudson, 2009a). In light of the weak consideration given to the resolution within official circles, it became evident that greater political will was needed to convince state-based security actors of this real and urgent threat. Indeed, one UN official described the years following 1325 as being at a "standstill" in which "we are all still trying to figure out how to move the agenda forward."[1] We argue that this political will was generated by the entry of new actors and audiences into the field of security. Looking at the case of advocacy around the SGBV situation in Congo, we show how non-state actors–activists, advocacy organizations, and celebrities adopted security discourses as a way of putting pressure on official mainstream security actors. This included the promulgation of a simplifying narrative, which narrowed women's experience with violence during armed conflict to strategic rape as a weapon of war, and gained traction with mass audiences.

How were these unofficial voices able to find entry points inside traditional security spaces to advance the WPS agenda? To what extent was this outsider engagement a contributing factor to further securitizing SGBV? This chapter takes up these questions, and in doing so, considers the ways in which western advocacy efforts, both in official and unofficial circles, broaden how we think about securitization, especially in terms of the question of who counts as securitizing actors and audiences. The focus on non-state actors and the issue of SGBV allows us to revisit securitization theory and provide a critical examination of its application to actors and issues of international relations that are often marginalized. Using the case of SGBV in Congo, we show how, starting in 2007, the 'strategic rape' narrative functioned as a security discourse that resulted in new gains in policy and political practice. By 2008–2009, the UN Security Council adopted a series of resolutions focusing specifically on sexualized violence; this period manifested the idea of women as consumers, drivers, owners, and subjects of security, and the WPS Agenda becoming the policy framework that shaped official responses to conflict-related harms experienced by women (Swaine, 2018). Adopting a security lens, we argue that rather than being solely the purview of state-centric actors, security discourses can be effectively adopted by new actors and audiences in ways that count as securitizing moves.

In order to situate the study of new actors and new audiences in securitization processes, this chapter begins by briefly examining traditional understandings of securitization. Then we offer our framework for analyzing actors, audiences, and security discourses. This research adopts a mixed method approach to capture how external and unofficial actors engaged with security discourses in order to strategically frame sexual violence in conflict for both mass and elite audiences.[2] Combining narrative analysis with a security lens, we show how messaging and communication strategies of unofficial actors serve as advocacy narratives that adopt security discourses in order to gain resonance both inside and outside mainstream security circles. Our case study is then laid out as follows: we distinguish three phases in the securitization process addressing the threat of SGBV in conflict in reference to the situation in the Democratic Republic of Congo.[3] We identify and discuss the interactions between new and old actors along with popular audiences.[4] Our data is drawn from media coverage, films, websites, campaign materials, reports, and semi-structured interviews with over 30 humanitarian practitioners, human rights advocates, and representatives of intergovernmental organizations in New York, London, Washington, D.C., and Boston from 2015–2017.

This work draws from existing scholarship on security studies, the expanding role of non-state actors in global governance, and the study of advocacy around SGBV. While some scholarship has examined the impact of legal processes on the securitization of sexual violence (Hirschauer, 2014) and of institutional shifts on the securitization of women's rights (Hudson, 2009b), a comprehensive understanding of the wider range of cultural, social and media-related activities by unofficial actors is lacking. There are gaps in our understanding of the actors and audience who were part of the discursive environment that grappled with SGBV in conflict-affected areas. To address these gaps, our analysis looks at official and unofficial actors as a means to better understand the interplay between cultural discourse and global politics in everyday life (Shepherd, 2012). Our case study deepens scholarship around why western activists, government officials, and international organizations have come to focus on the DRC above other cases (Coley, 2013). We also furnish new perspectives on how the narrative about rape in war became dominant, thus shaping policy shifts in the UN arena.[5] While this chapter does not discuss the ultimate impact of the security policies, we stress that the 'success' of these new securitizing actors in using particular advocacy narratives does not necessarily translate to effective measures dealing with SGBV. In the conclusion, we will consider what this means for security, especially regarding the limitations of advocacy narratives and the often problematic interventions by unofficial actors.

Applying securitization theory to advocacy around SGBV: prospects and problems

This research builds on securitization studies by drawing on analytical tools from political science, communications, social movement theory and human rights studies to better understand how advocacy uses a security lens, in what ways and to what effect. This multidisciplinary approach allows us to build on this literature in three ways that complicate the *who*, the *audience*, and the *where* of securitization practices. In this way, we adopt securitization theory as a "tool for practical security analysis" (Taureck, 2006, p. 53) in looking at the actors and narratives involved in raising attention and shaping policy-making around SGBV.

Securitizing discourses and processes

Discourses form the heart of security analysis, providing a way of understanding the material and symbolic effects of (re)presentations of security 'threats' as well as the effectiveness of responses. At its core, securitization is about the speech act – "the *word* 'security' is the act; the utterance is the primary reality" (Wæver, 1995, p. 55). Security, as a speech act, is "the move that takes politics beyond the established rules of the game and frames the issue either as a special kind of politics or as above politics" (Buzan, Wæver, & de Wilde, 1998, p. 23). According to Austin (1962, pp. 95, 107), certain statements do more than merely describe a given reality, and, while they cannot be determined as true or false, they can be perceived as such.

This understanding of the social construction of an issue has been effectively studied through the narrative analysis of the messages and communications of advocates and policy makers. For example, in their work on policy narratives, Shanahan, Jones, and McBeth distinguish the populating characters – hero, villain, beneficiary, allies, and opponents – as well as literary elements like setting and plot that combine to create moving story lines; crucially for a narrative used in the realm of advocacy, the "moral of the story" will encapsulate the policy solution or ask (2011, pp. 335–336). Thus, we see the discursive debates around issues like SGBV from diverse actors – both official and unofficial – as persuasive techniques using narratives that push state actors, as potential allies, to "do something." Paying attention to the power dynamics across different types of actors and audiences will guide thinking in how and when security discourses become accepted and implemented. When and how security discourses become convincing (and to whom) may help explain why certain conflicts and issue areas do not rise to the same level of consideration as others, also a key concern for human rights advocates.

Conventional thinking points to authoritative structures as the space where security happens. Along these lines, Wæver (1995) maintains that even a widened conceptualization of security like that of the Copenhagen School (CS) cannot be understood outside the context of authoritative structures of the state, most especially those of national security, such as the police or military.[6] For many, security as a speech act occurs in structured institutions where some actors are in positions of power by being generally accepted voices of security, and by having the power to define it. Thus, securitization is considered to be a power-laden, historically informed process that carries with it certain entrenched connotations related to notions of defense and institutions, like the military, the state, and nonstate actors recognized by the state. We challenge these assumptions by highlighting the ways in which discourses by unofficial actors can constitute securitizing moves that lead to changes in policy and implementation. The case in this chapter complicates thinking about *who* counts as a securitizing actor.

Gendered limits of securitization

The case of SGBV also reveals other limitations in securitization theory, in particular the presence of a gendered bias in the construction of voice. Lene Hansen's work is especially relevant here, particularly her insight that the securitization process operates under the (problematic) assumption that a speech act is in fact possible or equally available to all.[7] The experiences of women in armed conflict settings are often made invisible, and much of gender-based insecurity occurs in the private realm disconnected from (or ignored by) public discourse.[8] Hansen (2000) characterizes this barrier to gendering securitization as "security as silence," in which insecurity simply cannot be voiced because "raising something as a security problem is impossible or might even aggravate the threat being faced" (p. 287). Furthermore, securitization limits the speech act to verbal communication, and as feminists have long argued, communication is much more than verbal; it is often bodily and visual (Butler, 1997). From a feminist perspective, there is a blurring between public and private, and by extension official and unofficial – a distinction heretofore not accounted for by securitization theory.

While focusing on advocacy organizations and other non-state actors is nothing new for international relations or human rights scholarship (Nelson & Dorsey, 2008; Wong, 2012), within the realm of securitization theory it has the potential to shed light on how marginalized voices can and do engage in the process.[9] Within the strictures established by the Copenhagen School, marginal voices must adopt discourses that resonate with mainstream security circles, making it seemingly imperative for women's advocates to find entry points into policy-making circles. Going through the transnational advocacy community to influence national policy seems one of the few options available to organizations and activists in shaping international norms (Keck & Sikkink, 1998). To this end, the relationship between securitization as theory and process and international advocacy and activism is a compelling one, even in light of Hansen's important critiques. Securitization allows for the exploration of how security discourses are performed and what constraints or obstacles emerge for those involved. In the larger security studies debate, "it becomes apparent that what is at stake is not simply the question of whether the concept of security should be expanded or not, but how certain threats achieve such a political saliency that they become the subject of security policies" (Hansen, 2000, p. 306).

Revisiting securitization actors and audiences

As noted above, the study of securitization has focused on discourses emanating from state actors and institutions. Assumptions circulate on *who* possesses the power to securitize. Previous accounts of securitizing agents were "often reduced to the professionals of politics, such as the government, parliament, or the extra-parliamentarian opposition" (Balzacq, Basaran, Bigo, Guittet, & Olson, 2010, p. 2). This failed to take into account the myriad non-professional actors within and outside official settings who operate with some degree of authority and legitimacy that should be considered potential securitizing actors. Increasingly visible and influential in the field of global governance, we now recognize that non-state actors "have taken on authoritative roles and functions in the international system" addressing issues "traditionally and exclusively, associated with the state" (Hall & Bierstecker, 2002, p. 4). While there is some scholarship on non-state actors as securitizing agents in securitization, it is a more recent phenomenon (Dalaqua, 2013).

Within global civil society, non-state actors have been successful in persuading state actors to adopt new ideas or emerging norms. Finnemore and Sikkink conceptualized these actors as norm entrepreneurs, who can be either political and social actors who use expressive acts, such as speeches, letters, interviews, books, films, and photographs to raise awareness about issues and to 'frame' them in ways likely to elicit interest and concern from various bodies and suggest a course of action to take (Finnemore & Sikkink, 1998, p. 897).[10] The ultimate goal of norm entrepreneurs is to institutionalize favored courses of action in the form of norms accepted and adhered to by relevant parties.[11] Norm promotion and entrepreneurship may be undertaken by state and non-state actors, including advocacy organizations, celebrities, and filmmakers (see Keck & Sikkink, 1998; Lanz, 2011; Budabin, 2015; Majic, 2017).

While international and national policy-makers may be the target of securitization moves by non-state actors, approaches vary across different types of advocates. First, there are advocates who operate within the UN system and closely with official actors; this group is made up of established NGOs and networks who attain ECOSOC status. This status signifies access to debates at the UNSC and thereby entry points into the decision-making process of states. However, there is also a set of players within advocacy who operate outside the UN and ECOSOC system. These include smaller and younger organizations that often lack resources and any established channels of communication with state actors. These groups may focus on large-scale mobilization highlighting a different target audience (see de Waal, 2015; Budabin & Pruce, 2019). A separate category includes individuals such as activists and celebrities who may focus on the mass mobilization of publics but who also have the capacity to elevate issues to attention of the international community through the UN or Congress (see Cooper, 2008; Wheeler, 2013; Budabin & Richey, 2018). These high-profile people can use their celebrity platform as entry points into these places of power. This diverse pool of players is considered unofficial, given that they have not been elected, nor are they part of traditional sources of power, but operate with their own set of dynamics and hierarchies. Taking into account these different types of unofficial actors provides a more complete picture of how advocacy as well as securitization works.

The analysis which follows demonstrates in part how advocacy organizations have used outsider lobbying to bring new audiences to the security-making process. In what is often described as insider lobbying, pressure groups such as advocacy NGOs or human rights organizations persuade governments or international institutions to adopt particular norms in charters, constitutions, and other documents (Dellmuth & Tallberg, 2016). Others may look to the court of public opinion, or outsider lobbying, to build support for the application of previously adopted norms to new situations and scenarios (Dellmuth & Tallberg, 2016). Generally, advocacy organizations suffer from low visibility compared to state actors but shifts in transnational advocacy around conflict have made them both more visible and more controversial (see de Waal, 2015). Through outsider lobbying, advocacy organizations and celebrity figures draw on grassroots mobilization and deft use of 'impolitic' and 'impolite' behaviours to gain the attention of the media and then state actors and policy-makers (Budabin & Pruce, 2019; Cooper, 2008). The media is a critical "link in the larger chain of public acceptance essential to a successful securitizing move" (Vultee, 2010, p. 45).

Here, we argue that non-state actors have the freedom (and the challenge) to operate as unofficial security actors and therefore must be creative in how they utilize the security lens, who they target as their audience and under what context they operate. Their unofficial status renders them marginal in relative terms, but as the case below demonstrates, even marginal actors can exert power and gain influence under certain conditions. Also key for nonstate actors is their ability to take advantage of shifting political opportunity structures. As we examine in the next section, important changes have taken place both in terms of international jurisprudence, organizational practice, and empirical realities of violence in ongoing conflicts which reflect just such a shift.

Securitization at the margins: advocacy narratives around Congo and UNSCR 1325

As our methodological approach, we focus on the advocacy narratives that were circulated by state and non-state actors in promoting the issue of SGBV to further its securitization. Scholarship has shown that advocacy narratives are vital tools in interpreting situations as human rights violations, determining responsibility, and promoting solutions. Despite their simple storylines, narratives need to be considered "sites of the exercise of power" that, as Wibben (2011, p. 2) argues, enable us to "not only investigate but also invent an order for the world." Advocacy narratives are a key part of the discursive strategies of non-state actors, amplifying the voices of the voiceless. Indeed, for human rights actors, discourses operate as their main source of non-material power in global governance.

Deployed on behalf of human rights and humanitarian causes, narratives turn issues into problems and establish responsibility (Wilson & Brown, 2009, pp. 18–20). A narrative approach to understanding the power of ideas operationalizes the concept of norm entrepreneurship whereby the norm is being embedded in a storyline. In their work on policy narratives, Shanahan, Jones, and McBeth distinguish the populating characters (hero, villain, beneficiary, allies and opponents) as well as literary elements like setting and plot that combine to create moving story lines; crucially for a narrative used in the realm of advocacy, the "moral of the story" will encapsulate the policy solution or "ask" (2011, pp. 335–336). A similar cast and policy ask populates an advocacy narrative, where ideas of root causes, consequences, and solutions is imparted (see Autesserre, 2012). But advocacy around conflict often fails to reflect the on-the-ground realities, sometimes producing mixed results, as recently discussed in an edited volume by de Waal (2015).

In expanding the scope of securitizing actors to non-state actors such as advocacy organizations and celebrities, we are at the same time expanding the ambit for detecting narratives that differ from those advanced by official actors and texts customarily studied within securitization theory. Our research takes into account a wide variety of communication media, enabling us to examine the force of advocacy that inhabits visuals, films, and celebrity figures in mediating security aspects of SGBV. Following the approach of Brysk (2013, p. 6) who explores the narrative effects of human rights campaigns built upon the elements of voice, message, performance, media, and audience, we take seriously movies, performances, and campaign materials as meaningful 'texts' that merit our attention as securitizing devices. We explore how, first, these texts vary in terms of the speaker actor and his/her platform, broadening understanding of the securitization process to encompass both insider and outsider lobbying. Second, we examine the narratives for their adoption of security discourses, seeking resonance with the UNSCR 1325 as well as promoting notions of urgency and threat. Looking at the period 2007–2010 in three phases, we explore how the spheres of activity inside and outside the UN operated independently and sometimes overlapped. Our data is drawn from media coverage, films, websites, campaign materials, reports, and semi-structured interviews.

Phase 1: legal and institutional backdrop

As discussed above, the process of securitizing SGBV in armed conflict took shape in the 1990s and involved both official and unofficial actors. While sexual violence during armed conflict was a centuries-old practice (Brownmiller, 1995), it was only in 1995 that the silence surrounding wartime rape was suddenly broken. The first step occurred when transnational advocacy successfully linked women's experiences in conflict to human rights and international security and codified it in the Beijing Platform for Action. Then, during and after the wars in Bosnia and Rwanda, these conflicts and the subsequent ad hoc tribunals became critical points of departure for seeing women and women's bodies as referent objects for international peace and security (Hirschauer, 2014). Specifically, the international tribunal prosecutions of Duško Tadić in 1999 for crimes committed in the former Yugoslavia and of Jean-Paul Akayesu in 1998 for crimes committed in Rwanda codified 'systematic rape' as a category of international crimes, including as a crime against humanity and an instrument of genocide. Just before these two landmark rulings, the international community agreed to the draft of the Rome Statute, which included rape and other forms of sexual violence as part of the mandate of the International Criminal Court.

Accompanying the legal proceedings was extensive debate on the purpose and intent of sexual violence in conflict as either political or strategic, rather than the widespread appearance of that violence. What became generally accepted was that the purpose and intent of the violence are conceptually separate from the nature of the violence being widespread and systematic (Cohen, 2016).[12] Both tribunal judgements refer to the language of the Rome Statute, a legal framework that had given rape in conflict-affected areas a very specific meaning. "'Rape as a weapon of war' thus refers to sexual violence as having a systematic, pervasive, or officially orchestrated aspect, emphasizing that rapes are not random but appear to be carried out as deliberate policy" (Buss 2009, p. 145). While rape in war was not new, this particular understanding of a form of violence as strategic or tactical committed by a rational actor as opposed to an inevitable by-product of war was different (Askin, 2003; Buss, 2009). Hirschauer (2014) argues that Bosnia and Rwanda were the first signifiers of the securitization of women's protection needs during conflict in a process that resulted in the passing of UNSCR 1325. With wartime rape understood as part of a planned or targeted policy, this form of violence constituted a serious threat to international peace and security and therefore, demanded international intervention and extraordinary measures.

In this phase, there were a number of unofficial actors who contributed to and shaped these debates while also impressing upon official actors the urgency of the issue. Inal (2013, pp. 142, 164) credits NGOs with making sure that rape was "an unavoidable discussion topic that was taken seriously as a *legal* issue." In particular, she notes that women's groups were able "to reshape state interests by changing the normative context and by using (and to a certain extent creating) a normative shock – depicting rape as a repulsive, uncivilized practice that should be rejected by all civilized nations" (Inal, 2013, pp. 142, 164). This framing of sexual violence as not just a scourge but an existential threat shows the power of discourses in the securitization process. By 2000, a variety of human rights, peacebuilding and women's NGOs had influenced official actors—particularly a certain group of states that were sitting on the UN Security Council—to pass the UNSCR 1325.[13]

UNSCR was a critical first step in framing women's rights as essential to the maintenance of international peace and security, laying the foundation for securitizing sexual violence (Hudson, 2009a). This landmark resolution explicitly references rape and "calls upon all parties of armed conflict to take special measures to protect women and girls from gender-based violence," specifically "emphasizing the responsibility of all States to put an end to impunity and to prosecute those responsible for genocide, crimes against humanity, and war crimes including those relating to sexual and other violence against women and girls" (S/Res/1325). With this securitizing move, the responsibility to respond to and even address SGBV in conflict expanded from a purely humanitarian or post-conflict human rights issue to an issue central to international security.

What characterizes the securitization process in this period was the interaction between official and unofficial actors, operating within the bounds of the UN system, especially the Security Council. Actors such as NGOs and women's groups did not make a concerted effort at mobilization *outside* of the UN, but rather targeted their advocacy at state and state institutions. From the perspective of security, we can see how discourses promulgated in both official and unofficial texts debated the nature of the issue of SGBV in conflict – its violation of bodily integrity, its relationship to war, and its prevalence as an existential threat to international peace and security. Clearly, the invocation of security invested urgency in the issue to such a degree that an international resolution was passed. Yet, though the passing of the UNSCR 1325 might be regarded by some as the successful culmination of a securitization process, later events will reveal the limits of the resolution, in particular, the incomplete securitization of the issue of SGBV. The next section will examine efforts to close these gaps that came from a different set of actors that we argue reinforced security discourses through new means.

Phase 2: entrance of new actors and audiences from unofficial spheres

The high incidence of sexual violence in the Congo would emerge as one of the first test cases for the newly-passed resolution. Since 1996, numerous cases of rape and sexual torture of women and girls in the Congo had been reported. Sexual violence in conflict by armed forces, both regular and irregular, as well as the culture of impunity were considered an enduring problem in Congo (Berwouts, 2017, pp. 22–23). This dimension of the instability in the region of Eastern Congo began to attract wider attention in 2002 with the publication of a report by Human Rights Watch.[14] A close reading of this report reveals the early limitations in the international community's response to SGBV in conflict, particularly in a section directed to UN actors. For example, the HRW report recognized that official actors such as Secretary-General Kofi Annan and the Security Council

have devoted much attention to ending the Congo war and frequently denounced human rights abuses and the humanitarian crisis spawned by it.

They have also repeatedly stressed the importance of protecting women in armed conflict. But the strong language of the resolutions ordinarily lacked any effective mechanisms for implementation.[15]

Further on, the report acknowledges other efforts including an Open Session on Women and Armed Conflict and a major study being undertaken by the United Nations Development Fund for Women (UNIFEM) – all while concluding that "the council was unable to mobilize the political will to launch a major peace-keeping mission in the Congo."[16]

The lack of effective action on the situation in the Congo reflected a generally weak implementation of the Women, Peace, and Security agenda in terms of responding to SGBV in conflict. After the passage of UNSCR 1325, references to SGBV did emerge in the context of Security Council country-specific reso-lutions, but such violence was always linked to other forms of violence. For example, the Council condemned the use of sexual violence as a tool of warfare in the Congo with Resolution 1468 (2003), in Liberia with Resolution 1590 (2003), and in Sudan with Resolution 1590 (2005). Such references were included among other abuses and it was clear that SGBV was not a stand-alone security issue, nor enough to motivate intervention. One informant observed how "A few individuals who have been following through the development of the Women, Peace and Security mandate realized that conflict-related sexual viol-ence was absolutely not acknowledged."[17]

Outside of the UN, numerous humanitarian and human rights organizations were circulating reports focused specifically on SGBV in conflict, such as Amnesty International's 2004 report entitled, "Sudan, Darfur: Rape as a Weapon of War: Sexual Violence and its Consequences," and a Physicians for Human Rights 2004 report entitled, "The Use of Rape as a Weapon of War in Darfur." In 2005, the UN issued its own report entitled, "Broken Bodies, Broken Dreams." This flurry of reports, especially those concerning women in the Congo, were instrumental in the UN's decision to launch its Stop Rape Now Campaign. As recounted by one UN official, upon returning from Congo in 2005 and meeting with UNIFEM Executive Director Noleen Hayzner and UNDP offi-cial Kathleen Cravero, senior WHO official David Navarro exhibited an approach she likened to "Columbus discovering America" relative to his "dis-covery" of rape in Congo (Anonymous, 2015). Navarro likened the "rape epi-demic" to the HIV epidemic of the 1980s and the idea to launch a global campaign around rape and violence against women was born (interview, 2016). The concept note for that campaign was written by Douglas, who cites its foundation being laid in Beijing in 1995 and with UNSCR 1325 in 2000. She notes how the last item in 1325 "pointed to the lack of data and opened a space for the UN, NGOs and state to talk about how women are affected differently in conflict."

Run by the newly formed UN Action Against Sexual Violence in Conflict office, the Stop Rape Now Campaign was an attempt by institutional entities operating within the UN system to engage in outside lobbying.[18] We see how the campaign's asks (make a symbol, mobilize media, host and event, send a letter) focused on raising mass awareness, learning more about the meaning of SGBV, but with the final step being to write a letter to an elected official, the state actor that would be responsible for securitizing SGBV further. The Campaign included a website, social media platforms, and celebrities to broaden its reach beyond the UN; one insider described, "This campaign I think was very important, advocacy was really a key element of the work we were doing at the very beginning to make this [issue] feel known basically."[19] This push was further supported in 2006 when the UN Secretary-General submitted an in-depth study on all forms of violence against women mandated by the General Assembly.

While these institutional developments were clearly important, they alone did not lead to greater acceptance in mainstream security circles for an issue that had been part of human rights and humanitarian understandings of conflict since at least the mid-1990s. While some speech acts linking SGBV to security could be identified during this time, those speech acts were not reaching the target audience needed to elevate the issue demanding urgent action and justifying actions outside the normal bounds of UN human rights and humanitarian work. This is where non-state actors operating on non-traditional platforms and taking advantage of media and culture connections were able to use a securitized discourse to elevate the issue, construct a narrower narrative about SGBV in conflict, and frame the response from the international community.

In 2004 and 2005, human rights activists and journalists began to publish stories on the lack of attention to Congo. International Crisis Group's Andrew Stroehlein wrote about meta-narrative in the *Christian Science Monitor*, "a media story is currently developing around the Congo – focusing, paradoxically, on how the conflict is not a media story."[20] Stroehlein expressed his disbelief but then took comfort in the media story about a non-media story: "This is why the current coverage of Congo's noncoverage actually leaves me optimistic that the country might be the next distant disaster to capture broad media attention."[21] The tides began to turn for 'The Invisible War' in 2005 when journalist Lisa Ling visited Congo, setting in motion a domino effect of public engagement that would bring the issue of sexual violence in conflict to new heights, in Congo and beyond.[22]

As a special correspondent for *The Oprah Winfrey Show*, the popular Ling traveled to the Congo to do a piece on mass rape. She went on the Oprah Winfrey Show in January 2005 declaring before the large, mostly female, audience that "There's another Holocaust going on. This time, in the Democratic Republic of Congo" (Shannon, 2011, p. 36). She goes on, "Women in the Congo are considered "war booty," essentially. They are the ones who are suffering the most. The villages are attacked in the middle of the night by young soldiers. They violently rape the women. They've killed so many people already in six years. Four million people – and no one is paying attention. [...] This is happening right now."[23] Ling described Eastern Congo in stark terms, "I think it's the worst place on earth. And the most ignored" (Shannon, 2011, p. 37). The founder of Women for Women International, Zainab Salbi, was also on the show and offered a way for people to do something; audience members could sponsor a Congolese woman for $27 a month. The show with its 20-minute segment on Congo broke the previous record with nine million viewers and raised $2.5 million for women in Congo.[24]

The two messages of neglect of Congo's women and the possibility to help through fundraising reached Lisa Shannon, a small business owner, living in Portland, OR, who rushed to sponsor two women after viewing the report. She then organized a fundraising run for Women for Women in 2006 that eventually turned into its own organization, Run for Congo Women, which began coordinating runs taking place across the country, raising hundreds of thousands of dollars, in what she hoped would "spark a movement" (Shannon, 2011, p. 51). One of the women to join the run in Chicago was Lisa Jackson, who was in the process of putting together her documentary *The Greatest Silence: Rape in the Congo*. Along with Jackson, Shannon began to link with other activists working on Congo including the DC-based organization Friends of Congo. With just six other people, she engaged in a series of "Congo Lobby Days" to put pressure on policy-makers to support Congo legislation, and the bill passed with unanimous support and included a nod to Run for Congo Women (Shannon, 2011, p. 57).

Shannon made a five-and-a-half week trip to gather evidence and stories to strengthen her advocacy in DC and mobilization efforts. The focus on victims of sexual violence proved effective as thousands signed up to join the runs and donate money through Women for Women for a program called Restore Hope, which had been operating in Congo since 2004.[25] Shannon's own experience, however, in visiting the program and meeting the recipients is lukewarm. In her book published in 2010, Shannon would convey in an honest and direct manner the extent of her naiveté as well as the ineffectiveness of the cash programs that only benefited certain rape victims and left plenty in need, while failing to provide the protection needed. Still, the person-to-person connection of the Runs for Congo would introduce average Americans to the insecurities of women in the Congo and the notion that rape was a weapon of war.

It would be Jackson's documentary film that would take this movement into more elite circles (Anonymous, 2016a). Herself the survivor of gang rape, Jackson traveled to Congo in 2006 and 2007 to film a response to the "epidemic of sexual violence" that had been "getting little to no mainstream media coverage."[26] Jackson traveled across Congo, meeting with survivors, police forces, organizations, hospital staff, and even members of the militia. Reviews considered the documentary ground-breaking for "its willingness to hear from members of the militia who have repeatedly committed acts of rape" (Gibney, 2015, p. 49). Beyond the plaintive stories of the women, the landscape of Congo is revealed for its many gaps in prevention, protection, and prosecution. The relief and rehabilitation services for the survivors is wholly inadequate though there are sites of healing and support, which Jackson takes care to highlight. The film was made with the lofty expectations of human rights documentaries to draw attention to those without rights; the "greatest silence" is not only lack of mass awareness globally but even among UN officials. In its most powerful moments, the message to the audience is a call to action. One woman featured in the film expresses the hope that "our complaints will be heard at a higher level [...] and we will get some help." As part of the film's outreach among mass and elite audiences beyond the HBO viewings, festival appearances and screenings were held in sites including the US Senate, the UK House of Commons, the Belgian Parliament, and the Open Society.[27]

Observer accounts by policy-makers and human rights activists suggest that the impact of Jackson's film on the debate around sexual violence in Congo was wide-reaching. We can tie the influential nature of the film to the fact that it was seen by official actors. On the day of the UNSC debate on Resolution 1820 in 2007, NPR interviewed Lisa Jackson. NPR reported that the U.S. Ambassador to the UN, Zalmay Khalilzad, "says he was inspired to speak on this issue by a documentary chronicling the plight of rape victims in the Democratic Republic of the Congo."[28]Also important at this time was the activism of Eve Ensler – playwright of *The Vagina Monologues*. In 2007, OCHA, the UN's humanitarian agency asked Ensler to visit Eastern Congo, and her visit set off a chain reaction of activism.[29] First, her visit was followed by a fact-finding mission by the UN Under-Secretary General for Humanitarian Affairs who, upon his return, wrote an op-ed for the Los Angeles Times, in which he said that the Congo was the worst place in the world for women (Holmes, 2007). This report led to a lengthy segment on *60 Minutes* by Anderson Cooper of CNN. Eventually, Ensler testified before the Security Council during the debate that led to the resolution that renewed the mandate for the UN Peacekeeping force in the Congo (MONUC), which contained some of the strongest language condemning rape and sexual violence ever to appear in a resolution.

A U.S. Senate hearing on rape as a weapon of war in 2009 also featured Ensler among others. This hearing further demonstrated the entry of artists and documentarians (Lisa Jackson was another speaker) as norm entrepreneurs on behalf of women in Congo. It is an example of the rising prominence of new voices on behalf of Congo as well as with the singular focus on a very particular form of sexual violence. In the hearing, Ensler declared:

> Just this week I received an email that documented that Congolese soldiers are kidnapping and selling young Congolese girls between 12 and 16 years of age to Angolan soldiers. This impunity sends a signal to the world that the bodies of women and children will be the new battleground on which cheap wars will be fought.
>
> (Ensler, 2009)

Another witness from Congo at the 2009 hearing was Chouchou Namegabe, Founder of the South Kivu Women's Media Association. She too adopted the single narrative: "We ask the U.S. to join us in pressuring the Congolese government to stop giving amnesty to rebels who use rape as their war strategy."[30] While Western organizations and activists appear to dominate much of this advocacy, there is evidence of local Congolese actors adopting similar securitizing narratives. Collectively, these nonstate actors are very clearly engaging in a securitized discourse, first with wider public audiences and then with powerful state actors, showing how discursive moves by more marginalized nonstate actors can make their way into more official security spaces in meaningful ways.

This phase demonstrates the multiple ways that popular media, cultural dynamics, and individuals not traditionally part of international peace and security came together in a way that catapulted this particular issue onto the international agenda. Using celebrities, fundraisers, film, and media this case highlights the various mediums that nonstate actors use in their efforts to advocate and securitize their cause. At the same time, this case raises questions about where speech acts can emerge from and who has the authority and legitimacy to advance them. The securitization of SGBV in conflict was constructed by nonstate actors working both outside and inside the state system. Thus, their securitizing moves go beyond the political elite and are diffused in societal power relations and embedded in the cultural beliefs of a wider public.

Phase 3: moving the securitization of SGBV forward

Additionally, the case of securitizing SGBV in Congo pushes us to consider how the target audience of a securitization process can vary over time and to what effect. In March 2007, the UN launched UN Action Against Sexual Violence in Conflict (UN Action) which represented a "concerted effort of 13 UN entities to improve coordination and accountability, amplify advocacy, and support country efforts to prevent sexual violence and responds more effectively to the needs of survivors."[31] UN Action, chaired by the UNDP and the WHO to improve the quality of organizations' programming to better address sexual violence, reinforce coordination efforts among UN agencies for prevention and response services and improve accountability, became the driving force behind the Stop Rape Now and Get Crossed Campaign.

UN Action created space for advocates and policy-makers already officially part of the system to talk about sexual violence in conflict in ways they had not done before. One UN official recalled the creation of the Stop Rape Now website in 2008,

> At the beginning, I think it was needed to just have a place when you say, "okay, sexual violence in conflict? What are you doing?" You had this website. And it was much more dynamic at the beginning because it was the key, it was the main tool used for dissemination of information, advocacy. And then if you have a member state asking about, "you know I'm looking for these documents," you would refer them to the website.
>
> (Anonymous, 2016b)

It was a time of outreach and awareness-raising, and the campaign focused much of their efforts on the UN's Department of Peacekeeping Operations (DPKO) and the Department of Political Affairs (DPA) to make the case that sexual violence was a hard security issue, and therefore relevant to those agencies' mandates, rather than a softer humanitarian or development issue. DPKO and DPA are considered main security agencies within the UN to intervene in conflict-affected areas. The Stop Rape Now campaign operated on the slogan "There is no security without women's security."

In February 2008, the GA adopted resolution 62/134 without vote, entitled "Eliminating Rape and Other Forms of Sexual Violence in all their Manifestations, including in Conflict and Related Situations." This was a U.S.-led initiative, focusing on sexual violence whether or not committed during conflict, by state, non-state actors, or private individuals.[32] Subsequently, in May 2008, UNIFEM and the DPKO hosted a conference in Wilton Park, which brought together government officials, military and police personnel, UN peacekeepers, and representatives from women's civil society organizations. This unprecedented gathering of 'hard-core' security sector actors with gender specialists and women from various conflict zones around the world focused on the role that military peacekeepers must play in the prevention of widespread and systematic sexual violence in conflict and post-conflict societies. Of the 70 participants at Wilton Park, 27 came from military establishments (former Force Commanders, army personnel, staff of defense ministries); others included four MPs, four Permanent Representatives, seven DPKO staff, and a number of other UN personnel, peace activists, and academics. The rarity of having military officials hear from and speak with women survivors cannot be understated, especially in 2008.

Central to the conference was the acknowledgement that sexual violence is in fact a "security problem requiring a systematic security response" (Summary Report, 2008, p. 2). In this context, sexual violence was clearly situated within the security framework as an essential component to military and police work in UN peacekeeping. As Anne Marie Goetz, Director of UNIFEM's Governance, Peace and Security Program argued:

Even a few years ago, a gathering like this would have been unprecedented. Yet it is military peacekeepers now themselves that are demanding practical solutions to the types of conflict they encounter in theatre [...]. Military tactics have yet to catch up to changed realities on the ground. Security policy-makers and security institutions likewise have to catch up to new forms of conflict, and to the implications for their work of the arenas in which wars are fought, the methods used, and the groups targeted. Sexual violence is a matter for the Security Council, because conflict is its core business, and sexual violence is one way in which conflict is prosecuted. Sexual violence is a matter for governance and economic recovery, because it mars efforts to replace the rule of *war* with rule of *law*, and puts half the population out of commission for the important jobs of social, economic and political rebuilding, where a nation needs to call on every able person to pull itself back together. Post conflict peace, stability, democratic governance, and livelihoods recovery all require women's empowerment, and women's empowerment requires security from sexual violence, and a demonstrable end to the impunity that serves as incentive for continued violence.

(Wilton Park Conference Presentations, 2008, p. 7)

This argument not only emphasized women's rights as essential to establishing lasting peace and security, but also suggests that violence against women is generally new in the changing landscape of armed conflict and is now relevant to traditional security institutions at the national and international level. At the conference, Major General Patrick Cammaert argued, "It is more dangerous to be a woman than to be a soldier right now in Eastern Congo." Both Congo and Darfur were central to the conference, particularly in terms of understanding how violence against women may actually increase once the "situation is stabilized" (p. 2).[33] The simple fact that military and police commanders from various UN missions and offices were participating in such a conference and hearing from women's advocacy organizations about the realities of women's insecurities on the ground is noteworthy. It is these sorts of interactions that reshape identities and thus interest in ways that can redefine what constitutes a threat to security.

Building on the momentum of Wilton Park, the multiple injection of state actors and the various interventions of western-based advocacy on violence against women in the Congo, in June 2008 the U.S. (occupying the role of Security Council Presidency) issued a concept note (S/2008/364) suggesting an open debate on women, peace and security, and specifically sexual violence in armed conflict. The only conflict situation explicitly named in that report was the Congo, citing the Under-Secretary-General for Humanitarian Affairs John Holmes who claimed that more than 32,000 cases of rape and other forms of sexual violence had been registered in the South Kivu province alone. This document laid the conceptual foundation for UNSCR 1820, which explicitly recognizes the use of sexual violence as a weapon of war and stresses in its first operative paragraph that sexual violence is a war strategy and a self-standing security issue linked with reconciliation and durable peace. In sponsoring UNSCR 1820, U.S. Secretary of State Condoleezza Rice stated,

This world body now acknowledges that sexual violence in conflict zones is indeed a security concern. We affirm that sexual violence profoundly affects not only the health and safety of women, but the economic and social stability of their nations.[34]

Extraordinary measures taken in UNSCR 1820 include a new mechanism for protecting women and girls in and around UN-managed camps (para. 10), sexual violence relevant to country-specific sanction regimes (para. 5), other itemized measures aimed at improving protection and assistance (para. 13) and a global report mechanism (para. 15). As Aroussi highlights,

1820 uses stronger language regarding impunity than that used by Resolution 1325 [...] taking an even firmer position on accountability for gender-based violence by expressing in its operative paragraphs its readiness and

intention to take measures, including sanctions against parties that perpetuate sexual violence against women and girls.

(2011, p. 581)

This narrow concept of sexual violence in conflict connects with an equally
narrow concept of justice (sanctions and prosecutions). While this language was
in many ways a reiteration of established international legal principles, the fact
that these issues were now seen as relevant to the power and the authority of the
Security Council is significant, and reflective of the securitization process. This
resolution recognized sexual violence as an impediment to international stability
and, as such, sufficient to warrant response, even if clear intent cannot be established (Anderson, 2010).

UNSCR 1820 was also significant for its explicit statement on the need to
"debunk the myths that fuel sexual violence," recognizing that sexual violence is
not a natural expression of masculinity (S/Res/1820, para. 3). However, 1820
also reinforces important myths about sexual violence in conflict including the
notion that rape is the worst form of harm or suffering that women experience in
war, that sexual violence is perpetrated by men against women and girls, and
that women are helpless in the face of sexual violence. Otto argues,

In the absence of a commitment to gender equality, and despite its nod to
debunking myths, Resolution 1820 is grounded in the old script of biological certainties, which accepts women's inequality as natural and armed conflict as inevitable. The new language of 'gender' has not yet shifted the old
moorings of biology.

(2009, p. 24)

It has just shifted the narrative – where violence is reduced to SGBV (read rape),
the perpetrator is a male combatant with a strategic or tactical objective and the
victim is a female (even apolitical) civilian – from human rights and humanitarian policy to security policy.[35]

UNSCR 1820 set the nascent WPS agenda on a particular trajectory in its
powerful articulation of protection in relation to women's bodies (and women's
bodies alone), and specifically those bodies violated in sexual and gender-based
attacks (Shepherd, 2017). UNSCR 1888 adopted in 2009 continues the development of the protection pillar along similar lines, calling for: "[s]pecific provisions, as appropriate, for the protection of women and children from rape and
other sexual violence in the mandates of United Nations peacekeeping operations, including, on a case-by-case basis, the identification of women's protection advisers" (S/Res/1888, para. 12). The securitized narrative around SGBV in
conflict is quickly reinforced with UNSCR 1888 in 2009, explicitly linking
sexual violence as a tactic of war with the maintenance of international peace
and security. UNSCR 1960 (2010) reaffirms this link and establishes a "naming
and shaming" listing mechanism, sending a direct political message that there are
consequences for sexual violence including: listing in the Secretary-General's

annual reports, referrals to UN Sanctions Committees and to the ICC, international condemnation, and reparations.

As this section demonstrates, the period 2007–2010 represented a critical shift in the actors and audiences engaged in the securitization process, in which the securitization of a particular understanding of sexualized violence fully took hold as a result of advocacy efforts and strategic framings. Whereas the second phase involved a range of nonstate actors with varied access to mainstream security actors, this third phase was squarely situated in state-based institutions and in large part driven by states themselves. This kind of support by official security actors and organizations was clearly able to take the securitization process to the next level – beyond acceptance and awareness to actual implementation. At the same time, we can see how the gains in the third phase were impacted by the advocacy strategies of the unofficial nonstate actors in the second phase. Without the advocacy of a new set of actors adopting security discourses in their appeals to mass audiences, additional securitization of the WPS agenda might not have occurred. While we do not prove causation between the three phases, there is certainly correlation and more importantly, empirical evidence that pushes us to look more deeply at who the securitizing actors are and how they tend to operate.

Implications for securitization ... and security

This chapter adopted a multidisciplinary approach aimed at revealing deficiencies in existing uses of security, in particular to complicate conventional understanding around the *who*, the *audience*, and the *where* of securitization practices. By analyzing the securitization of SGBV in conflict in terms of three phases, we tracked how both state and nonstate actors navigate official and unofficial security circles taking an issue out of a realm of normal politics, making it urgent, and demanding extraordinary measures. Using a narrative analysis, we detected security discourses in new sources, beyond the speech-actors of officials. In this way, the use of securitization as an analytical device is illuminating in understanding how an issue comes to the fore in international policy-making circles *and* for understanding why it takes the form that it does.

We contend that those studying securitization theory would be well-served to more closely examine the securitizing moves of nonstate actors – including and especially those who do not have obvious or direct access to official security actors. In this case, we see the impact of intervening advocacy by nonstate actors, particularly those targeting public audiences and connecting to western cultural norms. Particularly in the second phase, the moves of these unofficial actors provided a critical understanding of how the securitization process works with respect to SGBV, and beyond. The ability to enter and shape mainstream security circles reveals new dynamics of power between and among these actors. Though limits remain on the amplification of marginalized voices, especially for those not taken up by advocacy organizations and allies, it is crucial to recognize the alternative mechanisms that can be (and here, were) used to attract and mobilize popular audiences. Examining the circulation of advocacy narratives and their meaningful engagement with security discourses pushes the boundaries of thinking around security processes to consider material such as films, activist testimonies, and social media platforms as security texts. Overall, the case of SGBV securitization during the period 2007–2010 shows us that the scholarship on human rights advocacy can be used to enhance our understanding of how unofficial actors thought to be external or new to the security field can and do strategize to communicate with various audiences to impact mainstream security discourse and policy.

It is essential to acknowledge that, while securitization may lead to increased attention to, resources for, and partnerships engaged on an issue like SGBV, such measures do not necessarily produce results with respect to increased protection for women and improved security. Indeed, when we look at the continued brutal targeting of women and girls in conflict zones across the globe, we are left to ponder the question of *securitization to what effect and for whom?* In fact, some scholars have found western advocacy's "fetishization" around rape as a weapon of war has led to a process by which "violence is divorced from its wider gendered and racialized political economy context and determinations and transformed into an object of global media and public fascinations" (Meger, 2016, p. 17). In this way, this incomplete and problematic narrative about women and security makes many forms of violence against women invisible, isolating sexual violence and assuming simplistic dichotomies in defining perpetrator and victim (Baaz & Stern, 2013). Further critique notes, "with an almost exclusive focus on rape women are seen as just that, raped—not as agents of change" (Coulter, 2012, p. 177). Rather than incorporating women's stories into mainstream narratives of conflict, Coulter argues, "the focus on the plight and fate of women as synonymous with rape" continues to marginalize women in what has become known as the "add-women-and-stir approach" (2012, p. 178).

In the last decade, funding for research, advocacy, and programs on sexual violence in conflict-affected areas has increased significantly. Many of our interviews (anecdotally) confirmed that donor support is available for work on sexual violence, particularly when it relates to international security concerns. In the media, we see journalists covering sexual atrocities like the thousands of Yazidis enslaved by the Islamic State of Iraq and the Levant (ISIL) with unprecedented regularity. One scholar even argues that conflict-related sexual violence "now rivals nuclear and biological weapons terrorism, and arms proliferation for receiving the most attention of security actors today" (Meger, 2016, p. 17). And yet, "conflict-related sexual violence continues to be pervasive, and the response from governments and the international community ranges from insufficient and inadequate at times, to scandalously negligent and complicit at others" (Castillo Diaz, 2017). In 2010 for example, in only three days, rebel groups raped close to 400 civilians in North Kivu, Eastern Congo, and to date no one has been brought to a domestic or international court for this atrocity.

These realities raise critical questions about the value and impact of the securitization process for women and girls in conflict-affected areas. This narrative on conflict-related sexual violence frames "rape as a weapon of war" as a clear-cut security issue, and as central to the WPS agenda. While raising attention and entrenching norms around the WPS agenda, the concerns of the securitization process for this case are numerous. For some, this violence is constructed as a masculine problem that can only be solved through the masculine solutions of military discipline or threat of punishment from a masculinized state (Otto, 2009). This process of framing violence against women in the existing security paradigm can serve an instrumental function in privileging and reinforcing traditional state-centric security prerogatives. For others, serious questions remain about whether or not even a 'successful' process will actually lead to increased security for women and girls in conflict-affected areas. Many practitioners note that strategic rape is not the only or even most common form of gender-based violence that women and girls experience. The ways in which advocacy narratives interact with securitization processes have thus produced limiting and obfuscating ideas around who and what needs to be securitized.

Still, many of the activists and even some survivors that we have interviewed maintain that an international focus on conflict-related sexual violence is as important now as it has ever been. It is not yet the time for desecuritization. Increased attention and funding for SGBV is noteworthy but still woeful for the challenges at hand; further, as the international community continues to retreat from international intervention and cut foreign aid, the needs are as serious as they have ever been. SGBV in conflict was and continues to be a significant security threat. As one UN official articulated:

> Far from being a specific niche issue, sexual violence is an indicator of the most severe breach of human security [...] it is closely related to food aid, firewood collection and HIV/AIDS. It directly affects women and girls but also men and boys – and destroys the fabric of families and communities. Punishing its perpetrators would contribute to restoring trust in the judicial system. Preventing it would spare disproportionate human and financial costs to reconstructing nations. Reducing sexual violence in all war-affected countries will be a true sign of national recovery.
>
> (Obaid, 2007, p. 5)

Of course, this expansive and holistic understanding of sexual violence and its consequences is very useful. It is not, however, the narrative of sexual violence that has emerged in the mainstream or the one analyzed throughout this chapter.

Notes

1 Interview with first author, 2006.
2 This chapter is part of a larger project that examines that nature, scope and power dynamics at work in transnational human rights advocacy around women's rights and violence experienced by women in conflict-affected areas. In addition to the security lens, we examine how advocacy narratives emerge, diverge and conflict and the impact of these narratives on the people who are the subjects of those discourses.

3 For the purposes of this paper and as is often done in popular media, references to the Democratic Republic of the Congo will be shortened to simply the Congo.

4 The main test cases in this period also include Darfur and Liberia, which we take up within the scope of our larger research project.

5 There exists much excellent analysis and critique of the "rape as weapon of war" narrative (Baaz & Stern, 2013; Meger, 2016; Swaine, 2018). This chapter does not examine the problematic nature of this narrative or its limitations in representing the harms experienced in conflict. Rather, we are focused on the 'successful' emergence and adoption of securitizing discourses for SGBV. Such success does not, of course, always mean positive (security-enhancing) outcomes for the subjects of security.

6 Wæver maintains that security "has to be read through the lens of *national* security" (1995, p. 49).

7 Hansen's critique also points to a second area of exclusion. Because gendered identities are intrinsically linked to other aspects of the subject's identity, specifically nationality, religion, and economic status, gender does not establish a cohesive neat group of individuals to serve as collective referent objects of security. Hansen refers to this "intimate inter-linkage between the subject's gender identity and other aspects of the subject's identity" as the "subsuming security" problem (2000, p. 287). This multidimensionality of identities makes gender a tough fit for the CS's qualification of referent object. In this sense, gendered identities are often characterized by their inseparability from other identities, creating great ambiguity. Yet, this is not a problem for SGBV, in fact the opposite. Women, and to a lesser extent, children, are considered the well-understood referents, but with the associated and negative implication of lacking agency, persisting victimhood, and lower prospects for empowerment. Further, those doing the advocacy also tend to identify as women. This theoretical tension and practical trend are outside the scope of this paper and something we take up in our larger research project.

8 Gender-based violence also occurs publicly in many situations. Honor killings in Pakistan are a vivid example of this. But even public gender-violence often silences its victims.

9 It should be noted that the advocacy organizations studied here are well-resourced and established in the Global North. Thus, they aim to 'speak on behalf of' stakeholders and marginalized voices elsewhere. The opportunities and limits for when and how these marginalized voices can enter security arenas and speak for themselves is deserving of further research and consideration.

10 It's worth thinking about the differences/similarities between expressive acts and speech acts. Expressive acts could include both discursive and nondiscursive forms of communication.

11 Finnemore and Sikkink's (1998) conceptualization of the norm life cycle can be particularly useful here, raising new questions for securitization theory as well.

12 For more on how rape and sexual violence serve symbolic, practical, and strategic objectives in war-making, see Kaufman and Williams, 2010 and Janie Leatherman, 2011.

13 The six founding members of the NGO Working Group on WPS were Women's International League for Peace and Freedom, Amnesty International, International Alert, Hague Appeal for Peace, Women's Commission for Refugee Women and Children, and Women's Caucus for Gender Justice. The NGO Working Group on WPS now has 18 members. www.womenpeacesecurity.org/.

14 www.hrw.org/reports/2002/drc/Congo0602.pdf.

15 www.hrw.org/reports/2002/drc/Congo0602.pdf, pp. 94–95.

16 Additional troops were deployed to the MONUC peacekeeping operation but this was inadequate and the mandate did not include civilian protection.

17 Interview October 27, 2016.

18 www.stoprapenow.org/about/.

19 Interview October 27, 2016.
20 www.csmonitor.com/2005/0614/p09s02-coop.html.
21 www.csmonitor.com/2005/0614/p09s02-coop.html.
22 Also in 2005 was the publication of "Not women anymore…: The Congo's rape survivors face pain, shame and AIDS" by S. Nolen in *MS Magazine*. Beverly Hills: CA.
23 www.oprah.com/oprahshow/reaching-out-to-the-world.
24 www.themaneater.com/stories/2009/9/18/lisa-ling-speaks-about-international-journalism/
25 https://web.archive.org/web/20080117034051/www.womenforwomen.org/congo_country.htm.
26 www.hbo.com/documentaries/the-greatest-silence-rape-in-the-congo/interview/lisa-f-jackson.html.
27 www.opensocietyfoundations.org/events/greatest-silence-rape-congo.
28 www.npr.org/templates/story/story.php?storyId=91692457.
29 www.glamour.com/story/rape-in-the-congo (2007, July) linked to PBS Lumo premiere www.pbs.org/pov/lumo/eve-ensler/.
30 For the full testimony of both women as well as others, see www.foreign.senate.gov/hearings/confronting-rape-and-other-forms-of-violence-against-women-in-conflict-zones-spotlight-drc-and-sudan.
31 http://mptf.undp.org/factsheet/fund/UNA00.
32 The U.S. support here and in the Security Council on this issue deserves further critique and analysis, particularly as we think about the impact of states and major powers as key actors in the securitization process, but what is important for this analysis is the fact these were major state powers contributing to the securitization of SGBV in conflict.
33 All conference documents, including the summary report and individual presentations can be found at www.peacewomen.org/assets/file/Resources/UN/unifem_targeted oraffectedbyarmedconflict_2008.pdf (Last accessed May 2017).
34 http://articles.latimes.com/2008/jun/20/world/fg-violence20.
35 It is worth noting that the ICC indictment of Sudanese President al-Bashir was announced in July 2008 right after the passage of 1820. He was charged with genocide, crimes against humanity, and war crimes in Darfur, and these charges included the subjection of "thousands of civilian women – belonging primarily to [various ethnic] groups – to acts of rape." For more see www.icc-cpi.int/darfur/albashir/pages/alleged-crimes.aspx.

Bibliography

Anderson, L. (2010). Politics by other means: When does sexual violence threaten international peace and security? *International Peacekeeping, 17*(2), 244–260.

Amnesty International. (2004). Sudan, Darfur: Rape as a weapon of war: Sexual violence and its consequences. AFR 54/076/2004. Retrieved from www.refworld.org/docid/4152885b4.html. Last accessed June 21, 2017.

Anonymous. (2015). Interview with UN official, May 2015, conducted by Natalie F. Hudson in New York City, NY.

Anonymous. (2016a). Interview with former NGO activist, March 2016, conducted by Natalie F. Hudson in Atlanta, GA.

Anonymous. (2016b). Interview with UN official, October 2016, conducted by Alexandra C. Budabin, New York City, NY.

Aroussi, S. (2011). Women, peace and security: Addressing accountability for wartime sexual violence. *International Feminist Journal of Politics, 13*(4), 576–593.

Askin, K. (2003). Prosecuting wartime rape and other gender-related crimes under international law: Extraordinary advances, enduring obstacles. *Berkeley Journal of International Law, 21*(2), 288–349.

Autesserre, S. (2012). Dangerous tales: Dominant narratives on the Congo and their unintended consequences. *African Affairs, 111*(443), 202–222.

Autesserre, S. (2014). *Peaceland: Conflict resolution and the everyday politics of international intervention.* Cambridge: Cambridge University Press.

Austin, J. L. (1962). *How to do things with words.* Oxford: Clarendon.

Baaz, M. E., & Stern, M. (2013). *Sexual violence as a weapon of war? Perceptions, prescriptions, problems in the Congo and beyond (Africa now).* New York: Zed Books.

Balzacq, T. (2005). The three faces of securitization: Political agency, audience and context. *European Journal of International Relations, 11*(2), 171–201.

Balzacq, T., Basaran, T., Bigo, D., Guittet, E. P., & Olson. C. (2010, January). Security practices. *International Studies Encyclopedia Online.* doi:10.1111/b.9781444336597.2010.x

Berwouts, K. (2017). *Congo's violent peace: Conflict and struggle since the Great African War.* London: Zed Books.

Breakey, H., Francis, A., Popovski, V., Sampford, C., Smith, M. G., & Thakur, R. (2012). *Enhancing protection capacity: Policy guide to the responsibility to protect and the protection of civilians in armed conflicts.* Queensland: Griffith University.

Brownmiller, S. (1995). The spoils of war. *War against women: The impact of violence on gender relations.* Report of the 6th annual conference, September 16–17, 1994. Berne: Swiss Peace Foundation.

Brysk, A. (2013). *Speaking rights to power: Constructing political will.* New York: Oxford University Press.

Budabin, A. C. (2015). Celebrities as norm entrepreneurs in international politics: Mia Farrow and the 'Genocide Olympics' campaign. *Celebrity Studies, 6*(4), 399–413.

Budabin, A. C., & Pruce, J. R. (2019). *New political science.* Forthcoming.

Budabin, A. C., & Richey, L. A. (2018). Advocacy narratives and celebrity engagement: The case of Ben Affleck in Congo. *Human Rights Quarterly, 40*(2), 260–286.

Buss, D. (2009). Rethinking rape as a weapon of war. *Feminist Legal Studies, 17*(2), 145–163.

Butler, J. (1997). *Excitable speech: A politics of the performative.* New York: Routledge.

Buzan, B., Wæver, O., & de Wilde, J. (1998). *Security: A new framework for analysis.* Boulder, CO: Lynne Rienner Publishers.

Castillo Diaz, P. (2017). Expert's take: A decade of efforts to combat sexual violence in conflict – Where are we now? UN Women. Retrieved from www.unwomen.org/en/news/stories/2017/6/experts-take-a-decade-of-efforts-to-combat-sexual-violence-in-conflict

Cohen, D. K. (2016). *Rape during civil war.* Ithaca, New York: Cornell University Press.

Coley, J. S. (2013). Theorizing issue selection in advocacy organizations: An analysis of human rights activism around Darfur and the Congo, 1998–2010. *Sociological Perspectives, 56*(2), 191–212.

Cooper, A. (2008). *Celebrity diplomacy. International studies intensives.* Boulder, CO: Paradigm Publishers.

Coulter, C. (2012). Plight and fate of women during and following genocide. *International Feminist Journal of Politics, 14*(1), 176–178.

Dalaqua, R. H. (2013). Securing our survival (SOS): Non-state actors and the campaign for a nuclear weapons convention through the prism of securitisation theory. *Brazilian Political Science Review, 7*(3), 90–117.

Dellmuth, L. M., & Tallberg, J. (2016). Elite communication and popular legitimacy in global governance. Retrieved from http://papers.ssrn.com/sol3/papers.cfm?abstract_id=2757650

de Waal, A. (Ed.). (2015). *Advocacy in conflict: Critical perspectives on transnational activism.* London: Zed Books.

Elbe, S. (2006). Should HIV/AIDS be securitized? *International Studies Quarterly, 50*(1), 119–144.

Finnemore, M., & Sikkink, K. (1998). International norm dynamics and political change. *International Organization, 52*(4), 887–917.

Gibney, M. (2015). *Watching human rights: The 101 best films.* London: Routledge.

Hall, R. B., & Bierstecker. T. J. (2002). *The emergence of private authority in global governance.* Cambridge: Cambridge University Press.

Hansen, L. (2000). The Little Mermaid's silent security agenda and the absence of gender in the Copenhagen School. *Millennium: Journal of International Studies, 29*(2), 285–306.

Hansen, L. (2012). Reconstructing desecuritisation: The normative-political in the Copenhagen School and directions for how to apply it. *Review of International Studies, 38*(3), 525–546.

Hirschauer, S. (2014). *The securitization of rape: Women, war and sexual violence.* London: Palgrave Macmillan.

Holmes, J. (2007, October 11). Congo's rape war (op. ed.). *Los Angeles Times.*

Hudson, N. F. (2009a). *Gender, human security and the United Nations: Security language as a political framework for women.* London: Routledge.

Hudson, N. F. (2009b). Securitizing women's rights and gender equality. *Journal of Human Rights, 8*(1), 53–70.

Inal, T. (2013). *Looting and rape in wartime: Law and change in international relations.* Philadelphia, PA: University of Pennsylvania Press.

Kaufman, J. P. & K. P. Williams. (2010). *Women and war: Gender identity and activism in times of conflict.* Sterling, VA: Kumarian Press.

Keck, M. E., & Sikkink, K. (1998). *Activists beyond borders: Advocacy networks in international politics.* Ithaca: Cornell University Press.

Kelly, J., King-Close, A., & Perks, R. (2014). Resources and resourcefulness: Roles, opportunities and risks for women working at artisanal mines in South Kivu, Democratic Republic of the Congo. *Futures, 26*(A), 95–105.

Lanz, D. (2011). Why Darfur? The responsibility to protect as a rallying cry for transnational advocacy groups. *Global Responsibility to Protect, 3*(2), 223–247.

Leatherman, J. (2011). *Sexual violence and armed conflict.* Cambridge: Polity Press.

Majic, S. A. (2017). Real men set norms? Anti-trafficking campaigns and the limits of celebrity norm entrepreneurship. *Crime, Media, Culture: An International Journal, 14*(2), 1–21.

Meger, S. (2016). *Rape, loot, pillage: The political economy of sexual violence in armed conflict.* Oxford: Oxford University Press.

Nelson, P. J., & Dorsey, E. (2008). *New rights advocacy: Changing strategies of development and human rights NGOs.* Washington, D.C.: Georgetown University Press.

Nolen, S. (2005, Spring). Not Women Anymore …: The Congo's rape survivors face pain, shame and AIDS. *MS Magazine.* Beverly Hills, CA.

Obaid, T. A. (2007). Sexual violence: Weapon of war, impediment to peace. *Forced Migration, 27*, 5. Retrieved from www.fmreview.org/sites/fmr/files/FMRdownloads/en/FMRpdfs/FMR27/full.pdf

Otto, D. (2009). The exile of inclusion: Reflections on gender issues in international law over the last decade. *Melbourne Journal of International Law, 10*(1), 11–26.

Physicians for Human Rights. (2004, October). The use of rape as a weapon of war in Darfur. Retrieved from http://physiciansforhumanrights.org/library/reports/darfur-use-of-rape-as-weapon-2004.html?referrer=www.google.com/. Last accessed June 1, 2017.

Shanahan, E. A., Jones, M. D., & McBeth. M. K. (2018). How to conduct a narrative policy framework study. *The Social Science Journal, 55*, 332–345.

Shannon, L. (2011). *A thousand sisters: My journey into the worst place on Earth to be a woman*. Berkeley, CA: Seal Press.

Sheehan, M. (2005). *International security: An analytical survey*. Boulder, CO: Lynne Rienner Publishers.

Shepherd, L. (2012). *Gender, violence and popular culture: Telling stories*. London: Routledge.

Shepherd, L. (2017). *Gender, UN peacebuilding, and the politics of space locating legitimacy*. Oxford: Oxford University Press.

Stroehlein, A. (2005, June). In Congo, 1,000 die per day: Why isn't it a media story? *Christian Science Monitor*. Retrieved from www.csmonitor.com/2005/0614/p09s02-coop.html. Last accessed June 15, 2017.

Swaine, A. (2018). *Conflict-related violence against women: Transforming transition*. Cambridge: Cambridge University Press.

Taureck, R. (2006). Securitization theory and securitization studies. University of Warwick institutional repository. Retrieved from http://wrap.warwick.ac.uk/1082/1/WRAP_Floyd_Securitization_theory_and_securitization_studies_WRAP.pdf. Last accessed June 15, 2017.

Vultee, F. (2010, February). Securitization. *Journalism Practice* [serial online]. *4*(1), 33–47. Available from: Communication & Mass Media Complete, Ipswich, MA. Last accessed June 12, 2018.

United Nations OCHA/IRIN. (2005). Broken bodies, broken dreams. Retrieved from http://peacewomen.org/node/89497. Last accessed June 15, 2017.

United Nations Security Council Resolution 1325. (2000).

United Nations Security Council Resolution 1820. (2008).

United Nations Security Council Resolution 1888. (2009).

United Nations Security Council Resolution 1889. (2009).

United Nations Wilton Park Conference Summary Report. (2008, May). *Women targeted or affected by armed conflict: What role for military peacekeepers* (pp. 1–24). Retrieved from www.unifem.org/attachments/events/WiltonParkConference_Presentations_200805.pdf. Last accessed January 2009.

Wæver, O. (1995). Securitization and desecuritization. In R. D. Lipschutz (Ed.), *On Security* (pp. 46–86). New York: Columbia University Press.

Wheeler, M. (2013). *Celebrity politics*. Cambridge: Polity Press.

Wibben, A. (2011). *Feminist security studies: A narrative approach*. London: Routledge.

Williams, M. (2003). Words, images, enemies: Securitization and international politics. *International Studies Quarterly, 47*(4), 511–531.

Wilson, R. A. & R. D. Brown (Eds.). (2009). *Humanitarianism and suffering: The mobilization of empathy*. New York: Cambridge University Press.

Wong, W. (2012). *Internal affairs: How the structure of NGOs transforms human rights*. Ithaca, New York: Cornell University Press.

5   Securitizing the environment

Climate change as first-order threat

Mark A. Boyer and Neil Oculi

Security: the state of being free from danger or threat[1]

From economic growth to the provision of basic human needs, the exploration of non-military conceptions of security and the security implications of non-militarized issues has grown exponentially in both policy and academic circles for the past few decades. But until relatively recently, environmental concerns have largely remained outside a security context, except when the realities of food scarcity or environmental disaster have been posited as at least partial impetus for armed conflict.[2] The relative marginalization of environmental security issues has changed significantly with the emergence and elevation of climate change on the local, national, regional, and global policy agendas.

Perhaps the highest profile example of the articulation of the security implications of climate change came from U.S. President Barack Obama in 2015 when he stated "I am here today to say that climate change constitutes a serious threat to global security, an immediate risk to our national security, and make no mistake, it will impact how our military defends our country."[3] But while President Obama continued to link climate change with its potential military implications, climate impacts pose independent, primary existential threats to people and countries around the world separate from the secondary, military, and conflict implications. Obama's arguments and imagery are reflective of the architecture of securitization as first laid out in Buzan, Wæver, and de Wilde (1998). Indeed, as climate change literally transforms our globe, securitization processes have thrust environmental concerns into the security frame and presented their implications and impacts as direct, first-order, threats. That conceptual argument will be further developed below, where we will discuss the elevation of climate change and its impacts in a security context through securitization moves and mechanisms. Following this, we provide an empirical assessment of climate change as first-order security threat through examination of recent and projected impacts of climate change on Caribbean island countries.

Climate security as a first order security threat

Context matters

Although the nascent stages of the intellectual discussion that would produce the concept of securitization is often dated to the publication of Richard Ullman's seminal article on 'redefining' security (1983), a broadened definition of security had implicitly been in place for decades. For instance, if one goes back to many of the early pronouncements regarding the creation of the Bretton Woods system at the end of World War II, the framing of the debate about the need for global institutions and governance was the linkage between economic prosperity and peace. The linkage was explicitly liberal in context, as figures like Cordell Hull and other policy-makers of the era viewed an open and liberal trading order as fundamental to the pursuit of peace. This explicit linkage between liberal economics and security begs the question of the origins of that linkage and why the leaders of the time perceived the need to reframe the dialogue of trade. In this reframing context, after centuries of global trade, why should the mid-twentieth century produce policy-making based on the economic causes of war and peace?

One set of arguments came from Alan Milward (1977), who drew our attention to the impact of the closing down of the world trading order in the 1920s and 1930s as a primary reason for World War II. Closing markets through increasing tariff barriers to trade arguably created the 'need' for armed conflict to obtain greater resources for continued economic growth. In other words, if you can't get what you want (and need) by trading for it, then you need to acquire those things through the use of force. This linkage of economics to war and peace, however, was still posed in a secondary context. Armed conflict emerged as the way to address economic needs. In this way, economic 'security' was inextricably linked to the ability to defend yourself militarily against threats in whatever form. But as we increasingly conceptualize security in the contemporary world system, it is apparent that there are venues where this pervasive linkage between a given issue area and the potential for military conflict no longer defines perceptions of security in the same way. This is indeed where context plays a significant role.

One illustrative contextual example draws on research about security perceptions among American adolescents (Boyer et al., 2005). These surveys were administered to respondents shortly after 9/11 and during the height of the Afghan and Iraq conflicts. Even during a time period fraught with overt physical security threats, when asked to define security in personal, national, and global terms, respondents offered the following:

- dominant responses on most important concerns for **personal** security – shelter, education, food, and defense (in that order)
- dominant responses on most important concerns for **national** security – strong economy, strong military, health care, and good diplomatic relations (in that order)

- dominant responses on most important concerns for **global** security – strong economy, eliminating weapons of mass destruction, education, health care, and a strong UN (in that order)

These results provide tangible empirical evidence on the contextual nature of security perceptions. Although the results are skewed by virtue of being drawn entirely from a sample of U.S. students, they nonetheless illustrate that even in times of heightened physical and militarized threats, other security concerns can and do rise above physical security. While these results might well be very different in other places around the globe, they serve to illustrate the contextual nature of security perceptions and the ways everyday people have come to view security in much more than military terms in their lived experiences.

As we will discuss below, this type of reframing has also happened recently around climate security, as the dialogue has moved from a focus on greenhouse gas mitigation to one of climate adaptation. As the other chapters in this volume help demonstrate, almost any issue and/or policy response can be securitized under the right conditions or situations. In the environmental realm, securitization has long centered on environmental conflict and the ways environmental problems such as famine, land degradation, extreme weather and the like lead to conflict over resources, the handling of migration flows, and other secondary impacts of environmental problems. These causal chains have led to well-established, research programs, but remain focused on the secondary causality of securitization in the environmental issue area (see Homer-Dixon, 1994, 1999; Gleditsch, 1998, 2012; Meierding, 2013). Hence, in this view, the 'environment' is not a security issue per se, but only becomes one when it generates causes for political-military conflict among global actors. But as Detraz and Betsill (2009) argue, in the age of attention to climate change, the discourse has shifted away from thinking about climate change as a cause for environmental *conflict* and into a realm where climate change is cast directly as a security issue just as Buzan et al. (1998) posited.

Securitizing climate change

The social, economic, and biophysical problems generated by climate change have been well-documented in the social and biophysical sciences as well as many other publications. Perhaps the most authoritative source on climate impacts are the recurrent assessments made by the Intergovernmental Panel on Climate Change (IPCC), whose most recent *5th Assessment* was published in 2014. Building on the path-breaking research on climate adaptation laid out in the *2007 4th Assessment*, the *5th Assessment* has tightened the focus on adaptation and vulnerability and has helped bring climate change more fully into the security frame. In fact, over the past two decades, culminating in the *4th Assessment*, researchers and policy-makers have moved into a sphere where adapting to climate change has arguably taken the policy foreground away from efforts on greenhouse gas (GHG) mitigation, long the primary focus on the environmental movement as it pertained to climate change. It is worth noting that originally the environmental movement was reticent to move away from the primary focus on greenhouse gas (GHG) mitigation for fear of losing sight of the root cause of the problem. Others, however, saw the focus on adaptation as both a political strategy and a policy urgency that would ultimately help the policy debate circle back to GHG mitigation (Boyer et al., 2017). As one set of authors put it, the *4th Assessment* and the policy discussions that followed led to a "lifting of the taboo on adaptation" and permitted action on the most urgent climate impacts (Pielke, Prins, Rayner, & Sarewitz, 2007, p. 597). The ongoing securitization of climate change played a vital role in that shift in both discourse and practice.

To that end, the securitization of climate change has centered on two forms. The first relies on authoritative scientific declarations about climate change that have largely been put forth globally through the IPCC. As Berling (2011, p. 392) puts it, "The scientific setting has given scientists a place from where to speak in the security field." Moving beyond the constraining binary (Derrida, 1981) of 'science/politics' or 'science/policy,' the scientific evidence produced by the IPCC has been mobilized in securitization claims relative to climate change impacts by securitizing actors, drawing on the appeal and credibility associated with the scientific vocation (Berling, 2011).

More specifically, the scientific contributions of the IPCC have been pushed into the global political realm through the UN Framework Convention on Climate Change (UNFCCC) process, which relies heavily on IPCC research and documentation. Hence, as Balzacq (2005) argues, translating the scientific work of the IPCC into the political realm of the UNFCCC is both a pragmatic and strategic practice that changes the audience and ultimately the power of the speaker and those who are listening. It is worth noting that even in the face of a U.S. Administration that is openly hostile to science in general and climate science in particular, the global community has continued to move forward with the larger climate agenda even without U.S. agreement about the issues at hand – a development largely attributable to the effective marshaling and use of 'science' and scientific expertise by securitizing actors.

The second important aspect of securitization to note in the climate change context is the switch from a focus on mitigation to one on adaptation. One can argue that this, too, is grounded in the scientific authority of the *4th* and *5th Assessments*. But this shift in focus also had profound implications for the broader debates in countries around the world, including the U.S.. This change in focus has also been aided by the reality of severe weather impacts in recent years in the U.S. from Hurricane Katrina in 2005 to 'Superstorm' Sandy in 2012, and more. These types of severe weather events have increasingly sensitized the average citizen to the fact that something new is indeed happening in our world's climate and weather. In this way, the central role of climate science and objective facts in the securitizing moves of those advocating for greater attention and response to climate change and its impacts have been reinforced by empirical realities. This mutually reinforcing, symbiotic dynamic between 'science-as-securitization' and the objective realities of climate change impacts is a topic we will revisit below, in our examination of the effects of climate change on Small Island Developing States (SIDS).

Risk, resilience, response

More fundamentally, with respect to securitization as a concept and process, the shift toward emphasizing adaptation has reframed much of the climate change political discourse. Arguably the chief result of this discursive move in policy terms has been a shift away from advancing policy remedies or proposed remedies with a longer (say, 50 year) time horizon to a focus on policies with immediate results. With the increased securitization of climate change and its associated impacts – defined as security threats – the logic underpinning policy responses has moved away from accepting the presumption that mitigation actions today will have little impact on temperature for many years to come; elevation of the threat driving immediacy of the response. Whether it is storm impacts, sunny-day flooding, new demands for storm water management inland, or changing tactics for agricultural production, such impacts are being felt now and in more direct ways than ever before.

Again, in returning to the interactive dynamics of (science-based) securitization and lived experiences, the intense, frequent, and direct effects of climate change for the average person has led him or her to focus on climate impacts at an individual, familial, and local community level – increasing and expanding the credibility and appeal of the 'moves' of securitizing agents in the process. In this way, as Trombetta (2008, p. 585) suggests more generally about environmental securitization, changes in discourse and context are changing policy as well, and transforming climate "security provisions and practices." Figure 5.1,

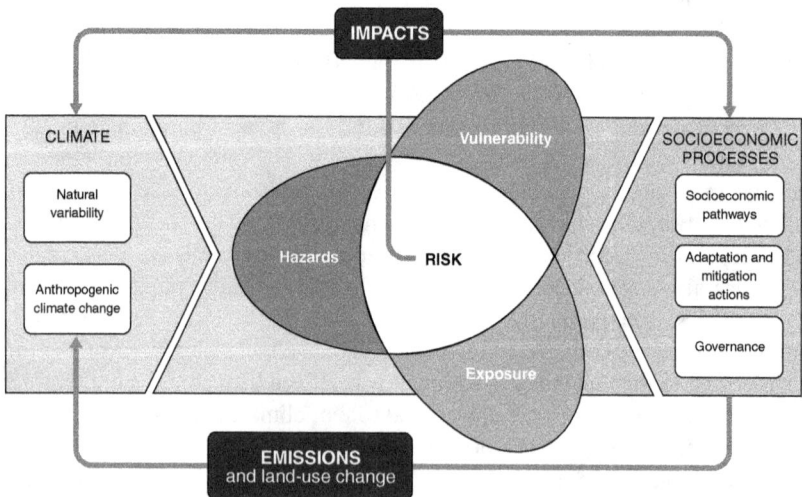

Figure 5.1 Conceptualizing climate risk.

drawn from the *5th Assessment*, depicts this securitization dynamic relative to climate change graphically.

The existence of risk sits centrally in nearly every security concern. Whether the risk of a terrorist attack, a traditional military incursion or – as depicted here – in climate impacts, the management of risk is acutely urgent within the development of strategies and tactics for enhancing security in any setting. The need to manage those risks becomes even more acute when we factor economic inequality into the equation. Although economic inequality might not affect the hazards portion depicted in Figure 5.1, it does impact both vulnerability and exposure. Vulnerability is a product of physical attributes as well as climate and emergency preparedness, and also the economic means at hand for use in preparedness and response. Exposure, while seemingly a product of physical attributes, is also conditioned by historic settlement patterns, the specific characteristics of the built environment (for example, type of construction: frame, brick, elevated or not) and quite directly the impact of colonialism on many countries in the Global South.

In this way, resilience can be seen as a luxury good, available (and largely affordable) only to those in the Global North. Resilience can be defined as the "capacity of a system to absorb disturbance and reorganize while undergoing change" (Adger, Brown & Waters, 2011, p. 698). As Corry (2014) puts it, resilience has moved into the void in security studies created when we move beyond "defense" as the primary operationalization. As he further argues, " 'risk' and 'resilience' have begun to constitute a conceptual pair in a similar way to 'threat' and 'defense' " (p. 256) as in the more traditional security venues. But as we will discuss further below, we argue that 'threat' remains a fundamental characteristic of the climate challenge for vast numbers of people and countries around the world.

Resilience and adaptive capacity come with significant economic costs and also a necessary degree of stability and flexibility in infrastructure that often does not exist in the Global South. Still, a lack of resilience does not, in and of itself, result in the transformation of climate change into a first-order security issue absent the purposive 'moves' of securitizing actors and agents. A lack of resilience might generate second order security concerns, where the problems generated might lead to internal or external conflict, but do not create security concerns in and of themselves. However, as we have moved into a more acute phase of climate impacts with our understanding of them increasing over the past decade, the existential security threat from climate change has become direct, and been translated as such through securitization. To this end, Table 5.1 displays a range of climate impacts as identified by the IPCC's *5th Assessment*.

As this table shows, many of the climate change impacts identified by the IPCC (and the threats they engender) might still be considered to fall in the 'second-order' threat category. But the threats generated by sea-level rise, storm surge, extreme and unpredictable weather, flooding and more, produce first-order security threats for people around the world. The climate threats are most acute for those in coastal areas and the Global South and are even more acute for the places where those two geographic categories intersect – and these threats in

Table 5.1 Observed and predicted impacts of climate change

Global physical indicators	Regional physical indicators	Socio-ecological indicators	Biological indicators
Global average combined land and ocean surface show a warming of 0.89°C [0.69 to 1.08]°C over the period 1901–2012, and about 0.72 [0.49° to 0.89]°C over the period 1951–2012.	Strong evidence suggesting an increase in the most intense tropical cyclones in the North Atlantic basin since the 1970s.	Farmers and foresters have had to adapt to different growing seasons and increase disturbance regimes.	Species ranges are moving towards the poles and upward in elevation.
The Ocean since the 1970s has stored about 93% of the excess energy absorbed by the climate system.	The Arctic is warming at the fastest rate. Annual mean Arctic sea ice extent from 1979 to 2012 decreased 3.5 to 4.1% per decade and 9.4 to 13.6% per decade during the summer.	Increase in sea level rise will displace people from islands.	Shift in migration and breeding patterns.
Decrease in ice contained in glaciers globally every year for the past 20 years.	Decrease in spring snow across the Northern Hemisphere since the 1950s.	Negative impacts on human systems, such as human health, food security, water security, and security of societal conditions.	Increase in coral bleaching and ocean acidification.
Global mean sea level (GMSL) has risen by 0.19 [0.17 to 0.21]m. over the period 1901–2010.	The largest precipitation changes over northern Eurasia and North America are projected to occur during the winter.	Loss of biodiversity will decrease important ecosystem services.	About 20–30% of species studied so far could face extinction.
Global-scale precipitation is projected to gradually increase in the 21st century.	The Mediterranean, southwestern U.S.A. and southern Africa will experience increased drying.	Coastal flooding due to sea level rise in 2005 accounted for loss of 5% of global GDP (U.S.$3,000 billion);estimated to increase by 9% in 2070.	Vegetated coastal habitats are declining globally.

Sources: IPCC (2013, p. 1535); IPCC (2014, p. 151); Wong, et al (2014, pp. 361–409).

particular have been, and remain, front-and-center in the efforts of actors engaged in the securitization of climate change.

Further complicating our understanding of climate change and its securitization are what Mayer (2012) calls "chaotic climate change" and Dyer (2014) calls "climate anarchy." Following Mayer's argument, we are faced with the unsettling fact that much of what we know about climate change is based on fundamentally sound science; but, as we move into the future, we are beginning to see signs that our climate future could be different, and perhaps significantly worse, than previously forecast. In 2016, for instance, the world received multiple reports of polar ice melting faster than originally expected.[4] Faster melting ice pack yields less reflective surface around the globe and greater ocean absorption of solar radiation further increasing rising temperatures and melting. In Mayer's conceptualization, then, the world may well face climate threats greater than expected and also those that are vexing in troubling and unanticipated ways. These shortcomings in terms of scientific projection and prediction could (and perhaps have) opened the door for those opposed to action on climate change to question and disparage the contributions of climate science that we have shown to be essential to the securitization process. On the other hand, the greater intensity and magnitude of the climate impacts that result are likely to override and trump the denialist position by (sadly) worsening the 'lived experience' (direct and personal impact) dimension of the securitization dynamic.

Dyer's constructs further underscore the chaotic biophysical nature of climate change while also highlighting the policy challenges they will create, given the reality that climate change policy-making does not fit well within existing global governance structures or neatly inside state-level policy-making. As a result, the world is faced with policy-making fragmentation over climate change that Dyer somewhat hopefully argues will provide the potential for policy innovation in the coming years. Much scholarly time and energy has been spent understanding this policy fragmentation over the past decade, but much of it points to the fundamental problem of policy coordination in tackling a complex and unpredictable problem.[5] Dyer's perspective here helps reveal that, while securitization processes may be well on the way to elevating climate change as a first-order security threat, they have made fewer inroads with respect to the specification and elevation of effective policy responses to that threat.

The inherent problem with the existence and the degree of policy fragmentation around climate change is that much of what needs to be done in coping with climate change requires macro-level securitization and, by extension, global policy decisions and actions, as so many of the impacts are boundary transcendent. In addition, devolution of climate governance to lower levels of government and even private or quasi-private entities underplays the limits to financial resources that exist below the global and state levels.[6] This policy fragmentation also raises significant concerns for coping with insecurity, especially when generated by climate impacts as we will discuss further below.

As argued here, and illustrated more concretely below, climate change generates both primary (direct), secondary, and even tertiary impacts that individually and collectively demonstrate the veracity of its securitization. But what sets climate change apart from other securitized policy issues is the direct way that it creates danger, jeopardizing the survival both of individuals and states. At the primary level, depending on the sea-level rise scenarios, some states may cease to exist in the relatively near future. Some of this will depend on topography, but even for those countries with higher elevations, coastal settlements will be impacted greatly. As a result, climate change will create climate refugees, which will undoubtedly impact the Global South asymmetrically (see Methmann, 2014). Moreover, these refugee flows will also exacerbate the incidence of state-lessness in parts of the Global South (see Belton, 2017). At a secondary level, refugees, statelessness, and disappearance of territory might also produce fertile ground for conflict as neighboring countries and the international community more broadly seek to cope with the realities of loss of homeland. In this way, climate threats intersect with human security concerns, with those interactions a crucial element of the securitization process.

Climate impacts and security: the case of Caribbean small island developing states

In seeking to further understand the primary threats associated with climate change in and of themselves, as well as the role they play in the construction of climate change as a first order threat via the securitization process, we turn here to an analysis of climate impacts on Caribbean Small Island Developing States (SIDS). The empirical evidence and discussion presented here provides an opportunity to evaluate the veracity of the argument that climate change is now the foundational example of environmental security, as well as its transformation into a first-order security concept. As Buzan et al. (1998) point out, the scientific agenda centers on the authoritative provision of evidence that climate change indeed threatens security on a near-daily basis in many parts of the world. They also argue, with particular relevance here, that "most successful securitization [...] is local (p. 92)." As the reader will see below, localized climate impacts abound and unfortunately emphasize the central irony of the climate security frame: climate change as a fundamental *global* problem yields impacts that are, and will continue to be, felt most acutely at the local level and will require local approaches to adaptation that are designed, scaled and in most cases paid for at the local level.

We begin by conducting a longitudinal analysis of past loss and damage caused by storms in the Caribbean. This analysis uses data from the International Disaster Database (EM-DAT), located at the Center for Research on the Epidemiology of Disasters (CRED). The main purpose of the database is to help facilitate humanitarian action at both national and international levels. CRED aims to provide useful and reliable data for disaster preparedness, as well as an objective base for vulnerability assessments and policy-making. EM-DAT consists of data from various sources including UN agencies, non-governmental organizations, insurance companies, research institutes and press agencies. This dataset focuses on the impacts of storms for the Caribbean Region from 1960 to 2010. In our analysis, we look at four different categories:

1   Total population affected
2   Total damage in U.S.$
3   Number of deaths
4   Total number of storms

In presenting and analyzing this data, we employ both traditional and geospatial techniques.

The first type is a comparative analysis of the data though various graphical representations. In examining the Caribbean, we will see that the increasing intensity of storms create both human and national security crises throughout the region. The Caribbean is the focal point for our analysis because of the concentration of Small Island Developing States (SIDS). In addition, the region has a long history of storm impacts that have accelerated in recent decades. As a result, the Caribbean region provides a convenience sample of climate impacts, but a sample that we argue is also representative of the broader picture globally.

The Caribbean region consists of countries inside and surrounding the Caribbean Sea, but this group is not homogenous. As shown in Figure 5.2, the region is located in the southwest of the Gulf of Mexico and North America. The region

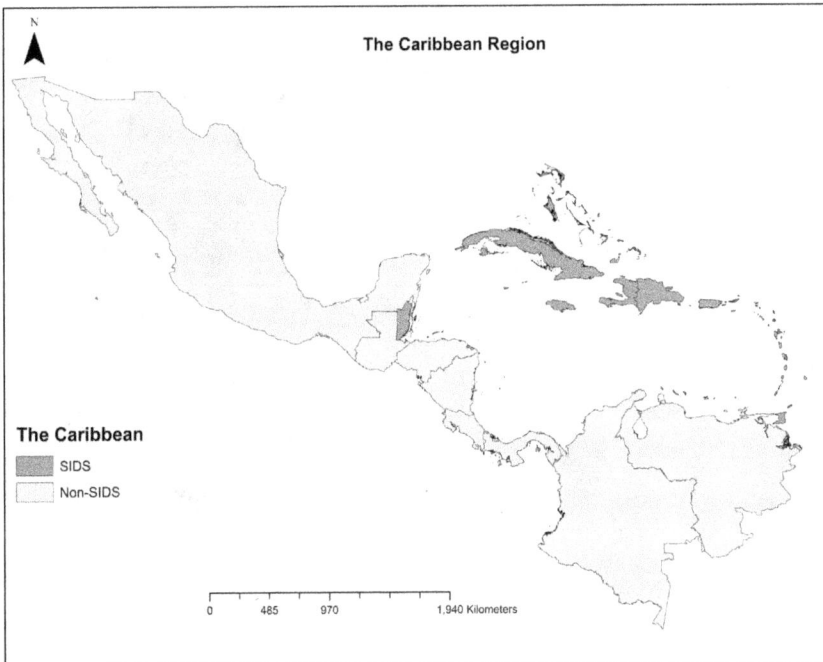

Figure 5.2 Map of the Caribbean.

also borders the east of Central America and the northern part of South America. As noted above, we focus here on SIDS within the Caribbean Region as they are among the most vulnerable to the impacts of climate change, most notably rising sea levels and extreme events (Sim, 2011).[7]

Spatial and temporal analysis of loss and damage as a security issue[8]

Our first analytical concern is measuring the relationship between the total number of people who died from 1970 to 2010 as a result of storms in the Caribbean region and the number of storms for the same period. As shown in Figures 5.3 and 5.4, there is a clear increase in both the number of storms and storm-related deaths from the 1980s onwards. For instance, from 1970 to 1980 there were 32 storms, resulting in a total of 1,819 deaths. By 2010 the number of storms had quadrupled compared to the total number of storms that occurred from 1970 to 1980. Even within this time period, there is a notable intensification in terms of storm-related deaths; as indicated in Figure 5.4, 1979 accounted for 1,451 of the 1,819 (80 percent) storm-related deaths occurring during the decade. Moreover, based on the EM-DAT data, four islands experienced storm-related deaths in 1979: Dominica, 40; Dominican Republic, 1,400; Haiti, eight; and Puerto Rico, three. This was chiefly attributable to the destructive force of Hurricane David, which first made landfall in the Lesser Antilles, sweeping

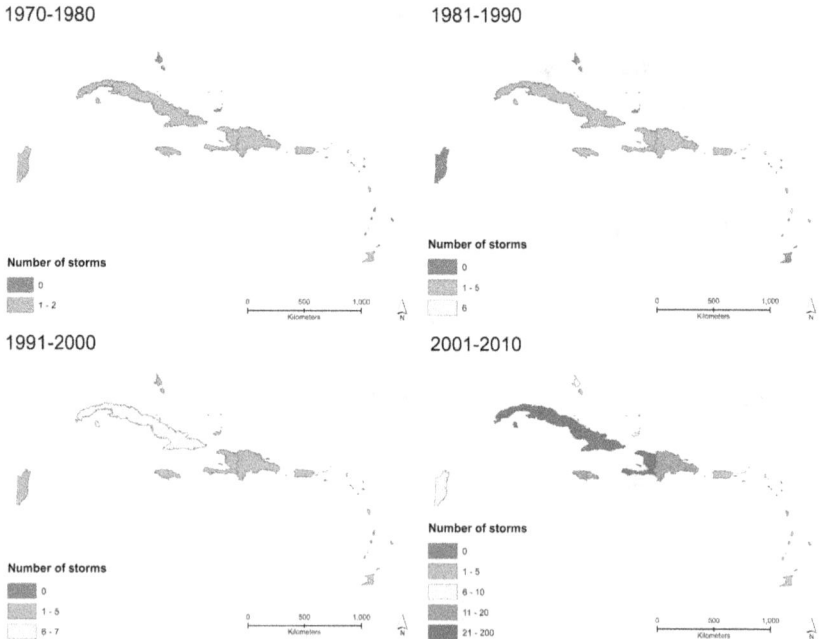

Figure 5.3 Number of storms by decade per country in the Caribbean region, 1970–2010.

1970-1980   1980-1990

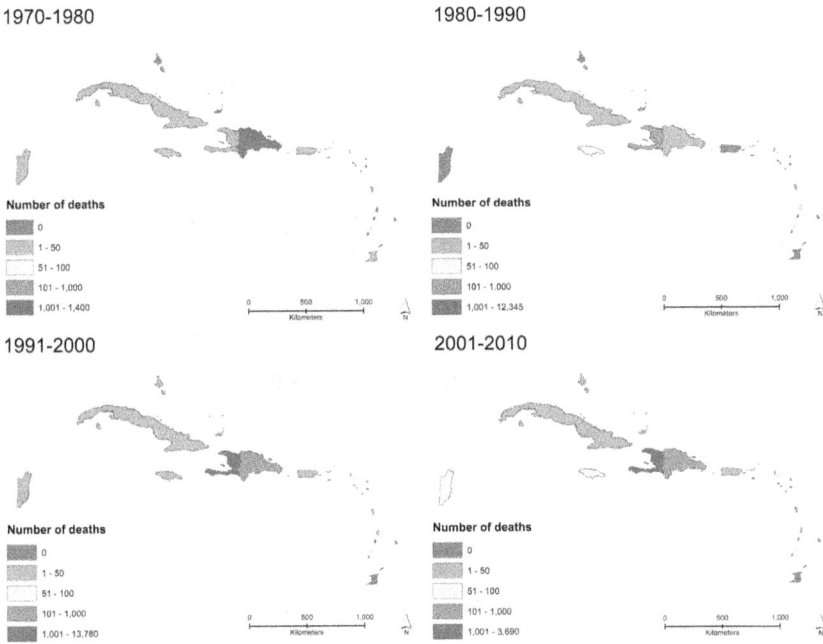

Number of deaths
- 0
- 1 - 50
- 51 - 100
- 101 - 1,000
- 1,001 - 1,400

Number of deaths
- 0
- 1 - 50
- 51 - 100
- 101 - 1,000
- 1,001 - 12,345

1991-2000   2001-2010

Number of deaths
- 0
- 1 - 50
- 51 - 100
- 101 - 1,000
- 1,001 - 13,780

Number of deaths
- 0
- 1 - 50
- 51 - 100
- 101 - 1,000
- 1,001 - 3,690

Figure 5.4 Number of storm-related deaths by decade per country in the Caribbean region, 1970–2010.

through the Greater Antilles, the Bahamas and the U.S. Figure 5.4 shows the impact of Hurricane David in 1979 on the Dominican Republic, though significant deaths also occurred in Haiti and Jamaica.

The relationship between occurrence of storms and the number of deaths (depicted graphically in Figure 5.5) also demonstrates the relatively high security risk resulting from the frequencies of these storms. The other major death count was in 2004, when the Caribbean region was hit by a series of deadly storms. While there were 23 storms during this year, four major Hurricanes caused the greatest destruction in the Caribbean in 2004. The first was Hurricane Charley, killing four people in Cuba, followed subsequently by Frances, Ivan, and David. In the Caribbean, David was a Category 5 hurricane, with recorded wind speeds of 160 mph from a location just south of the Dominican Republic; on two occasions the minimum pressure fell to 910 mb. Ivan killed 39 people in Grenada, seven in Jamaica, four in the Dominican Republic, three in Venezuela, two in the Cayman Islands, and one each in Tobago and Barbados. The largest share of deaths in 2004 resulted from Hurricane Jeanne, which took the lives of 2,754 Haitians. In sum, this consideration of storm frequency and storm-related deaths shows a substantial increase in the number and impact of storms especially in Cuba, Haiti, Dominican Republic, and the Bahamas during the period of concern.

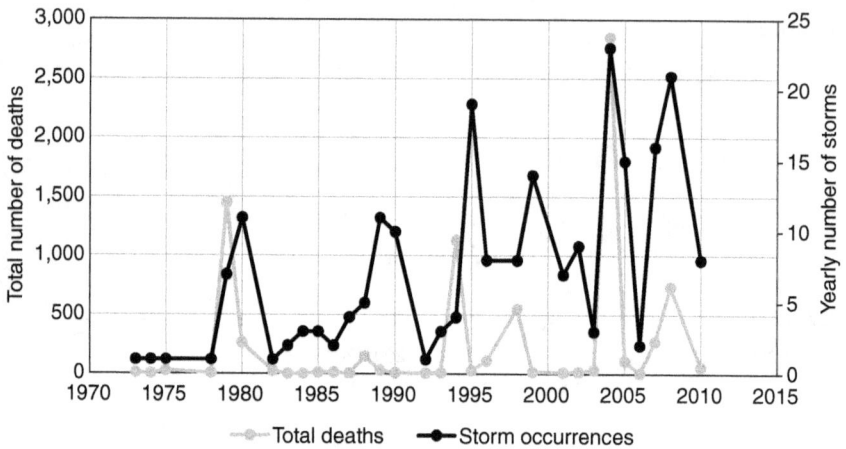

Figure 5.5 Total storm and total deaths for the Caribbean region, 1970–2010.

The next focal point in the analysis is a consideration of the combined impact of human causalities with the extent of property damage caused by the storms. A comparison of the number of storms and aggregate storm-related damage totals is displayed in Figure 5.6.

As with the death tolls, from the 1980s onwards there has been a notable increase in the amount of property damage. One significant example is the case of Cuba, as demonstrated in the maps in Figure 5.7. While the Greater Antilles suffer the most damage, the Lesser Antilles has incurred increased property damage and, because of their size, has had a greater burden on its socio-economic welfare. For

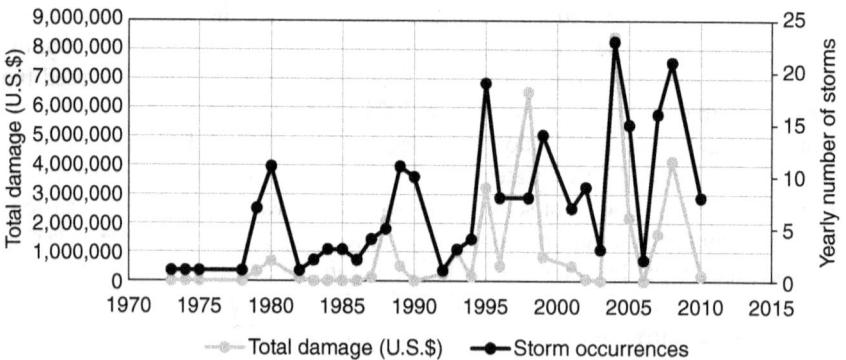

Figure 5.6 Number of storms in relation to total damage for the Caribbean region, 1970–2010.

1970-1980   1981-1990

Damage ('000 USD)
■ $0.00
▨ $0.01 - $1,000.00
□ $1,000.01 - $100,000.00
▨ $100,000.01 - $150,000.00

Damage ('000 USD)
■ $0.00
▨ $0.01 - $1,000.00
□ $1,000.01 - $100,000.00
▨ $100,000.01 - $1,000,000.00
■ $1,000,000.01 - $1,070,200.00

1991-2000   2001-2010

Damage ('000 USD)
■ $0.00
▨ $0.01 - $1,000.00
□ $1,000.01 - $100,000.00
▨ $100,000.01 - $1,000,000.00
■ $1,000,000.01 - $1,599,144.00

Damage ('000 USD)
■ $0.00
▨ $0.01 - $1,000.00
□ $1,000.01 - $100,000.00
▨ $100,000.01 - $1,000,000.00
■ $1,000,000.01 - $9,663,452.00

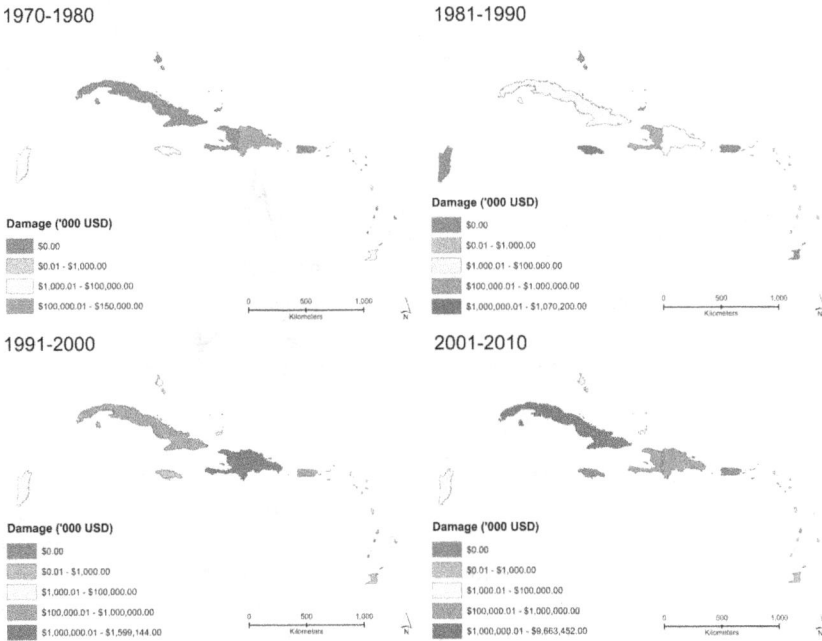

Figure 5.7 Total damage caused by storms per decade for the Caribbean region, 1970–2010.

example, the case of Grenada with Hurricane Ivan in 2004 and Hurricane Thomas in Saint Lucia of 2010, exemplifies the impact of one storm on these Caribbean islands.

As indicated by the World Bank, the financial damage caused by Hurricane Ivan crippled Grenada's economy and amounted to more than U.S.$900 million, more than twice the country's GDP, causing damage to more than 80 percent of the buildings, including 73 of the 75 public schools.[9] The total cost of losses and damage by Hurricane Thomas was estimated at U.S.$336.2 million representing 43.3 percent of the country's GDP.[10] Belize has incurred significant property damage throughout three of the four decades of analysis, with the exception of the 1990s. Similarly, Jamaica has experienced significant storm-related property damage throughout the period, with the 1980s showing the most severe and, again, the 1990s representing something of an outlier.

The third component of the analysis looks at the total population affected in relation to the total cost of damage. Again, from the late 1980s, the data show trends of major increase in the cost of damage (see Figure 5.8). The data also indicated a concentration of substantial damages in particular individual storm events. The Caribbean region is very vulnerable because of the threat from coastal flooding due to storm surge. This is particularly significant as a major

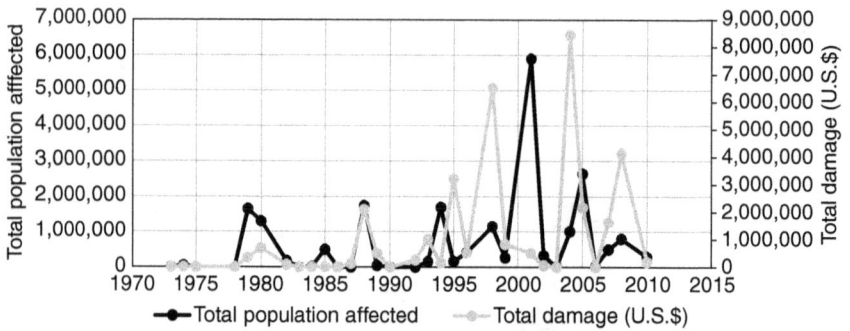

Figure 5.8 Total population affected in relation to damage for the Caribbean region, 1970–2010.

component of the region's economy is tourism, in which most of the businesses are located on the coastal region. It is worth noting though that at times, damage and casualties are not correlated, for instance in situations of low damage but high causalities (affected population), such as instances of coastal flooding. The year 2001 was instructive in this regard. The results depicted in Figure 5.8 reveal an outlier in 2001, where the total population affected was far greater than the cost of damage. That is because of the impact of Hurricane Michelle over Cuba. During this period, over 590,000 people were evacuated across the country, with coastal tourism resorts cleared. The storm affected many people and required a mass mobilization of resources and more than 24,000 volunteers to help the civil defense team in evacuating those who were affected by the storm. However, due to the efforts and preparedness by the Cuban government, the damage was lessened, and according to the EM-DAT database the death count was limited to five.

Another similar outlier revealed in careful analysis of the data occurs when one storm's impact in terms of damages skews the data across a longer time period, particularly when that time period features multiple other storms. For instance, in comparing Figures 5.9 and 5.10, one can see that while there was little change in the Dominican Republic for the 1970s because of the severity of Hurricane David in 1979, there are slightly different results for the same country during the 1980s.

Likewise, the maps showing the impact of storm-related damage on the total population in Figure 5.9 overestimate the impact of storms occurring in the Dominican Republic in the 1980s in comparison to the results depicted in the maps in Figure 5.10 (i.e., total population affected per storms). The same result is seen for other countries through the four decades, such as Cuba in the 2000s and Jamaica in the 1990s. In an attempt to control for this, we considered how many people died in relation to how many people that were affected. The data shown in Figure 5.11 below are consistent with the assumption that generally

1970-1980   1981-1990

1991-2000   2001-2010

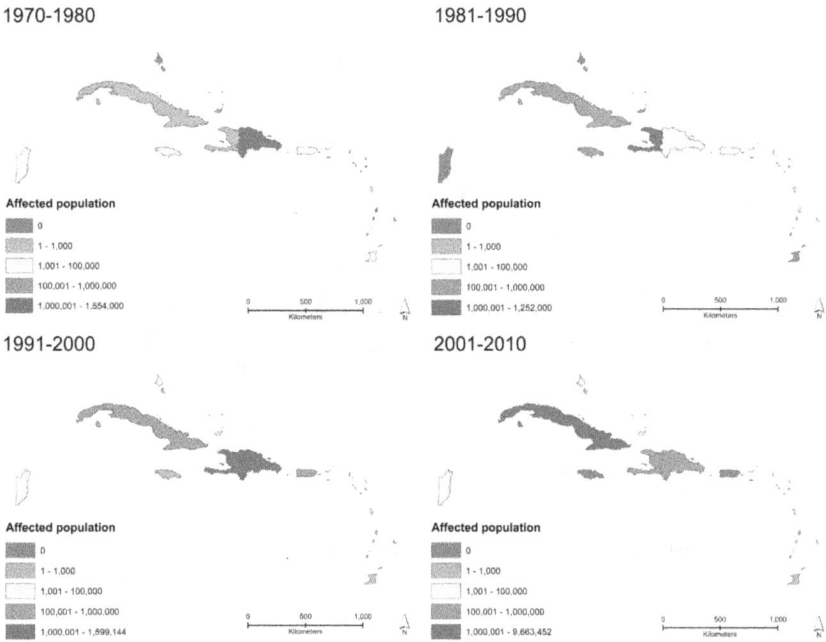

Figure 5.9 Total population affected in reference to the total cost of damage for the Caribbean region, 1970–2010.

more people will be affected as opposed to those who die during any natural disaster. Since the data provides the population affected for all the storms occurring in a given decade, to be able to visualize the severity of individual storms, we normalize the number of the population affected from individual storm (in ArcGIS) to the total population affected by the total storm in the same decade.

In order to evaluate the most impacted areas in the region, we examined the directional distribution of the dataset. This method uses the standard deviational ellipse in ArcGIS to calculate the standard deviation of the x-coordinates and y-coordinates from the mean center. The goal of this is to explain the directional relationship of the data in order to examine its spatial dynamics. The directional distribution covers on standard deviation about 63 percent of the data shown below. The map below (Figure 5.12) illustrates that in terms of total damage, the Greater Antilles (Puerto Rico, Hispaniola, Cuba, and Jamaica) incur about 63 percent of the total damage. Hispaniola and Cuba had 63 percent of the total affected population as well as the total deaths. Finally, as it relates to the number of storm events, the directional distribution indicates that most of the Caribbean islands except Trinidad and Tobago and Belize fall within the distributional directional ellipse. This provides clear evidence that climate-related events such as storms provide major security threats for the Caribbean region.

1970-1980   1981-1990

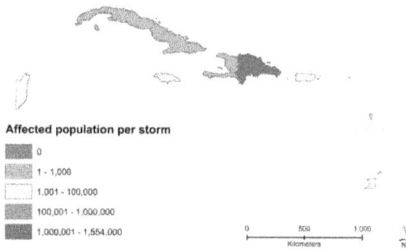
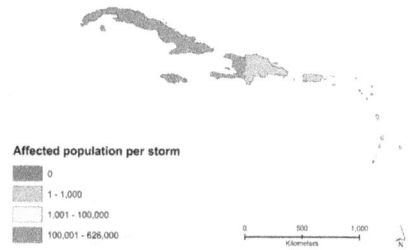

Affected population per storm

0
1 - 1,000
1,001 - 100,000
100,001 - 1,000,000
1,000,001 - 1,554,000

1991-2000   2001-2010

Affected population per storm

0
1 - 1,000
1,001 - 100,000
100,001 - 626,000

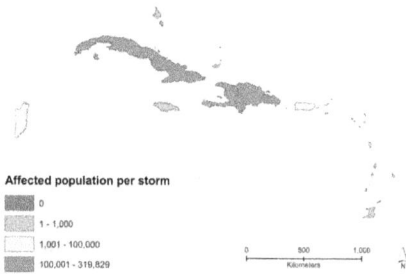
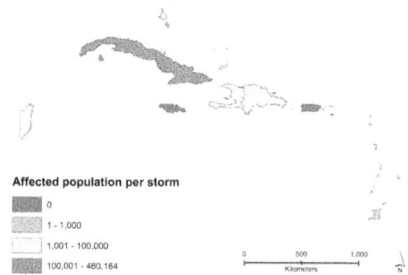

Affected population per storm

0
1 - 1,000
1,001 - 100,000
100,001 - 319,829

Affected population per storm

0
1 - 1,000
1,001 - 100,000
100,001 - 480,164

Figure 5.10 Affected population per storm for the Caribbean region, 1970–2010.

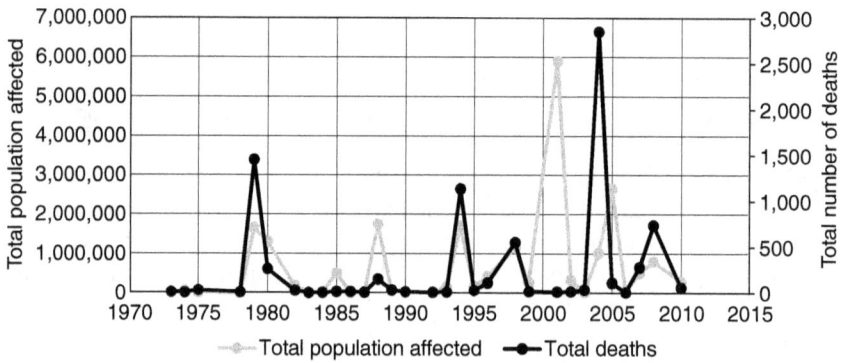

Figure 5.11 Total deaths in relation to total population affected for the Caribbean region, 1970–2010.

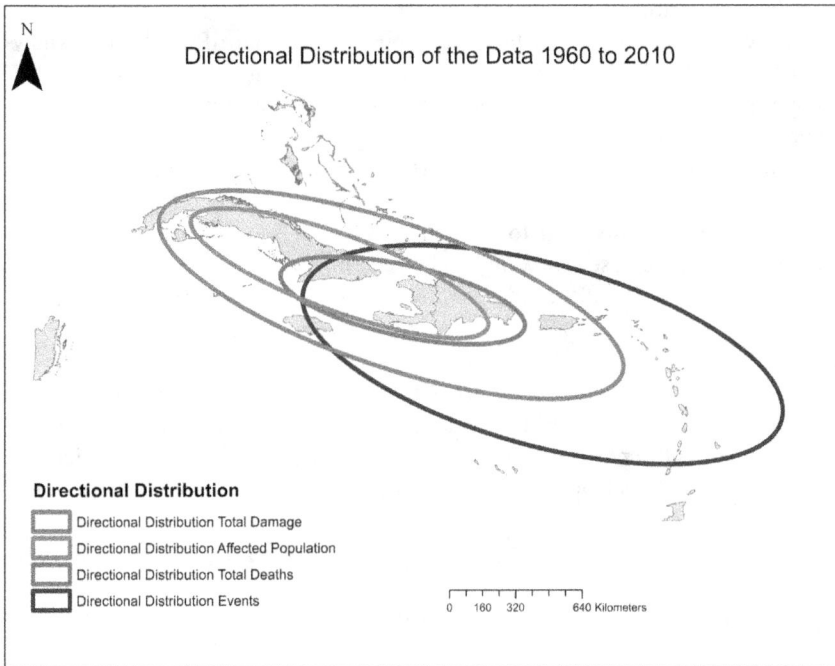

Figure 5.12 Directional distribution of the data 1970 to 2010.

Spotlight: sea level rise

As discussed above, climate change poses an acute and existential threat to the security of Small Island Developing States (SIDS), and sea level rise (SLR) is perhaps the most pressing direct climate change-related threat they face. Indeed, Nurse et al. (2014, p. 1616) explain that "SLR poses one of the most widely *recognized* climate change threats to low-lying coastal areas on islands and atolls" (emphasis added; see also Cazenave & Llovel, 2010; Nicholls & Cazenave, 2010; Church & White, 2011). Political leaders representing SIDS have repeatedly called for global action on climate change and SLR, with the first Small States Conference on Sea Level Rise held in Male, Maldives in 1989. The conference brought together

> a small, but representative group of island States [...] including non-self-governing territories from the Pacific, Caribbean, Mediterranean and Indian Ocean. The discussion in Male centered on the need for a common strategy on SLR and on how to protect SIDS from the effects of global warming.
>
> (Oculi, 2014, p. 24)

Since then, SIDS have played a pivotal role in contributing to the securitization of SLR at international, regional, and local levels.

At the international level, both the UNFCCC and the IPCC have acknowledged that "small islands do not have uniform climate change risk profiles" (Nurse et al., 2014, p. 1616). Not surprisingly, the physical characteristics of some SIDS along with their demographic and social composition make them much more vulnerable than others to the adverse effects of climate change and SLR because of their low adaptive capacities. The frequencies of weather and climate-related hazards lead to challenges such as salinization of freshwater, coastal erosion, increased flooding, and forced migration – all issues which have featured in the efforts of the IPCC and other securitizing actors. As indicated in the *Working Group II to the Fifth Assessment Report of the IPCC*,

> the key climate and ocean drivers of change that impact small islands include variations in air and ocean temperatures; ocean chemistry; rainfall; wind strength and direction; sea levels and wave climate; and particularly the extremes such as tropical cyclones, drought, and distant storm swell events.

> (Nurse et al., 2014, p. 1619)

These climate and ocean drivers produce differential impacts related to SIDS biophysical, socio-economic, and political characteristics. Additional important factors are the magnitude, frequencies, temporal, and spatial extents of these drivers, as illustrated in Figure 5.13.

Moreover, SLR affects the livelihood and lifestyle patterns of many communities in SIDS. One of the biggest socioeconomic impacts of SLR is its direct effect on economic drivers of coastal communities. One of these economic drivers is the impact on coastal tourism. AR5 WGII put that

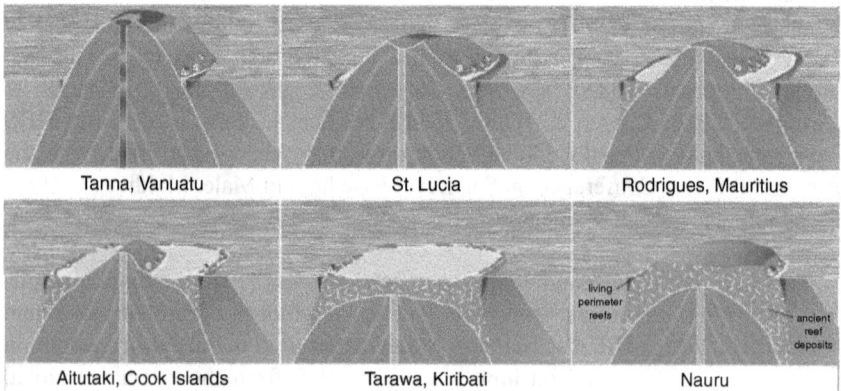

Figure 5.13 Representative tropical island typologies.

developing countries and small islands within the tropics dependent on coastal tourism will be impacted directly not only by future sea level rise and associated extremes but also by coral bleaching and ocean acidification and associated reductions in tourist arrivals.

Ironically, many visitors are drawn to these coastal areas for the same scenic qualities that make SIDS so fragile.

SLR also have a great impact on infrastructure due to floods and storm surges. Fisheries play an important role in the social and economic development of many SIDS; given that these ecosystems are already very fragile, climate change and SLR greatly amplify the vulnerabilities of fisheries in SIDS. For instance, SLR has negative impacts on mangroves and their capacity to serve as nurseries for smaller fish. The health of both mangroves and coral reefs are very important for local communities because they provide provision services such as fisheries; habitat services for wildlife such as migratory birds; cultural services such as ecotourism; and regulatory services such as the first line of defense against storms and hurricanes by serving as windbreakers for coastal and inland communities.

Here we have employed ArcGIS in order to simulate SLR and depict the extent of security threats it poses in the Caribbean region.[11] We begin with Hispaniola (see Figure 5.14). Hispaniola is the second largest Caribbean island

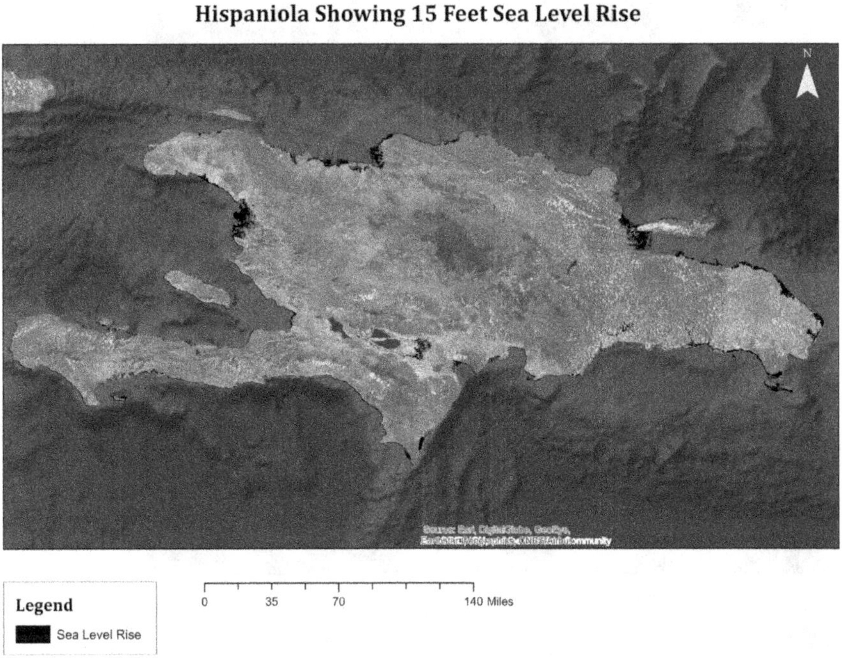

Hispaniola Showing 15 Feet Sea Level Rise

Legend
Sea Level Rise

0   35   70   140 Miles

Figure 5.14 Map of Hispaniola showing 15 feet sea level rise.

covering about 29,418 m^2. Our analysis indicates that a 15 ft or 4.6 m sea level rise would inundate about 493 m^2 of Hispaniola, an area larger than Antigua and Barbuda (232 m^2) and Barbados (166.4 m^2) combined. That amount of inundation is 1.67 percent of the island.

A similar depiction of Antigua and Barbuda is provided in Figure 5.15. Both are very small islands in the Leeward area of the Caribbean and because of their size, topography, and geographic location, are very vulnerable. As a result, even small amounts of sea level rise present grave security threats for this country. As Figure 5.15 demonstrates, a 15 ft sea level rise would inundate much of the

Antigua and Barbuda Showing 15 Feet Sea Level Rise

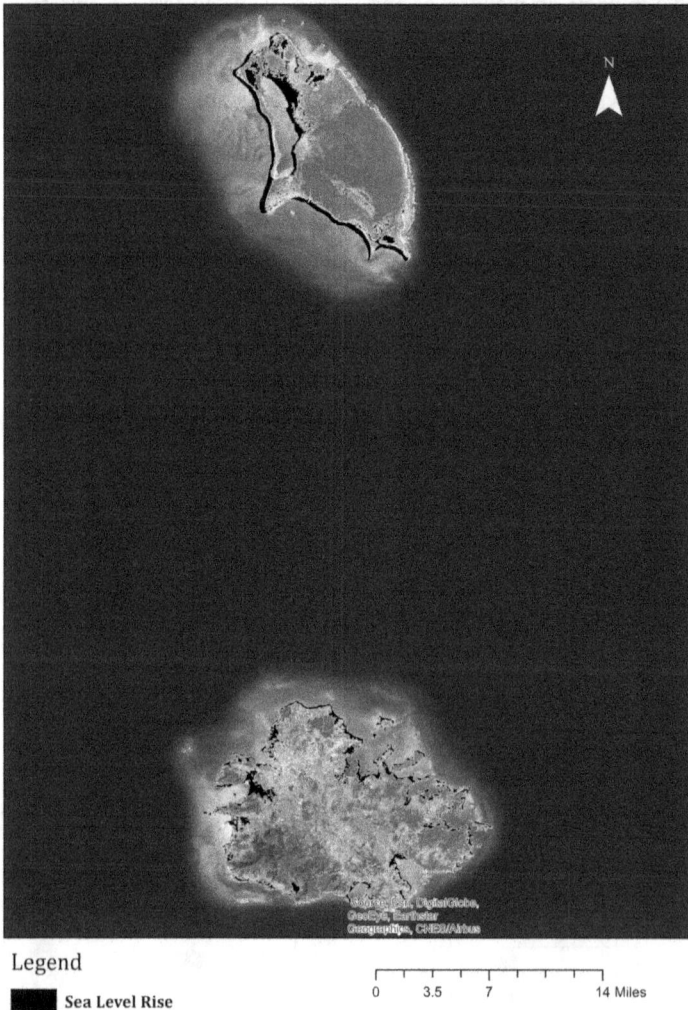

Legend

◼ Sea Level Rise

0   3.5   7   14 Miles

Figure 5.15 Map of Antigua and Barbuda showing 15 feet sea level rise.

Barbados Showing 15 Feet Sea Level Rise

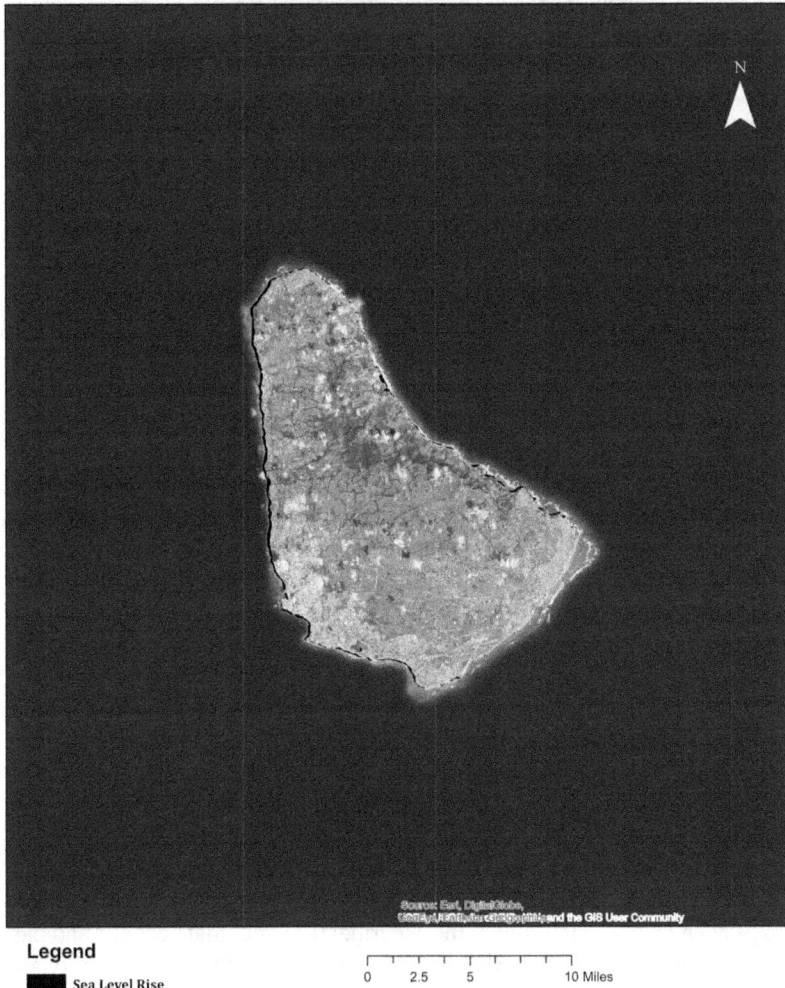

Legend

■ Sea Level Rise

0   2.5   5   10 Miles

Figure 5.16 Map of Barbados showing 15 feet sea level rise.

eastern part of Barbuda. However, in Antigua, the entire island would be affected by such an increase in sea level. Like Antigua, most of Barbados will experience a sea level rise that will have significant impacts on urban areas (see Figure 5.16). As each of these cases illustrate, the existential threat posed by SLR to SIDS in the Caribbean (and beyond) makes it among the most direct and acute security threats associated with climate change. In light of the many implications and ramifications associated with SLR – some of which were depicted here – it is not surprising that it has become a central focus of securitizing agents.

Conclusions

In this chapter we have provided clear evidence of the direct, first-order security threats posed by climate change. These are threats which play a crucial role in the process by which climate change has been and is being securitized, especially given the importance of both scientific knowledge and expertise, and lived experience with climate change impacts to the securitization of climate change. In our view, the evidence presented here also provides an important illustration of the merits of securitization both in terms of advancing the scholarly debate concerning climate change (and environmental security more broadly), and in potentially providing for mitigation of the negative impacts of climate change on people and economic assets. No longer should environmental security issues such as climate change be considered as 'merely' a second-order effect at most; rather, the risks it engenders – as shown empirically here – threaten the very survival of people and in many cases the states in which they live.

To the extent that the securitization process can and does transform debates over environmental issues such as climate change, it also has the potential to advance and support the construction of a new set of policy initiatives to confront the direct outcomes of climate change in the short-run, as well as those related outcomes (such as climate refugees) that will need to be engaged in the coming years. This is not to say that the securitization of climate change should be understood as a panacea. On the one hand, the public and policy attention that results from efforts to underscore the fact that climate change is an imperative is likely to be beneficial. Yet, as is well-chronicled, the responses that result from securitizing moves tend to emphasize coercive, statist-militarist 'solutions' that emerge from, and are largely contained within, the domain of established 'security professionals' – the so-called 'security trap' (C.A.S.E. Collective, 2006).

In sum, as demonstrated by the analysis in the latter portion of this chapter, climate threats are significant, growing, and apparently accelerating. This is particularly true for the countries like those in the Caribbean region profiled here. In order to cope with the adverse effects of climate change, SIDS will have to continue to play an instrumental role in the securitization of climate change and particular dimensions of it, such as SLR, in order to highlight their vulnerability and the grave security threats they face. As sea level inevitably creeps upwards, as storm surge and extreme events become more acute and more frequent, the security threats will come faster and more often. The issue as posed early on, however, is whether the global community is equipped to adapt to the policy challenges being thrust upon it by climate change, such that the ultimate result of the securitization of climate change will be effective responses and not just greater attention.

Notes

1 https://en.oxforddictionaries.com/definition/security.
2 See Homer-Dixon (1994, 1999), Gleditsch (1998, 2012) and Meierding (2013).

3 McCain Nelson, C. (2015, May 20). Obama says climate change endangers national security. *Wall Street Journal.* Available at www.wsj.com/articles/obama-to-cast-climate-change-as-a-national-security-threat-1432126767.Last accessed May 23, 2017.

4 See for instance, Harvey. C. (2016, April 5). It's not just Antarctica – Why Greenland could also melt faster than expected. *Washington Post.* Last accessed June 6, 2017.

5 A wide range of studies have focused on non-state level climate governance, including Betsill and Bulkeley (2004, 2006), Boyer (2013), Hoffman (2011), Rabe (2004, 2008), and many others.

6 For a much more developed discussion of the implications of the locus of climate change decision-making, especially as it reflects the nature of the public (and impurely public) goods endemic to this policy-making realm, see Boyer (2013), and Boyer, Meinzer and Bilich (2017).

7 While some islands such as Martinique and Guadeloupe are not classified as SIDS by the UN (see: https://unstats.un.org/unsd/methodology/m49/), for this project we classify all island states within the Caribbean as being part of SIDS. Belize and Guyana are also considered as part of SIDS by the UN and in our analysis.

8 We employed spatial analysis and representation of loss and damage through ArcGIS. The base map was downloaded from the Data Basin website (https://databasin.org/). The Data Basin provides free and open source access to biological, physical, and socio-economic datasets. From the Data Basin database, we downloaded a map of Erosion statistics for watersheds in the wider Caribbean Region. The map highlighted statistics for relative erosion rate, river flow, and sediment delivery estimated for each of over 3,000 watersheds draining into the Caribbean Sea and Gulf of Mexico. The map represents a combination of the region-wide 1 km analysis and the higher resolution 270 m analysis for the islands of the eastern Caribbean. The data was developed by the World Resource Institute through the Reefs at Risk in the Caribbean project. Since the scope of analysis focused on the loss and damage in the entire Caribbean and not in each of its watersheds, we manipulated the map through ArcGIS to retrieve the necessary data required for further analysis. The first task was to merge all the polygons (about 3,500) into one single polygon to encompass the entire Caribbean. In order to represent our four sets for data (total population affected; total damage in U.S.$; number of deaths; total number of storms), we use a decadal approach for each of the dataset. Because the dataset as explained above focused on the impacts of storms for the Caribbean Region from 1970 to 2010, we then downloaded another map from Natural Earth (www.naturalearthdata.com/), which had the necessary attributes of the Caribbean Region and overlaid it onto the first map. Our spatial representation of losses and damages are represented in four different maps.

9 http://web.worldbank.org/WBSITE/EXTERNAL/NEWS/0,,contentMDK:22324886" pagePK:34370 "piPK:34424"theSitePK:4607,00.html.

10 www.finance.gov.lc/resources/download/290.

11 In order to evaluate the impacts of sea level rise, we applied a Bathtub Method (BTM) inundation analysis, which included four steps: one, collect and generate the Digital Elevation Model; two, pre-processing the DEM which includes geo-referencing the data and validating the vertical values of the DEM; three, various analysis of the DEM, which includes selecting the area of interest and reclassification of the DEM; four, various inundation analyses such as processing of maps, graphical analysis of inundation, and spatial calculation of areas of inundation. The BTM itself was processed in ArcGIS 10.5 to generate inundation maps for different Caribbean islands. The DEM of the Caribbean was downloaded from the USGS Earth Explorer: http://earthexplorer.usgs.gov/, *Shuttle Radar Topography Mission (SRTM),* 1 Arc-second data (~30 m resolution) and then mosaic in ArcMap for further analysis. Various SLR conditions were attributed to the raster using the Spatial Analyst Tool Map Algebra. The raster was then reclassified to create only inundated areas. From this reclassified raster, inundated areas could be seen from the results in the attribute table. To get rid

of the anomalies (the areas that are not connected to the coast) the inundated raster was converted to a polygon, where it was easier to remove the inundated areas that meet SLR conditions but are not hydrologically connected to the coastline.

Bibliography

Adger, W. N., Brown, K., & Waters, J. (2011). Resilience. In J. S. Dryzek, R. B. Norgaard, & D. Schlosberg (Eds.), *Oxford handbook of climate change and society* (pp. 696–710). New York: Oxford University Press.

Balzacq, T. (2005). The three faces of securitization: Political agency, audience and context. *European Journal of International Relations, 11*(2), 171–201.

Belton, K. A. (2017). *Statelessness in the Caribbean: The paradox of belonging in a postnational world*. Philadelphia: University of Pennsylvania Press.

Berling, T. V. (2011). Science and securitization: Objectivation, the authority of the speaker and mobilization of scientific facts. *Security Dialogue, 45*(4–5), 385–397.

Betsill, M. M. & Bulkeley, H. (2004). Transnational networks and global environmental governance: The cities for climate protection program. *International Studies Quarterly, 48*, 471–493.

Betsill, M. M. & Bulkeley, H. (2006). Cities and the multilevel governance of global climate change. *Global Governance, 12*, 141–159.

Boyer, M. A. (2013). Global climate change and local action: Understanding the Connecticut policy trajectory. *International Studies Perspectives, 14*, 79–107.

Boyer, M. A., Brown, S. W., Butler, M., Florea, N., Johnson, P., & Lima, C. (2005). Understanding security through the eyes of the young. In P. Dombrowski (Ed.), *Guns and butter: The political economy of security* (pp. 205–230). Boulder, CO: Lynne Reinner Publishers.

Boyer, M. A., Meinzer, M., & Bilich, A. (2017). The climate adaptation imperative: Local choices targeting global problems? *Local Environment, 22*(1), 67–85.

Buzan, B., Wæver, O., & de Wilde, J. (1998). *Security: A new framework for analysis*. Boulder: Lynne Reinner Publishers.

C.A.S.E. Collective (2006). Critical approaches to security in Europe: A networked manifesto. *Security Dialogue, 37*(4), 443–487.

Cazenave, A., & Llovel, W. (2010). Contemporary sea level rise. *Annual Review of Marine Science, 2*, 145–173.

Cazenave, A., & Remy, F. (2011). Sea level and climate: Measurements and causes of changes. *Wiley Interdisciplinary Reviews: Climate Change, 2*(5), 647–662.

Church, J. A. & White, N. J. (2011). Sea-level rise from the late 19th to the early 21st century. *Surveys in Geophysics, 32*(4–5), 585–602.

Corry, O. (2014) From defense to resilience: Environmental security beyond neoliberalism. *International Political Sociology, 8*, 256–274.

Derrida, J. (1981). *Positions* (Trans. Bass, A.). Chicago: University of Chicago Press.

Detraz, N. & Betsill, M. M. (2009). Climate change and environmental security: For whom the discourse shifts. *International Studies Perspectives, 10*, 303–320.

Dyer, H. C. (2014). Climate anarchy: Creative disorder in world politics. *International Political Sociology, 8*, 182–200.

Gleditsch, N. P. (1998). Armed conflict and the environment: A critique of the literature. *Journal of Peace Research, 35*, 381–400.

Gleditsch, N. P. (2012). Whither the weather: Climate change and conflict. *Journal of Peace Research, 49*, 3–9.

Guha-Sapir, D., Below, R., & Hoyois, P. (2014). *EM-DAT: International Disaster Database*. Retrieved from www.emdat.be. Brussels, Belgium: Université Catholique de Louvain.

Hawkins, S. J., Moore, P. J., Burrows, M. T., Poloczanska, E., Mieszkowska, N., Herbert, R., Jenkins, S. R., Thompson, R. C., Genner, M. J., & Southward, A. J. (2008). Complex interactions in a rapidly changing world: Responses of rocky shore communities to recent climate change. *Climate Research, 37*(2–3), 123–133.

Hoffman, M. J. (2011). *Climate governance at the crossroads: Experimenting with a global response after Kyoto*. Oxford: Oxford University Press.

Homer-Dixon, T. F. (1994). Environmental scarcities and violent conflict: Evidence from cases. *International Security, 19*, 5–40.

Homer-Dixon T. F. (1999). *Environment, security and violence*. Princeton: Princeton University Press.

IPCC. (2013). T. F. Stocker, D. Qin, G.-K. Plattner, M. Tignor, S. K. Allen, J. Boschung, A. Nauels, Y. Xia, V. Bex, & P. M. Midgley (Eds.). *Climate change 2013: The physical science basis. Contribution of working group I to the fifth assessment report of the Intergovernmental Panel on Climate Change*. Cambridge & New York: Cambridge University Press.

IPCC. (2014a). Technical Summary. *Climate change 2014: Impacts, adaptation and vulnerability*. New York: IPCC & Cambridge University Press.

IPCC. (2014b). Core Writing Team R. K. Pachauri & L. A. Meyer (Eds.). *Climate change 2014: Synthesis report. Contribution of working groups I, II and III to the fifth assessment report of the Intergovernmental Panel on Climate Change*. IPCC, Geneva, Switzerland.

Mayer, M. (2012). Chaotic climate change and security. *International Political Sociology, 6*, 165–185.

Meierding, E. (2013). Climate change and conflict: Avoiding small talk about the weather. *International Studies Review, 15*, 185–203.

Methmann, C. (2014). Visualizing climate-refugees: Race, vulnerability and resilience in global liberal politics. *International Political Sociology, 8*, 416–435.

Milward, A. (1977). *War, economy and society: 1939–1945*. Berkeley: University of California Press.

Nicholls, R. J. & Cazenave, A. (2010). Sea-level rise and its impact on coastal zones. *Science, 328*(5985), 1517–1520.

Nurse, L. A., McLean, R. F., Agard, J., Briguglio, L. P., Duvat-Magnan, V., Pelesikoti, N., Tompkins, E., & Webb, A. (2014). Small islands. In V. R. Barros, C. B. Field, D. J. Dokken, M. D. Mastrandrea, K. J. Mach, T. E. Bilir, M. Chatterjee, K. L. Ebi, Y. O. Estrada, R. C. Genova, B. Girma, E. S. Kissel, A. N. Levy, S. MacCracken, P. R. Mastrandrea, & L. L. White (Eds.), *Climate change 2014: Impacts, adaptation, and vulnerability. Part B: Regional aspects. Contribution of working group II to the fifth assessment report of the Intergovernmental Panel on Climate Change* (pp. 1613–1654). Cambridge & New York: Cambridge University Press.

Oculi, N. (n.d.) *Vulnerability and resilience of The Alliance of Small Island States AOSIS: To access their climate change strategies at the climate change negotiations* (Unpublished manuscript). University of Connecticut.

Pielke, R., Prins, G., Rayner, S., & Sarewitz, D. (2007). Lifting the taboo on adaptation. *Nature, 445*, 597–598.

Rabe, B. G. (2004). *Statehouse and greenhouse*. Washington, D.C.: Brookings Institution.

Rabe, B. G. (2008). States on steroids: The intergovernmental odyssey of American climate policy. *Review of Policy Research, 25*(2), 105–128.

Sim, R. (2011). *Assessing the impacts of sea level rise in the Caribbean using geographic information systems* (Master's Thesis in Environmental Science). University of Waterloo, Canada.

Trombetta, M. J. (2008). Environmental security and climate change: Analyzing the discourse. *Cambridge Review of International Affairs, 21*(4), 585–602.

Ullman, R. (1983). Redefining security. *International Security, 8,* 129–53.

World Bank (2017). Grenada: Dealing with the aftermath of Hurricane Ivan. (n.d.). Retrieved from http://web.worldbank.org/WBSITE/EXTERNAL/NEWS/0,,contentMD K:22324886"pagePK:34370"piPK:34424"theSitePK:4607,00.html. Last accessed June 10, 2017.

Wong, P. P., Losada, I. J., Gattuso, J.-P., Hinkel, J., Khattabi, A., McInnes, K. L., Saito, Y., & Sallenger. A. (2014). Coastal systems and low-lying areas. In C. B. Field, V. R. Barros, D. J. Dokken, K. J. Mach, M. D. Mastrandrea, T. E. Bilir, M. Chatterjee, K. L. Ebi, Y. O. Estrada, R. C. Genova, B. Girma, E. S. Kissel, A. N. Levy, S. MacCracken, P. R. Mastrandrea, & L. L. White (Eds.), *Climate change 2014: Impacts, adaptation, and vulnerability. Part A: Global and sectoral aspects. Contribution of working group II to the fifth assessment report of the Intergovernmental Panel on Climate Change.* Cambridge & New York: Cambridge University Press.

Part III

Mechanisms of desecuritization

6 Conflict management redux

Desecuritizing intractable conflicts

Siniša Vuković

Introduction

The theoretical notion of 'securitization' most commonly refers to a discursive dynamic through which a particular issue gets transformed into a security threat. So far, this concept has had an impressive level of applicability, as it has been used to explain the creation of security concerns in a wide variety of areas, stemming from immigration and minority rights, to political dissidence and even health. While a growing number of studies have explored the link between securitization and conflict emergence (Diez, Stetter, & Albert, 2006; Stetter, Herschinger, Teichler, & Albert, 2011; Zeitoun, Talhami, & Eid-Sabbagh, 2013), we still lack an overarching conceptual framework which would expound the extent to which securitization can be used to craft more appropriate conflict management strategies. The aim of this chapter is to fill this conceptual gap, by exploring whether and how securitization can be applied to the complex world of conflict management.

It is widely understood that conflicts are an essential feature of everyday social life, where two or more parties perceive their interests as mutually incompatible and irreconcilable (Mitchell, 1989; Rubin, Pruitt, & Kim, 1994; Kriesberg, 2012). This perception in turn is fueled by incomplete information which prevents the parties from fully understanding each other's essential interests and needs, and creates self-enforcing images of enmity (Kriesberg, 1993; Fearon 1995). In cases where parties show an inability or unwillingness to manage their differences, conflicts may become more protracted and destructive. Such conflicts are commonly characterized by recurring violence, psychological manifestations of animosity, intense mutual feelings of fear and distrust, amplified stereotypes, and reservations over each other's intentions. Moreover, the issues at stake become ingrained in each party's identity, because each side develops a system of beliefs that reflects their understandings and perceptions of the conflict and past events (Coy, Woehrle, & Dayton, 2000; Bar-Tal, 2013). With the passing of time, conflict becomes ingrained in peoples' daily routines and such behavior even becomes institutionalized. In such intractable conditions, the persistence of the status quo provides a unique opportunity for some parties to maintain their socio-political and economic power. The increased saliency of issues, coupled with a conflict's potentially profitable nature, encourages leaders to accept higher costs. Sunk costs become sources of entrapment, which cannot easily be disregarded. As a consequence, parties tend to be less inclined to compromise, making any conflict management activity extremely elusive.

The formative process of conflict eruption and escalation is preceded by an act which transfers the perception of incompatibility to a specific type of confrontational behavior. This act is commonly verbalized through a 'call and response' dynamic: where an actor presents the incompatibility as a matter of pressing urgency that poses an existential threat to their interests and the audience responds with acceptance of such formulation. When an issue is framed or presented as an existential threat, the authorities may decide to employ special measures to manage the issue. If this 'speech act' successfully posits an issue as a security concern, and consequently justifies moves "which take politics beyond the normal rules of the game," then this issue is securitized (Buzan, Wæver, & de Wilde, 1998, p. 23).

So how does securitization as a process contribute to and fuel protracted conflicts, and can that process be reversed through the use of conflict management? There is a clear, yet largely overlooked, link between conflict processes and securitizing speech acts. On the one hand, speech acts unequivocally generate mutually exclusive perceptions, which replace trust and increase suspicion and uncertainty, leading parties to resort to confrontational and often destructive strategies as a way of protecting and/or promoting their particular interests. On the other hand, speech acts are frequently exploited as a strategic tool that consolidates and furthers the status quo for those who are profiting from a protracted conflict.

Consequently, the link between conflict emergence and securitization calls for a better conceptual understanding of whether, and if so how, desecuritization processes and conflict management activities may inform one another. To desecuritize implies a process of unmaking securitization, opting for an alternative way to regulate security issues. According to Wæver, there are three fundamental ways to desecuritize: one, not talking about the issue in terms of security, two, if an issue gets securitized then to avoid employing measures that may generate a security dilemma, and three, bringing those security issues back into "normal politics" (Wæver, 1995). Wæver warns that the last two face significant resistance due to the "self-reinforcing character" of securitized issues as they become embedded in the narratives of existential threats to collective identities (Wæver, 2000). Although comprehensive in scope, Wæver's taxonomy has not yet been operationalized in order to expound specific techniques that may reverse the speech act and desecuritize an issue.

In order to fill this conceptual gap, the present chapter explores how different forms of conflict management activities fit with, and enhance, our understanding of desecuritization as a concept and process. By addressing escalating conflicts, conflict management activities aim to affect parties' antagonistic perceptions of each other and of the issues at stake, and thus minimize the potential of a speech act or other securitizing 'move' to elicit or perpetuate a security dilemma between the parties. The chapter will also indicate how these adverse perceptions have a tendency to become self-perpetuating when peacemaking, peace-building, or peacekeeping efforts fail. The sense of insecurity and lack of trust are the core aspects that any conflict management activity needs to deal with. Irrespective of the point in the conflict cycle in which a certain activity is undertaken – be it peacemaking, peacekeeping, or peacebuilding – the success of conflict management efforts rests on the ability to provide sufficiently credible commitment by external parties, which can take forms of security guarantees, (promises of) implementation assistance and political cover for the parties to perceive the utility of a mutually acceptable peaceful solution to their problem.

The relationship between conflict management and desecuritization processes is not one-sided, but rather intertwined and reciprocal. A more nuanced exploration of various desecuritization techniques may offer a new way of structuring and juxtaposing various conflict management activities, which so far have been subject to scholastic parochialism. Therefore, by focusing on methods that are designed to manage speech acts, this chapter will assume a holistic approach and look at all conflict management practices (either as a sequence or as a specific combination of methods), and create a three-step approach to prevent, mitigate, and reverse conflict escalation using desecuritization as a benchmark. As such, this chapter offers a comprehensive, hybridized conflict management approach as a means of desecuritizing intractable conflicts.

Securitizing intractable conflicts

Among all social processes, conflicts are commonly perceived as the most sinister and harmful. Yet, as experience shows, not all conflicts are violent or destructive. On the contrary, to the extent that they epitomize social interactions where two or more actors perceive their interests and goals as irreconcilable, conflicts can be observed on nearly all social levels. As noted by Ramsbotham, Miall and Woodhouse, conflicts represent a universal feature of human society, exemplified through processes of economic differentiation, social change, cultural formation, psychological development, and political organization (Ramsbotham et al., 2016, p. 7). All of these dynamics are conflictual by nature, as participating actors may express their disputing views over the issues that are being contested. However, this is generally done through the rules and procedures that parties have agreed to in advance, making such processes predictable and routinized. These 'constructive' conflicts are regulated through a set of pre-existing political and judicial institutions and, as such, represent an essential feature of democracy (Kriesberg, 2012). They can be observed on daily bases on various levels, from traffic regulation, to elections, from the request for tenders and public procurement procedures, to job hiring processes. In such circumstances, participating actors resort to persuasion, compromise, and positive inducements in order to achieve outcomes that are mutually acceptable. As a consequence, such conflicts can 'construct' new social value both in the short and long term.

Nevertheless, many conflicts are not channeled through pre-existing institutional systems. This is particularly common for conflicts that take place at the international level, or have a capacity to become internationalized. In an international system that lacks an overarching authority and enforcement mechanisms comparable to the ones on the domestic level, conflictual relations may assume a destructive and intractable character. Such conflicts may last for a long period of time during which the parties resort to severe and harmful methods, show complete disregard for the other parties' interests and needs, focus on unilateral solutions, and resort to escalatory tactics (Crocker, Hampson, & Aall, 2005). Moreover, they imply a systematic application of various forms of violence, ranging from physical to cultural and structural (Galtung, 1969, 1990). The human casualities and material damage resulting from such destructive conflicts are generally considered the most significant type of socio-political costs (Gartner & Segura, 1998; Berinsky, 2007; Gartner, 2008). Not surprisingly, there is an increasing demand for managing conflicts coming from the same (political) actors that are involved in them, accompanied by pressures from both local and global civil society.

Unmanaged and destructive conflicts are fostered by parties' incomplete information about the other side's actual interests, capabilities, and levels of resolve (Fearon, 1995; Powell, 2006). In turn, impaired communication exacerbates mutual suspicion and distrust, reducing the parties' willingness and ability to establish a cooperative regime that would deliver them from the predicament. Failed attempts at managing the dispute reduce the appeal for any future efforts at finding a compromise solution. As conflicts become self-perpetuating, the parties look for ways to justify the inevitability of staying in a conflict. This is manifested through the establishment and perusal of appropriate military, economic, and political measures, which help the parties cope with imminent intractability of their conflict. According to Bar-Tal, such measures are grounded in a set of societal beliefs which include: justness of one's own goals, security, the adversary's delegitimization, positive self-image, own victimization, patriotism, unity, and one's own wish for peace:

> [...] what makes these beliefs special in time of intractable conflict is their complementary wholeness, unidimensionality extremism, black and white view, blind adherence to them, strong belief in their validity, and their intensive and extensive use in the society.
>
> (Bar-Tal 1998, p. 26)

Securitizing logics

As securitization theory tells us, conflict protraction is contingent upon conflicting parties' premeditated rhetorical action (Balzacq, 2005, 2014). As noted by Huysmans (2006, p. 25), "security rhetoric defines existential challenges which endanger the survival of the political order. As a result it alters the premises for all other questions; they become subjugated to the security question." Building on this argument, Balzacq (2010, p. 36) argues that "every securitization requires a prior politicization, even if the consequence of securitization is depoliticization." An effective securitization process presupposes that a securitizer's claim defines an existential threat, which in turn through audience's (i.e., constituency's) consent enables emergency measures and suspension of "normal politics" (McDonald, 2008).

In conflict dynamics such as these, each party constructs and furthers a master narrative of self-victimization through discourse and speech which in turn becomes a central theme in their respective collective memories about the conflict (see Rosoux, Chapter 8 in this volume). These master narratives are used to transmit a sense of injustice inflicted by the other sides' actions, which is then translated into an unequivocal devotion to pursue unilateral solutions, and loyalty to the group cause (Bar-Tal et al., 2009). Throughout time, such devotion becomes a routinized and institutionalized part of everyday life (Kriesberg, 2005). Parties in conflict accept the sunk costs of an ongoing conflict, gradually perceiving it as bearable and necessary. For the elites – the ones responsible for constructing and maintaining such master narratives – conflicts become an indispensable source of political legitimacy (Zartman, 2005).

Mitzen argues that "where conflict persists and comes to fulfill identity needs, breaking free can generate ontological insecurity, which states seek to avoid" (Mitzen, 2006, p. 343). Challenging the state-centric approach to security, McSweeney notes that

> security cannot be reduced to defense, to a balance of threats and vulnerabilities, or to any such objective and material equation [...] security and insecurity are a quality of a relationship, and reflect stability or change in the identity of the collectives involved.
>
> (McSweeney, 1999, p. 101)

In other words, the referent object of security is not just the state (i.e., government, or a territorially defined entity), but the shared identity that defines a social 'we,' or as Wæver and his colleagues put it, "the security of a society can be threatened by whatever puts its 'we' identity into jeopardy" (Wæver, Buzan, Kelstrup, & Lemaitre, 1993, p. 42; Williams, 1998, p. 435).

Securitizing mechanisms

In intractable conflicts, the master narratives deployed through speech-acts become ingrained in groups' collective identities, thereby securitizing intergroup relations and the social environment in which they take place. The conflict is presented as an existentialist struggle, often associated with historical grievances. In such conflicts, new generations are socialized into a grudge culture and conspiracy thinking. Through the employment of a targeted speech-act, the securitizers (i.e., the elites) exploit the process of 'othering,' presenting the other side as evil, dangerous and threatening (Marsella, 2005). On the other hand, a sense of superiority is promoted, based on a particularly affirmative reading of one's own historical legacy (Greenfeld, 1992). Critical interpretations of the past are strongly discouraged, as they may produce uncertainty and put in question the policies aimed at countering the security threat coming from the Other.

The resulting sense of superiority, coupled with the perception of a security threat, often yields policies aimed to undermine or suppress the Other (McManus, 2017). Even if a group constructs its superior in-group identity around a strong sense of liberal and democratic values, these values can be compromised in the name of security (Brewer & Higgins, 1998). As a way of countering a perceived threat from the Other, various measures that promote the spirit of segregation, inequity and oppression may be employed. Paradoxically, these measures are frequently intended to strengthen the negative images of the Other as intolerant and repressive.

When the securitizing rhetoric is translated into specific domestic policies that discriminate, persecute and vilify members of the Other group, such policies represent a very vivid manifestation of institutionalized violence. As previously mentioned, conflicts are often associated with violence that is expressed in a direct and physical form, where parties employ measures intended to inflict harm on their rivals, thus limiting them from meeting their basic needs. However, as such direct violence is both costly and impractical in the long term, securitized conflicts may inspire a different type of violence, more institutionalized in its form, and routinized in application. This structural violence – where discrimination and persecution are embedded in the existing social structures, and legalized through an existing institutional framework – protracts the conflict, as securitized policies become a societal standard (Galtung, 1969; Coleman, 2000).

In order to avoid conceptual ambiguity, it is important to specify that the policies or mechanisms of securitization of conflict may consist of a variety of tools and instruments. Balzacq defines tools (or instruments) of securitization as an "identifiable social and technical 'dispositif' or device embodying a specific threat image through which public action is configured in order to address a security issue" (Balzacq, 2008, p. 79; see also Linder & Peters, 1984; Salamon, 2002, p. 19). According to his conceptualization, "not all instruments of securitization are securitizing tools," the latter consisting of instruments which, by their very nature or by their very functioning, transform the entity (i.e., subject or object) they process into a threat; in other words they represent a substitute for the discursive logic of securitization (Balzacq, 2008, p. 80). While securitizing tools are certainly technical in nature, they carry a strong political and symbolic securitization message which explains how the securitizing agent perceives the issue, and how the intention of a policy can be translated into operational activity (Balzacq, 2008, p. 81). For Balzacq, "selection and use, as well as the effects of securitization instruments depend on political factors and, in turn, require political mobilization" (Balzacq, 2008, p. 81; Peters, 2002, p. 552).

In intractable conflicts, securitization tools aim to routinise the interaction both within a given society and between conflicting parties, define issues identified as threats, and specify a suitable method for addressing that threat. Such tools may be imbedded in a broad range of policies, ranging from trade (Sohn & Koo, 2011), to migration (Ibrahim, 2005; Adamson, 2006; Watson, 2009), border control (Diez et al., 2006, Côté-Boucher, Infantino, & Salter, 2014), health (Maclean, 2008; Hanrieder & Kreuder-Sonnen, 2014), development (Stern & Öjendal, 2010), distribution of resources (Stetter et al., 2011), and foreign affairs (Roe, 2008). Building on a taxonomy developed by Salamon (2002, p. 20), Balzacq suggests that, in order to be effective, these policy tools ought to have four fundamental facets: one, a type of good or activity (such as reconnaissance, interdiction, education, etc.), two, a delivery mechanism (such as various forms of media, digital devices, etc.), three, a delivery system (such as educational systems, public agencies, etc.), and four, a set of rules, either formal or informal, which define the relations between entities in the delivery system (Balzacq, 2008, p. 81). In intractable conflicts, the routinization of structural violence occurs once the rules have been defined, accepted, and repeated to the point of making discrimination, marginalization, and alienation a new normalcy. As securitizing tools become more widely implemented, societal complacency toward securitization becomes more apparent, which in turn enables the existentialist interpretation of an identified threat that swiftly intensifies the conflict.

Conflict management and desecuritization

As noted above, over-investment in creating and maintaining a security regime traps the parties in a conflict. The more they commit to countering a perceived security threat from the Other, the costlier a compromise solution becomes. As such, conflicts are frequently characterized by a sense of entrapment. According to Meerts:

> entrapment means increasing efforts, expanding demands, adding unilateral issues, upping investments, drawing in other actors, demonizing the other party, enhancing risks, increasing expenditures, and making stronger commitments.
>
> (Meerts, 2005, p. 112)

In other words, entrapment is a race to the bottom, where parties increasingly diminish their range of possible alternatives. Not surprisingly, due to their over-commitment in securitizing the Other, parties are frequently either unable or unwilling to find a compromise solution to their dispute on their own. For this reason, the responsibility to peacefully manage their conflict is necessarily delegated to a distinct third party.

Depending on the third party's interests, commitment, and resources, conflict management activities may range from very passive verbal appeals for peaceful solutions, to more active diplomatic approaches such as mediation, institutionalized judicial processes, administrative assistance in peacebuilding efforts, and the use of military force either for peacekeeping purposes or to enforce peace (Frazier & Dixon, 2006; Butler, 2009; Melin, 2014; Diehl & Regan, 2015).

Looking at practice, despite their evident diversity, all conflict management activities demonstrate a significant degree of interdependence. Particularly inter-linked are verbal appeals and mediation efforts, where the former is often pro-jected with an offer to conduct the later (Greig & Diehl, 2012). According to Oswiak, third parties are most inclined to use (and reuse) less costly methods, while in more than 50 percent of cases, mediation efforts were followed by verbal action through which violence was denounced and parties were called to reach a cease-fire, and mediators were more reluctant to resort to more costly strategies such as economic sanctions or military intervention (Oswiak, 2014).

Despite an evident link between securitization and conflict escalation, thus far the literature pertaining to each has largely overlooked or ignored the related link between conflict management and desecuritization. A notable exception to this trend has been a conceptual reflection developed by Bonacker and his colleagues (2011), who reviewed the applicability of this link in relation to the articulation of human rights in ethno-political conflicts. They observed that conflict manage-ment approaches view "desecuritization largely as a process of agreeing on or upon new institutional arrangements that allow for peaceful management of con-flict through the provision of information and the stabilization of mutual expec-tations through the codification of rules" (Bonacker, Diez, Gromes, Groth, & Pia, 2011, p. 22). Unfortunately, their study did not provide an in-depth analysis of how specific conflict management approaches treat information provision and codification of rules, nor did their study look at the sequencing of specific con-flict management activities as a way of maximizing the effectiveness of desecu-ritizing instruments. Therefore, building on their claim that the range of desecuritization strategies pertinent to conflict management activities include primarily coercive measures (such as power mediation, sanctions, and arbit-ration), the following section aims to expound a more comprehensive taxonomy of conflict management activities, which will include any form of third-party involvement in managing the dispute.[1]

The involvement of third parties inevitably shapes conflict dynamics. Their behavior and resources influence the conflicting parties' preferences and prior-ities in an escalating conflict. At the same time, third-parties' ideas and agendas frame the range of potential solutions conflicting parties may subse-quently explore as viable solutions to their conflict (Vuković & Hopmann, 2019). Although their involvement is not associated with the root causes of conflict which have shaped the initial speech-acts and related securitization tools employed by conflicting parties, third parties assume a specific role of a 'party to the conflict.' As such, they may explore ways to contain and reverse further escalation though targeted desecuritization instruments. These meas-ures may not only mitigate the conflict, but help the parties address the under-lying causes that generated various forms of violence, and guide them toward a more robust transformation of their relations, through new structures and rules that promote desecuritized discourse and practices. Having in mind this phased approach, it is important to look at the most common type of conflict management, i.e., mediation, and explore how it may be expanded to include other forms of third-party involvement in order to promote a more holistic approach to desecuritization.

Mediation as a tool for desecuritization

In line with its popularity in practice, mediation has been deemed the most efficient method of managing conflicts through peaceful means. As experience shows, a large number of internationalized conflicts were not as often and as easily handled by other modes of conflict management, such as legal tribunals, arbitration, or the use of force (Bercovitch & Houston, 1996; Frazier & Dixon, 2006; Grieg & Diehl, 2012). In fact, compared to other forms, mediation represents a relatively low-cost alternative to the options of doing nothing and conducting a large-scale military intervention. Mediation represents a form of 'assisted negotiation' in which an external actor enters the peacemaking process in order to influence and alter the character of previous relations between the conflicting sides (Touval & Zartman, 2001; Bercovitch & Jackson, 2009). It does so by providing new narratives that reduce the perception of insecurity, downplay the need for extraordinary measures, and – most relevant to this research – delegitimize securitizing tools employed by conflicting parties.

Publicly, third parties often justify their involvement on humanitarian grounds (Blechman, 1995; Dowty & Loescher, 1996; Regan, 1998). Yet, given the sheer variety of international actors and mediation contexts, it would be implausible to expect that mediators are only driven by humanitarian concerns to intervene. Keeping in mind the considerable investment of resources that mediation calls for, it is reasonable to presume that mediators are no less motivated by self-interest than by humanitarian impulses (Touval & Zartman, 1985, p. 8). These interests may range from preventing adverse spill-over effects of an escalating conflict – ranging from unmanageable refugee flow, to illicit economic activities conducted in conflict-affected areas, from rebel incursions across porous borders, to potential unwanted importation of terrorist activities – to improvement of a mediator's international reputation. At the same time, for many peacemaking is the *raison d'être* for the existence of many international and regional organizations, which are interested in promoting norms, principles, and values that have peace and security at their core. Lastly, many non-governmental organizations and prominent individuals are prompted to get involved in order to assert their expertise on a disputed issue, or knowledge of a context in which the conflict is unfolding (Vuković, 2014, 2015a).

This variety of motives that induce mediators to intervene generate an equally diverse set of tools that they may employ in order to achieve their goals in the peacemaking process. By extension, four strategies of desecuritization, as identified by Hansen (2012) – stabilization, silencing, rearticulation, and replacement – can find practical applicability in mediation. **Stabilization** entails a process through which parties may step away from the explicit security discourse. Facilitative mediation, which posits a carefully assisted form of information exchange, aims to help the parties transform the negative perceptions and reduce hostile rhetoric (Touval & Zartman, 1985; Bercovitch, Anagnoson, & Wille, 1991). Similarly, the second desecuritization strategy, **silencing**, through which parties are discouraged from using language of security, may find its applicability both in preventive mediation efforts and in previously described facilitative mediation strategies which alter the way parties communicate with one another (Beardsley, Quinn, Biswas, & Wilkenfeld, 2006). The third desecuritization strategy, **reart-iculation**, implies a process through which an issue is 'unmade' and 'decon-structed' from a security threat to a completely new formula (Huysmans, 1998). From a mediation perspective, mediators are frequently tasked with the role of formulating specific solutions which parties themselves are either unable or unwilling to do, and are ready to accept those formulas only because mediators provide (domestic) political cover and international legitimacy for such dis-course (Bercovitch & Wells, 1993; Beardsley, 2011) As Zartman and Touval noted, "formulas are the key to a negotiated solution to a conflict; they provide a common understanding of the problem and its solution or a shared notion of justice to govern an outcome" (Zartman & Touval, 1996, p. 454). Finally, the strategy of **replacement** assumes the possibility of substituting one issue with another, and can be found in mediators' most assertive types of activities that prescribe the alteration of pay-off structures and inclusion of new issues into the discourse, so that the parties may recalibrate their cost-benefit calculus (Beards-ley et al., 2006; Vuković, 2015a).

Evidently, the link between desecuritization and mediation strategies requires further scrutiny. As the information exchange and provision of incentives stand at the core of mediation activities, they may also expound in greater detail how certain issues can eventually be desecuritized. More importantly, they may provide a more nuanced explanation of specific desecuritization tools that can be part of various desecuritization strategies. As mentioned earlier, tools imply a good/activity, a delivery mechanism and system, and rules that regulate relations within those systems. Since mediation activities are ad-hoc, non-coercive and legally non-binding, they will potentially operate outside of existing systems and related rules. Nevertheless, through the provision of information and incentives, mediators offer specific goods/activities, delivered through both direct and indi-rect communication and through the provision of tailor-made incentives. These activities will address the nature of existing securitized systems and their rules, and offer new formulas that will regulate relations between the parties.

Mechanisms: how mediation desecuritizes

While mediators are motivated by their self-interests, the demand for mediation is based on an expectation that mediators will transform the existing conflict between the parties and desecuritize their relations. This does not imply that all mediation efforts will result in full conflict settlement, or that all parties that invite or accept mediators' initiatives will be fully committed to transforming their securitized policies. On the one hand, mediation needs to produce a solu-tion that is better than that which parties can achieve through confrontational methods; on the other, mediators still need to project a higher utility of a proposed solution that desecuritizes their relations, at least higher than the one parties can negotiate on their own. When mediators are unable or unwilling to deliver such outcomes, parties may resort to accepting mediation for purely devious reasons: trying to 'catch a breath' from an ongoing conflict, rally international support, regroup and rearm for subsequent conflict dynamics, etc. (Richmond, 1998).

In other words, accepting mediation is a useful, yet insufficient, indicator that desecuritization may be initiated or underway. Therefore, the level of commitment mediators project is contingent on their interests and capabilities. The commitment can vary from a passive (albeit essential) facilitation of communication, so that the parties can reframe their conflictual positions and start realizing a zone of possible agreement (ZOPA), to a more active formulation of potential solutions within a facilitated ZOPA, to the most assertive provision of side payments that alter the parties' cost benefit calculations to further pursue their conflict and explore options within a newly-created ZOPA (Touval & Zartman, 1985; Bercovitch et al., 1991; Beardsley et al., 2006; Vuković, 2015b). Consequently, such commitments translate into specific mechanisms that mediators can apply to 'de-securitize' an issue.

Information control

Mediators may provide, manage and manipulate the information which can undermine or eliminate the perception of a security threat. Mutual distrust, hatred, suspicion, and fear generated by conflict are both the source and the result of incomplete information parties have about the Other's preferences and capabilities (Rauchhaus, 2006; Savun, 2008; Halperin, Bar-Tal, Nets-Zehngut, & Drori, 2008). The perception of a security threat and related security provisions aimed at countering those threats are thus reinforced throughout the conflict due to incomplete information that parties possess. Therefore, the ability to desecuritize an issue is directly related to the availability of missing and necessary information, which can help the parties gain a better understanding of each other's interests, capabilities, and resolve.

Information provision by a mediator may diminish a sense of uncertainty, and eliminate the perception of a security threat. As parties get locked in a conflict, facing a complete breakdown of communication, the responsibility of providing desecuritizing information falls on the mediators. As mediators provide the relevant information, they embark on a process of improving mutual perceptions between the parties, creating the necessary momentum in the peacemaking process where talking, exploring viable options, and committing to a specific formula are no longer perceived as signs of treason. As a result, as parties soften up to diplomacy and start humanizing each other, previously established security policies may lose practical significance and political legitimacy, to the point of becoming obsolete and unnecessary.

Incentivizing

Even when mediators apply the best facilitation techniques, and help the parties realize that they have more in common than they initially perceived, parties may still be reluctant to settle on a specific solution on their own. The dominant zero-sum perceptions and hard-liner bargaining strategies, coupled with increased levels of distrust, enmity, and perceived threat, induce the parties to still view potential solutions as mutually exclusive and unacceptable, even though the solutions are actually in line with everyone's interests (Beardsley et al., 2006; Wilkenfeld et al., 2007). In such situations, mediators may propose specific formulas, giving guidance and structure to the parties on which solutions will merit mediators' backing. Zartman and Touval argue: "formulas are the key to a negotiated solution to a conflict; they provide a common understanding of the problem and its solution or a shared notion of justice to govern an outcome" (Zartman & Touval, 1996, p. 454). Although formulas diminish uncertainty regarding the future relations of the parties, parties will commit to such formulas if they are perceived as more attractive than continuing a conflict. More importantly, formulas provide a novel framework through which the issue can be desecuritized, either by dismissing the securitizing speech-act that existed until then, or by prescribing measures that bring the issue back to 'normal politics.'

In order to increase the appeal of proposed formulas, mediators may provide enticing incentives (Cortright, 1997; Fey & Ramsay, 2009; Beardsley, 2011). These incentives may take the form of a *political cover* for policies intended to replace previous ones stemming from securitized narratives; *conferral of international legitimacy* for a new approach that abandons previous security provisions; *implementation assistance* through various types of economic aid, humanitarian relief, and development support intended to reduce the profitability of the previously securitized regime; and *security guarantees* through peacekeeping, peace enforcement, and peacebuilding provisions which undermine or eliminate the perception of a security threat, and assist the parties in maintaining a regime of trust.

Mediation and desecuritization: a question of timing?

The application of different desecuritization tools via mediation will inevitably have differing effects depending on the stage of the conflict in which they are employed. In their study on the relevance of articulating human rights as a security issue in ethno-political conflicts, Bonacker and his colleagues found that a timely recognition of damaged relations, and subsequent application of measures that address structural causes of conflict, may contribute to the creation of institutions that desecuritize relations between parties in the long-term (Bonacker et al., 2013, p. 41). At the same time, the invocation of human rights at the early stages of conflict may be viewed as a genuine securitizing move, which may further intensify the conflict on the short and medium-term (Bonacker et al., 2013, p. 38). Evidently then, the appropriate timing of specific mediation initiatives becomes a crucial challenge in managing relations in a securitized and/or (potentially) securitizing environment.

The decision to manage intractable conflicts is never random nor unilateral, but rather a result of a careful analysis by all sides of whether or not a conflict has become "ripe" for resolution (Zartman, 1989, 2001). According to Zartman's ripeness theory, the parties first need to perceive that they are locked in a 'mutually hurting stalemate,' (MHS) which is an unbearable, painful and costly impasse experienced by both parties in which neither party is able to escalate the conflict unilaterally to achieve victory, and in which both parties can expect an impending catastrophe if confrontational strategies continue. They gradually start perceiving the futility of their securitization policies, and realize that they are approaching a precipice that will lead them to an even more destructive catastrophe. Under such conditions, the parties may begin to perceive mediators' initiatives as a preferable alternative to the continuation of belligerent activities and see them as a 'way out' (WO) of the impasse (Zartman, 2001, p. 8).

Given the prevailing concern here with securitization and desecuritization, it is essential to point out that both conditions – 'mutually hurting stalemate' and 'way out' – are based on the conflicting parties' subjective perceptions: they have to recognize that they are at a painful impasse (no matter what the 'evidence' on the ground says and/or how the situation is perceived by other actors), and develop a sense of seeing a compromise solution as an alternative to continued fighting. While the mutually hurting stalemate pushes the parties out of the conflict, and the perception of a way out pulls them into a negotiation process, a third element is required to keep them locked in and committed to compromise and reaching a mutually acceptable solution. Parties will perceive the utility of a negotiated agreement if they are presented with 'mutually enticing opportunities' (MEO). These enticements are: *exclusively* tied to the ongoing peacemaking process and unavailable elsewhere, and *mutually* beneficial, and subject to the parties' willingness to embrace *cooperation* both in the short and long term in order to sustain the regime of *interdependency* they are creating (Vuković, 2019). Moreover, MEOs offer new narratives, ideas and rules that deconstruct existing securitizing policies, leading the parties to desecuritize their relations.

All three elements – mutually hurting stalemate, way out, mutually enticing opportunities – are a matter of perception. Even though they are based on objective inputs, they are still socially constructed and embedded in a master narrative projected by elites. As a consequence, ripeness theory also assumes the existence of a strong leadership or a 'valid spokesman,' that can bring their parties into compliance and compromise (Zartman, 1989, 2001, p. 11). The role of a mediator is to engage with valid spokespersons and promote a sense of ripeness by constructing a de-securitized narrative characterized by the spirit of cooperation with the other side.

The appropriate timing of mediation initiatives to de-securitize the relations between conflicting parties is subject to considerations that fall into three broad categories.

Proactive (or preventive)

Mediators are seldom mere bystanders who passively observe the unfolding of a conflict. In fact, given the high material and non-material costs conflicts can generate, mediators are frequently inclined to tackle the issue at hand before it escalates into physical violence (Lund, 1996; Jentlson, 1999; Ackermann, 2003; Zartman, 2015). Preventive efforts are aimed at addressing the existing structural arrangements which have been developed by the securitization speech act, and that gradually provide a legal and legitimate baseline for conflict escalation. By detecting early warning signals – an indication that a certain policy, activity or decision may create a sense of discrimination, marginalization, or violation of existing rights among members of a specific community – mediators may tackle specific issues that have the potential to become securitized. As a result, mediators offer new frames through which the issues can be viewed, and consequently assist the parties in developing new and desecuritized narratives which can reduce the sense of insecurity and the need for extraordinary measures to mitigate potential security threats.

An important limitation to any preventive action arises from the counterfactual nature of early warning signals, making it very difficult to document prevention (Zartman, 2015). For this reason, academics and policy-planning experts have devoted much of their attention to finding statistically verifiable sources of conflict. Although the bulk of these indicators have been associated with economic factors (Homer-Dixon, 1994; Barbieri, 1996; Collier, 2003), recent studies have emphasized the significance of political elites as instigators of violence (Chiozza & Goemans, 2011; Horowitz, Stam, & Ellis, 2015). Regardless of the type, violence (i.e., against civilians, terrorism, ethnic cleansing, genocide, etc.) is seldom irrational and/or random, nor is it caused solely by existing socio-economic cleavages. It is a premeditated tactical choice devised by political elites and influential leaders as a way of realizing concrete political or military objectives (Valentino, 2014). In order to justify the inevitability of conflict escalation, and consequently galvanize and mobilize communities to commit to 'the cause,' leaders intentionally use 'ethnically-loaded rhetoric' that has the potential to create a sense of intercommunal distrust and suspicion (Wennmann, 2016).

Detecting this type of rhetoric at the earliest stages may offer an entry point for mediators to provide alternative narratives and technical assistance that may reduce the need for further securitization of the issue (Crisis Group, 2016). Furthermore, mediators' early engagement may reduce the likelihood that the securitizing speech-act assumes a self-reinforcing character. In the earliest stages, when securitizing narratives are still not coupled by extraordinary measures, mediators may break the securitizing pattern by assisting the parties in reducing the inflammatory rhetoric, and help parties refrain from talking about the issue in terms of security. At the same time, by detecting specific structural arrangements that may have the potential of legitimizing securitizing policies, mediators may offer new formulas and ideas of how a seemingly looming existential threat may be treated by reformed and improved institutions and policies.

Reactive

If prevention does not yield results, and conflict still escalates into either sporadic episodes or full-blown systemic use of direct violence, then mediators are tasked with the responsibility of defusing the escalation in the short-term (Hopmann, 1996; Sisk, 1996; Bercovitch & Diehl, 1997; Gartner & Bercovitch, 2006). Preventive activities embody measures that Wæver identifies as the principal way an issue may be desecuritized, i.e., "not talking about the issue in terms of security." However, reactive activities are employed in circumstances that Wæver associates with the second method of desecuritization; i.e., "if an issue gets securitized then avoid employing measures that may generate a security dilemma" (Wæver, 1995).

Mediators are often called upon to address the security concerns parties project when conflictual activities are suspended. On the one hand, in such circumstances, mediators may commit security guarantees, through peacekeeping and peace enforcement measures. On the other, they can also assist the parties to downplay the usage of securitized rhetoric, and develop narratives that are aimed at establishing integrative solutions to the conflict. While the former is intended to create conditions which can promote a spirit of cooperation, the latter aims to help parties internalize the change so they don't relapse into violence. Moreover, mediators also provide political cover and international legitimacy for policies that can avert the political intentions to implement extraordinary measures (Beardsley, 2011). This is particularly important in circumstances where such measures yield high political benefits for specific elites. Conferral of external political cover and international legitimacy for non-extraordinary measures may serve as an essential trade-off, which can deter political elites from acting upon an already securitized issue.

Interactive

Long-term measures that abate the securitization narrative are those that help to undermine the utility of any and all self-victimization narratives. Mediators may set the tone for comprehensive peacebuilding and reconciliation policies, which promote the spirit of cooperation and generate new structures that diminish the sense of security threats coming from the Other (Hampson, 1996; Doyle & Sambanis, 2000; Jarstad & Sisk, 2008; Rosoux, 2013; Rosoux & Anstey, 2017). While mediation is by definition intended to primarily manage a situation from further escalating, peacebuilding and reconciliation take the entire process a step further, each one aspiring to achieve the ultimate aim of conflict resolution: full transformation of relations between the parties (Butler, 2018).

Both peacebuilding and reconciliation aim to overcome structural violence between the parties. This is most frequently tackled through the employment of provisions that foster a new sense of security, economic interdependence, and political cooperation between the parties. While these provisions are predominantly manifested through institutional reform and/or creation of new systemic features (i.e., legal procedures, institutions, and decision-making practices), they also contribute to what Wæver (1995) identifies as "bringing back particular security issues into 'normal politics'". These structural changes provide a new platform through which new narratives may be promoted, while at the same time marginalizing or fully eliminating those speech-acts that fostered the sense of insecurity and uncertainty between the parties. As a consequence, for these structures to have a long-term effect, they require continuous interaction between the parties, and their commitment to make these policies work.

Alongside structural changes, true transformation is only possible if socio-psychological aspects of the past conflictual relations are also addressed. Parties are encouraged and assisted in restoring their broken relations, and supported to find ways through which they may learn to live non-violently, despite their past radical differences (Rosoux, 2009). This process is much lengthier than the structural changes. The transformation requires 'reframing the other': developing a sense of empathy about the other's victimhood, and accepting one's own responsibility for possible past transgressions (Halpern & Weinstein, 2004; Kelman, 2004). During the conflict, each party engages in a process of self-glorification and self-praise, while at the same time intentionally dehumanizing the other in order to avoid viewing oneself as the victimizer (Kelman, 1999). Jackson notes that, although it may be a lengthy and politically costly process, deconstructing discursive structures that reinforce violence and conflict is both possible and necessary (Jackson, 2009).

Accepting the past for what it is, and not for what it should be, is the ultimate aspiration of the reconciliation process. Breaking away from the institutionalized images of the enemy and narratives that demonize the other may take several steps, and the responsibility of undergoing these efforts falls primarily on the elites that have established, reinforced, and defended discursive structures that ignited conflict in the first place. As noted by Rosoux, due to initial resistance from the population to embrace full transformation of the discourse, leaders may opt for "partial amnesia" or "willful ignorance" (Rosoux, 2009, p. 550; Bargal & Sivan, 2004). This may give enough time for the elites to gradually reflect on their own side's responsibilities for past offenses, and decide on the best way this may be projected publicly. These may take the form of various 'reconciliatory events,' ranging from symbolic gestures of visiting sights of past atrocities, to formal and informal apologies, to concrete legal acts that may provide a sense of justice for the former opponents (Rosoux, 2009, p. 551). Such events have both a rational and emotional component, as they provide a much-needed signal through which parties indicate a credible commitment to transform their relationships (Long & Brecke, 2003; Kaufman, 2006).

Moreover, on the socio-psychological level, these events imply a significant shift in the way past events are portrayed. Through new speech-acts – such as apologies, emphasis on past episodes of cooperation, calls for resetting relations, acknowledgement of the others' victims and pain, etc. – the issue that ignited the conflict is gradually no longer portrayed as a security concern, and the existence of the other is not deemed an automatic existential threat. While these gestures may bring back the securitized issue into normal politics, in order to be effective, the parties need to have a basic level of trust, which may be grounded in previously established institutions and structures that may reduce the sense of insecurity between them.

Conclusion

The aim of this chapter was twofold. On the one hand, it explored if and how securitization – a discursive dynamic through which an issue is transformed into a security threat – applies to conflict dynamics, and in particular intractable conflicts. On the other, this chapter explored how different forms of conflict management activities may enhance our understanding of desecuritization as a concept and process using insights from conflict management. By addressing intensifying and protracted conflicts, conflict management activities aim to affect parties' antagonistic perceptions of each other and issues at stake, and thus minimize the potential of a speech act to perpetuate a security dilemma between the parties.

Evidently, there is a significant link between conflict management activities and measures aimed at desecuritizing an issue. Due to an imminent breakdown in communication, third parties are commonly tasked with the role of providing relevant information which may reduce the sense of insecurity and help parties refrain from labeling a contentious issue as a security threat. At the same time, in order to help parties maintain a sense of trust and security, external actors may offer specific inducements in the form of political cover, implementation assistance, and international legitimacy.

As shown above, depending on the degree to which an issue has been securitized, third parties may act either preventively, in order to help parties refrain from addressing a specific issue in terms of a security threat; reactively, by halting further escalation of bellicose rhetoric in case an issue has already been securitized, so that extraordinary measures would not be employed; or interactively, to assist the parties in bringing back the issue into normal politics, by offering assistance in creating new structures, institutions and fostering a sense of ripeness. With all this in mind, existing studies in conflict management may offer ample insight on how to desecuritize an issue, how to time those initiatives, and which types of provisions are most suitable given the stage of securitization. This chapter provided a first step in conceptualizing this link, expecting that future studies may deepen our knowledge of this nexus in a more nuanced manner.

Note

1 It should be noted that the emphasis will be on activities intended to manage and abate further escalation of conflict, and as such should not be equated with the more elusive notions of conflict resolution and conflict transformation.

Bibliography

Ackermann, A. (2003). The idea and practice of conflict prevention. *Journal of Peace Research, 40*(3), 339–347.

Adamson, F. B. (2006). Crossing borders: International migration and national security. *International Security, 31*(1), 165–199.

Balzacq, T. (2005). The three faces of securitization: Political agency, audience and context. *European Journal of International Relations, 11*(2), 171–201.

Balzacq, T. (2008). The policy tools of securitization: Information exchange, EU foreign and interior policies. *JCMS: Journal of Common Market Studies, 46*(1), 75–100.

Balzacq, T. (2010). Enquiries into methods: A new framework for securitization analysis. In T. Balzacq (Ed.), *Securitization Theory* (pp. 45–68). London & New York: Routledge.

Balzacq, T. (2014). *Contesting security: Strategies and logics.* London & New York: Routledge.

Barbieri, K. (1996). Economic interdependence: A path to peace or a source of interstate conflict? *Journal of Peace Research, 33*(1), 29–49.

Bargal, D., & Sivan, E. (2004). Leadership and reconciliation. In Y. Bar-Siman-Tov, *From conflict resolution to reconciliation* (pp. 125–148). Oxford: Oxford University Press.

Bar-Tal, D. (1998). Societal beliefs in times of intractable conflict: The Israeli case. *International Journal of Conflict Management, 9*(1), 22–50.

Bar-Tal, D. (2013). *Intractable conflicts: Socio-psychological foundations and dynamics.* Cambridge: Cambridge University Press.

Bar-Tal, D., Chernyak-Hai, L., Schori, N., & Gundar, A. (2009). A sense of self-perceived collective victimhood in intractable conflicts. *International Review of the Red Cross, 91*(874), 229–258.

Beardsley, K. (2011). *The mediation dilemma.* Ithaca: Cornell University Press.

Beardsley, K. C., Quinn, D. M., Biswas, B., & Wilkenfeld, J. (2006). Mediation style and crisis outcomes. *Journal of Conflict Resolution, 50*(1), 58–86.

Bercovitch, J. (2005). Mediation in the most resistant cases. In C. A. Crocker, F. O. Hampson, & P. R. Aall, *Grasping the nettle: Analyzing cases of intractable conflict* (pp. 99–121). Washington, D.C.: U.S. Institute of Peace Press.

Bercovitch, J., Anagnoson, J. T., & Wille, D. L. (1991). Some conceptual issues and empirical trends in the study of successful mediation in international relations. *Journal of Peace Research, 28*(1), 7–17.

Bercovitch, J., & Diehl, P. F. (1997). Conflict management of enduring rivalries: The frequency, timing, and short-term impact of mediation. *International Interactions, 22*(4), 299–320.

Bercovitch, J., & Houston, A. (1996). The study of international mediation: Theoretical issues and empirical evidence. *Resolving international conflicts: The theory and practice of mediation,* 11–35.

Bercovitch, J. & Jackson, R. D. W. (2009). *Conflict resolution in the twenty-first century: Principles, methods, and approaches.* Michigan: University of Michigan Press.

Bercovitch, J., & Wells, R. (1993). Evaluating mediation strategies: A theoretical and empirical analysis. *Peace & Change, 18*(1), 3–25.

Berinsky, A. J. (2007). Assuming the costs of war: Events, elites, and American public support for military conflict. *The Journal of Politics, 69*(4), 975–997.

Blechman, B. M. (1995). The intervention dilemma. *Washington Quarterly, 18*(3), 63–73.

Brewer, J. D., & Higgins, G. I. (1998). *Anti-Catholicism in Northern Ireland, 1600–1998. The mote and the beam*. New York: St. Martin Press.

Bonacker, T., Diez, T., Gromes, T., Groth, J., & Pia, E. (2013). Human rights and the (de) securitization of conflict. In R. Marchetti & N. Tocci (Eds.), *Civil society, conflicts and the politicization of human rights* (pp. 13–46). New York: United Nations University Press.

Butler, M. J. (2009). *International conflict management*. London & New York: Routledge.

Butler, M. J. (2018). Context, process, and structure: Correlates of conflict management in foreign policy crisis. *Journal of Global Security Studies, 3*(2), 163–180.

Buzan, B., Wæver, O., & de Wilde, J. (1998). *Security: A new framework for analysis*. Boulder, CO: Lynne Rienner Publishers.

Chiozza, G., & Goemans, H. E. (2011). *Leaders and international conflict*. Cambridge: Cambridge University Press.

Coleman, P. T. (2000). Intractable conflict. In M. E. Deutsch & P. T. Coleman (Eds.), *The handbook of conflict resolution: Theory and practice* (pp. 428–450). San Francisco, CA: Jossey-Bass.

Collier, P. (2003). *Breaking the conflict trap: Civil war and development policy*. Washington, D.C.: World Bank Publications.

Cortright, D. (1997). *The price of peace: Incentives and international conflict prevention*. Lanham, MD: Rowman & Littlefield.

Côté-Boucher, K., Infantino, F., & Salter, M. B. (2014). Border security as practice: An agenda for research. *Security Dialogue, 45*(3), 195–208.

Coy, P. G., Woehrle, L. M., & Dayton, B. W. (2000). *Social conflicts and collective identities*. Lanham, MD: Rowman & Littlefield.

Crisis Group. (2016). *Seizing the moment: From early warning to early action*. Special Report N°2. Brussels. Retrieved from www.crisisgroup.org/global/seizing-moment-early-warning-early-action. Last accessed July 16, 2018.

Crocker, C. A., Hampson, F. O., & Aall, P. R. (2005). *Grasping the nettle: Analyzing cases of intractable conflict*. Washington, D.C.: US Institute of Peace Press.

Diehl, P. F., & Regan, P. (2015). The interdependence of conflict management attempts. *Conflict Management and Peace Science, 32*(1), 99–107.

Diez, T., Stetter, S., & Albert, M. (2006). The European Union and border conflicts: The transformative power of integration. *International Organization, 60*(3), 563–593.

Doyle, M. W., & Sambanis, N. (2000). International peacebuilding: A theoretical and quantitative analysis. *American Political Science Review, 94*(4), 779–801.

Dowty, A., & Loescher, G. (1996). Refugee flows as grounds for international action. *International Security, 21*(1), 43–71.

Fearon, J. D. (1995). Rationalist explanations for war. *International organization, 49*(3), 379–414.

Fey, M., & Ramsay, K. W. (2009). *Uncertainty and incentives in mediation*. APSA 2009 Toronto meeting paper.

Frazier, D. V., & Dixon, W. J. (2006). Third-party intermediaries and negotiated settlements, 1946–2000. *International Interactions, 32*(4), 385–408.

Galtung, J. (1969). Violence, peace, and peace research. *Journal of Peace Research, 6*(3), 167–191.

Galtung, J. (1990). Cultural violence. *Journal of Peace Research, 27*(3), 291–305.

Gartner, S. S. (2008). The multiple effects of casualties on public support for war: An experimental approach. *American Political Science Review, 102*(1), 95–106.

Gartner, S. S., & Bercovitch, J. (2006). Overcoming obstacles to peace: The contribution of mediation to short-lived conflict settlements. *International Studies Quarterly*, *50*(4), 819–840.

Gartner, S. S., & Segura, G. M. (1998). War, casualties, and public opinion. *Journal of Conflict Resolution*, *42*(3), 278–300.

Greenfeld, L. (1992). *Nationalism: Five roads to modernity*. Cambridge, MA: Harvard University Press.

Greig, J. M., & Diehl, P. F. (2012). *International mediation*. Cambridge: Polity.

Halperin, E., Bar-Tal, D., Nets-Zehngut, R., & Drori, E. (2008). Emotions in conflict: Correlates of fear and hope in the Israeli-Jewish society. *Peace and Conflict: Journal of Peace Psychology*, *14*(3), 233.

Halpern, J., & Weinstein, H. M. (2004). Rehumanizing the other: Empathy and reconciliation. *Human Rights Quarterly*, *26*, 561.

Hampson, F. O. (1996). *Nurturing peace: Why peace settlements succeed or fail*. Washington, D.C.: U.S. Institute of Peace Press.

Hanrieder, T., & Kreuder-Sonnen, C. (2014). WHO decides on the exception? Securitization and emergency governance in global health. *Security Dialogue*, *45*(4), 331–348.

Hansen, L. (2012). Reconstructing desecuritisation: The normative-political in the Copenhagen School and directions for how to apply it. *Review of International Studies*, *38*(3), 525–546.

Homer-Dixon, T. F. (1994). Environmental scarcities and violent conflict: Evidence from cases. *International Security*, *19*(1), 5–40.

Hopmann, P. T. (1996). *The negotiation process and the resolution of international conflicts*. Columbia, SC: University of South Carolina Press.

Horowitz, M. C., Stam, A. C., & Ellis, C. M. (2015). *Why leaders fight*. Cambridge: Cambridge University Press.

Huysmans, J. (1998). The question of the limit: Desecuritisation and the aesthetics of horror in political realism. *Millennium: Journal of International Studies*, *27*(3), 569–589.

Huysmans, J. (2006). *The politics of insecurity: Fear, migration and asylum in the EU*. London & New York: Routledge.

Ibrahim, M. (2005). The securitization of migration: A racial discourse. *International Migration*, *43*(5), 163–187.

Jackson, R. (2009). Constructivism and conflict resolution. In J. Bercovitch, V. Kremenyuk, & I. W. Zartman (Eds.), *The SAGE handbook of conflict resolution* (pp. 172–189). London: SAGE.

Jarstad, A. K., & Sisk, T. D. (2008). *From war to democracy: Dilemmas of peacebuilding*. Cambridge: Cambridge University Press.

Jentlson, B. W. (1999). *Opportunities missed, opportunities seized: Preventive diplomacy in the post-Cold War world*. Lanham, MD: Rowman & Littlefield Publishers.

Kaufman, S. J. (2006). Escaping the symbolic politics trap: Reconciliation initiatives and conflict resolution in ethnic wars. *Journal of Peace Research*, *43*(2), 201–218.

Kelman, H. C. (1999). Transforming the relationship between former enemies: A social-psychological analysis. In R. L. Rothstein (Ed.), After the peace: Resistance and reconciliation (pp. 193–205). Boulder, CO, & London: Lynne Rienner Publishers.

Kelman, H. C. (2004). Reconciliation as identity change: A social-psychological perspective. In Y. Bar-Siman-Tov (Ed.), *From conflict resolution to reconciliation* (pp. 111–124). Oxford: Oxford University Press.

Kriesberg, L. (1993). Intractable conflicts. *Peace Review*, *5*(4), 417–421.

Kriesberg, L. (2005). Nature, dynamics, and phases of intractability. In C. A. Crocker, F. O. Hampson, & P. R. Aall (Eds.), *Grasping the nettle: Analyzing cases of intractable conflict* (pp. 65–98). Washington, D.C.: US Institute of Peace Press.

Kriesberg, L. (2012). *Constructive conflicts: From escalation to resolution*. Lanham, MD: Rowman & Littlefield.

Linder, S. H., & Peters, B. G. (1984). From social theory to policy design. *Journal of Public Policy, 4*(3), 237–259.

Long, W. J., & Brecke, P. (2003). *War and reconciliation: Reason and emotion in conflict resolution*. Cambridge, MA: MIT Press.

Lund, M. S. (1996). *Preventing violent conflicts: A strategy for preventive diplomacy*. Washington, D.C.: U.S. Institute of Peace Press.

Maclean, S. J. (2008). Microbes, mad cows and militaries: Exploring the links between health and security. *Security Dialogue, 39*(5), 475–494.

Marsella, A. J. (2005). Culture and conflict: Understanding, negotiating, and reconciling conflicting constructions of reality. *International Journal of Intercultural Relations, 29*(6), 651–673.

McDonald, M. (2008). Securitization and the construction of security. *European Journal of International Relations, 14*(4), 563–587.

McManus, C. P. (2017). Dealing with the legacy of ethnic conflict: Confronting 'othering' through transformative adult education—A Northern Ireland case study. *Ethnopolitics, 16*(4), 411–429.

McSweeney, B. (1999). *Security, identity and interests: A sociology of international relations* (Vol. 69). Cambridge: Cambridge University Press.

Meerts, P. W. (2005). Entrapment in international negotiations. In I. W. Zartman, & G. O. Faure (Eds.), *Escalation and negotiation in international conflicts* (pp. 111–141). Cambridge: Cambridge University Press.

Melin, M. M. (2014). Commitment problems: Understanding variation in the frequency of international conflict management efforts. *International Negotiation, 19*(2): 221–256.

Mitchell, C. R. (1989). *The structure of international conflict*. New York: Springer.

Mitzen, J. (2006). Ontological security in world politics: State identity and the security dilemma. *European Journal of International Relations, 12*(3), 341–370.

Owsiak, A. P. (2014). Conflict management trajectories in militarized interstate disputes: A conceptual framework and theoretical foundations. *International Studies Review, 16*(1), 50–78.

Peters, G. B. (2002). The politics of tool choice. In L. Salamon (Ed.), *The tools of government: A guide to the new governance*. Oxford: Oxford University Press.

Powell, R. (2006). War as a commitment problem. *International Organization, 60*(1), 169–203.

Ramsbotham, O., Miall, H., & Woodhouse, T. (2016). *Contemporary conflict resolution*. Cambridge: Polity.

Richmond, O. (1998). Devious objectives and the disputants' view of international mediation: A theoretical framework. *Journal of Peace Research, 35*(6), 707–722.

Rauchhaus, R. W. (2006). Asymmetric information, mediation, and conflict management. *World Politics, 58*(2), 207–241.

Regan, P. M. (1998). Choosing to intervene: Outside interventions in internal conflicts. *The Journal of Politics, 60*(3), 754–779.

Roe, P. (2008). Actor, audience(s) and emergency measures: Securitization and the UK's decision to invade Iraq. *Security Dialogue, 39*(6), 615–635.

166   *S. Vuković*

Rosoux, V. (2009). Reconciliation as a peace-building process: Scope and limits. In J. Bercovitch, V. Kremenyuk, & I. W. Zartman (Eds.), *The SAGE handbook of conflict resolution* (pp. 543–63). London: Sage.

Rosoux, V. (2013). Is reconciliation negotiable? *International Negotiation, 18*(3), 471–493.

Rosoux, V., & Anstey, M. (2017). *Negotiating reconciliation in peacemaking: Quandaries of relationship building.* New York: Springer.

Rubin, J. Z., Pruitt, D. G., & Kim, S. H. (1994). *Social conflict: Escalation, stalemate, and settlement.* New York: McGraw-Hill.

Salamon, L. (2002). The new governance and the tools of public action: An introduction. In L. Salamon (Ed.), *The tools of government: A guide to the new governance* (pp. 1–47). Oxford: Oxford University Press.

Savun, B. (2008). Information, bias, and mediation success. *International Studies Quarterly, 52*(1), 25–47.

Sisk, T. D. (1996). *Power sharing and international mediation in ethnic conflicts.* Washington, D.C.: U.S. Institute of Peace Press.

Sohn, Y., & Koo, M. G. (2011). Securitizing trade: The case of the Korea–US free trade agreement. *International Relations of the Asia-Pacific, 11*(3), 433–460.

Stern, M., & Öjendal, J. (2010). Mapping the security—development nexus: Conflict, complexity, cacophony, convergence? *Security Dialogue, 41*(1), 5–29.

Stetter, S., Herschinger, E., Teichler, T., & Albert, M. (2011). Conflicts about water: Securitizations in a global context. *Cooperation and Conflict, 46*(4), 441–459.

Touval, S., & Zartman, I. W. (1985). *International mediation in theory and practice.* Boulder, CO: Westview Press with the Foreign Policy Institute, School of Advanced International Studies, Johns Hopkins University.

Touval, S., & Zartman, I. W. (2001). International mediation in the post-Cold War era. In C. A. Crocker, F. O. Hampson, & P. Aall (Eds.), *Turbulent peace: The challenges of managing international conflict* (pp. 427–443). Washington, D.C.: U.S. Institute of Peace Press.

Valentino, B. A. (2014). Why we kill: The political science of political violence against civilians. *Annual Review of Political Science, 17*, 89–103.

Vuković, S. (2014). International mediation as a distinct form of conflict management. *International Journal of Conflict Management, 25*(1), 61–80.

Vuković, S. (2015b). *International multiparty mediation and conflict management: Challenges of cooperation and coordination.* London & New York: Routledge.

Vuković, S. (2015a). Soft power, bias and manipulation of international organizations in international mediation. *International Negotiation, 20*(3), 414–443.

Vuković, S. (2019). Mediating closure: Driving toward mutually enticing opportunities. In I. W. Zartman (Ed.), *How negotiations end.* Cambridge: Cambridge University Press.

Vuković, S., & Hopmann, P. T. (2019). Satisficing in international mediation: Framing, justifying and creating outcomes in peacemaking. In J. Wilkenfeld, K. Beardsley, & D. Quinn (Eds.), *Research handbook on mediating international crises.* Cheltenham, UK: Edward Elgar.

Watson, S. D. (2009). *The securitization of humanitarian migration: Digging moats and sinking boats.* London & New York: Routledge.

Wennmann, A. (2016). The political economy of violent conflict. *Armed Conflict Survey, 2*(1), 20–35.

Wilkenfeld, J., Young, K., Quinn, D., Young, K., Msn, R. N., & Asal, V. (2007). *Mediating international crises.* London & New York: Routledge.

Williams, M. C. (1998). Modernity, identity and security: A comment on the 'Copenhagen controversy.' *Review of International Studies, 24*(3), 435–439.

Wæver, O. (1995). Securitization and desecuritization. In R. Lipschutz (Ed.), *On Security* (pp. 46–86). New York: Columbia University Press.

Wæver, O. (2000). The EU as a security actor: Reflections from a pessimistic constructivist on post-sovereign security orders. In M. Kelstrup & M. Williams (Eds.), *International relations theory and the politics of European integration: Power, security, and community* (pp. 250–294). London: Routledge.

Wæver, O., Buzan, B., Kelstrup, M., & Lemaitre, P. (1993). *Identity, migration and the new security agenda in Europe*. London: Pinter.

Zartman, I. W. (1989). *Ripe for resolution: Conflict and intervention in Africa*. Oxford: Oxford University Press.

Zartman, I. W. (2001). The timing of peace initiatives: Hurting stalemates and ripe moments 1. *The Global Review of Ethnopolitics, 1*(1), 8–18.

Zartman, I. W. (2005). Analyzing intractability. In C. A. Crocker, F. O. Hampson, & P. R. Aall (Eds.), *Grasping the nettle: Analyzing cases of intractable conflict* (pp. 47–64). Washington, D.C.: U.S. Institute of Peace Press.

Zartman, I. W. (2015). *Preventing deadly conflict*. Cambridge: Polity.

Zartman, I. W., & Touval S. (1996). International mediation in the post-Cold War era. In C. A. Crocker, F. O. Hampson, & P. R. Aall (Eds.), *Managing global chaos: Sources of and responses to international conflict* (pp. 445–461). Washington, D.C.: U.S. Institute of Peace Press.

Zeitoun, M., Talhami, M., & Eid-Sabbagh, K. (2013). The influence of narratives on negotiations and resolution of the upper Jordan river conflict. *International Negotiation, 18*(2), 293–322.

7 Beyond the speech act

Contact, desecuritization, and peacebuilding in Cyprus

Katerina Antoniou

Introduction

Achieving security has been one of the principal end goals of society, both within the boundaries of sovereign states as well as in other forms of organized in-groups. Moving beyond the broader definition of security as the assurance of survival and the absence of existential threats, security's evolution through constructivist and post-structuralist research has shifted the attention of scholars to evaluating the societal context in which security is conceptualized, as well as the methodological tools employed in analyzing it. As was discussed in the introduction to this volume, the scholarly examination of security finds its roots in positivist and realist accounts. Nonetheless, securitization has been widely heralded as a constructed process, due to the underlying assumption that the act of identifying or perceiving an actor or a situation as threatening is subjective in nature. Dannreuther (2013) suggests that the Copenhagen School's "constructivist-inspired approach of securitization" (2013, p. 48) is in fact democratizing the scholarly examination of security, as it goes beyond the state level to include the general public as a protagonist in the formulation of an existential threat.

At the same time, a number of accounts have dealt with the limitations of the Copenhagen School's securitization theory, leading the way towards its refinement. As Emmers (2013) notes, the line between securitization and politicization is blurry, and the subjectivity with which the two are pursued (and assessed) can be restrictive. Dannreuther (2013) highlights the epistemology of securitization and argues that the Copenhagen School has isolated the speech act from the socio-political influences and contexts that also impinge upon securitization processes and relevant audience(s) and agent(s). Further to this point, a number of scholarly accounts have critiqued the Copenhagen School for its inability to embrace the interactive nature of securitization processes and the catalytic role of the audience (Stritzel, 2007; Côté, 2016; Wilhelmsen, 2016). The result is an over-emphasis on the agency of the securitizing actor which overlooks the power of the audience in accepting or rejecting the articulated threat – what Wilhelmsen (2016) refers to as a 'public consent' to securitization provided by the audience.

This chapter addresses this critique by focusing on the agency of the audience. Drawing on Gordon Allport's (1954) contact hypothesis, this chapter examines how intergroup contact can reduce prejudice between rival groups. Intergroup contact has been widely accepted for its ability to shift perceptions between members of rival communities, and is for this reason a prominent peacebuilding tool in intergroup conflicts – settings in which societal security is severely compromised. As such, this chapter examines how intergroup contact as a non-discursive practice influences patterns of societal securitization in intergroup conflict. To the extent that intergroup contact alleviates societal insecurity by reducing prejudice between groups in conflict, the contention raised here is that it can also play a major role in reducing an audience's receptivity to the securitization of group identity and intergroup enmity.

The particular empirical focus here is the case of Cyprus, a frozen and protracted conflict with both interstate and intrastate dimensions. Cyprus provides an important ground for testing the supposition of intergroup contact's desecuritizing dimension, given its extensive record of peacebuilding and social reconciliation initiatives over the span of more than two decades, as well as the incorporation of intergroup contact within its peacebuilding initiatives. The peacebuilding timeline in Cyprus offers insight to the emergence of an intercommunal peacebuilding civil society movement, which, unlike the island's partitioned communities, is defined by normalized intergroup interaction and negligible levels of societal securitization. Thus, the Cypriot peacebuilder audience portrays what Foucault (1984) referred to as 'heterotopic' behavior in comparison to the island's partitioned communities – making it a worthy testing ground for examining patterns and effects of continuous intergroup contact.

However, examining the relationship between intergroup contact and (de) securitization is impossible without also breaking out of the methodological strictures associated with most securitization research. As speech acts have monopolized the attention of securitization research, it comes as no surprise that discourse analysis has been a popular methodological route for conducting examinations of securitization processes and applications (Wilhelmsen, 2016; Greussing & Boomgaarden, 2017; Vollmer & Karakayali, 2018). Nevertheless, the disproportionate attention given to discourse and language risks leaving other parameters that are potentially influential to securitization and desecuritization underexplored, such as audience agency and intergroup prejudice. Karyotis and Patrikios (2010) challenge the discourse analysis approach by employing mixed methods to examine religion, securitization, and anti-immigration attitudes in Greece, while Balzacq, Léonard, and Ruzicka (2016) acknowledge methodology as one of the three main challenges faced by securitization theory that scholars should work on overcoming. A second critique regarding the need for increased methodological diversity in securitization studies is offered by Jarvis and Holland (2015), who highlight the personal bias authors bring into the analysis of security processes, suggesting that authors ought to be as transparent as possible regarding their "normative commitments" (2015, p. 221) in order not to compromise the validity of their findings.

Inspired by to these two methodological critiques, this chapter adopts a critical autoethnography approach in order to collect and analyze qualitative field observations from Cyprus beyond the confined framework of discourse analysis, while also acknowledging the author's personal bias as a member of the audience explored – an approach often adopted in the case of native ethnographers (Reed-Danahay, 1997; Foley, 2002). Data on intercommunal interactions between Greek and Turkish Cypriots are presented in the form of direct quotes, hence achieving the empowerment of the population under study (Foley, 2002), or the Habermasian emancipatory intent (Habermas, 1971). These quotes are combined with a case study analysis providing a narrative history of Cyprus' peacebuilder community emergence, as well as my autoethnographic reflections as a co-performer in a mixed methodological approach.

Societal securitization and intergroup relations

The process of societal securitization as articulated by the Copenhagen School enables a securitizing agent to selectively identify a single identity, convince the recipient audience of the existential threat against it, and prioritize it over other identities. This often transpires in light of a power imbalance between the in-group and out-group that justifies the proposed threat (Simon, Aufderheide, & Kampmeier, 2003).[1] Societal securitization can be detected in examples of interethnic and identity-based conflict, with the example of continuous interethnic animosity between Serbs and Albanians of Kosovo (Demjaha, 2017) and the escalated rivalry of Ukrainians against Russia (Janmaat, 2007). Societal insecurity has also prevailed on a macro-scale, through what Huntington (1993) referred to as the Clash of Civilizations, with the West confronting the Islamic world in the post-9/11 War on Terror, in an era of far-right politicians rising to power (Wodak, 2013; Ellinas, 2013) and with an international migration crisis provoking anti-migration attitudes (Karyotis & Patrikios, 2010). The study of societal securitization therefore requires greater attention be paid to social psychological conditions such as in-group/out-group dynamics, patterns of in-group favoritism and out-group hostility, and conditions of intergroup reconciliation – factors and conditions that are not always adequately addressed by discourse analysis.

Insights from social psychology

In response to the amplification of societal securitization in the occasion of inter-group conflict, intergroup reconciliation practices can be perceived as tools for societal desecuritization, or the process of bringing issues back to the "normal haggling of politics" (Buzan, Wæver, & de Wilde, 1998). The relationship between intergroup interaction and constructed threats against an external 'other' is best captured by social psychology research. According to Howard (2000), two prevalent assessments of social psychology are social cognition (the process of acquiring and processing information) and symbolic interaction (the meaning people assign to incidents of social interaction). Both social cognition and symbolic interaction are considered key perspectives for the social psychological analysis of group and individual identity (Howard, 2000), and therefore can be directly associated with societal securitization.

Oakes (2004) introduces categorization, in the form of category activation and category-based construal, as a primary step towards the emergence of intergroup discrimination and hostility. Brewer and Gaertner (2004, p. 304) also acknowledge categorization as a source of in-group bias and intergroup discrimination through the "de-individualization of members of the out-group." Categorization can be seen as a dominant form of social bias and a prevalent factor in individual subjectivity, the latter being a defining principle in social psychology (Oakes, 2004). Turner and Reynolds (2003, p. 267) distinguish in-group bias from in-group favoritism, a form of bias that reflects an "irrational, indiscriminate, reality-distorting psychological bias" that favors the in-group over other out-groups; ethnocentrism, or the favoritism of an ethnically defined in-group, can be seen as a form of in-group favoritism.

Newcomb (1947) considered autistic hostility (defined as the process of hostility amplification) to be an unavoidable outcome of intergroup conflict. This approach purports that members of antagonistic parties choose to remain in isolation from one another, leading negative assumptions and stereotypes across them to amplify. Intergroup hostility and antagonism can also be products of a comparative power imbalance between the in-group and the out-group, a dynamic particularly evident in minority-majority relations (Simon et al., 2003). One compelling response to autistic hostility comes from Allport's Contact Hypothesis (1954). Allport contended that intergroup contact could serve as a method of preventing the amplification of intergroup hostility and under certain preconditions reduce prejudice against members of a rival out-group. In an extension, Brewer and Gaertner (2004) suggest de-categorizing the in-group and re-categorizing inclusively with the out-group by employing intergroup contact for the step of de-categorization and encouraging a common identity for achieving re-categorization. Establishing a common identity between former rivals would inevitably indicate the elimination of societal securitization, as formerly threatened social identities would have merged into a unifying one. Societal re-categorization through meaningful intergroup contact and shared cognition can therefore be a valid indicator of successful societal desecuritization – a means of "retrieving the normality of politics" (Huysmans, 1998).

The 'contact hypothesis' and desecuritization

The concepts of autistic hostility and the Contact Hypothesis highlight the catalytic role of intergroup contact in processes of securitization. As the absence of contact can amplify intergroup hostility and reaffirm the security threat one group poses to the other, so too might its presence enhance the likelihood for desecuritization and, by extension, potential reconciliation. The direct connection between securitization and contact not only reinforces the need to rethink the securitization process beyond the speech act, but to examine contact as a variable in processes of desecuritization.

Revisiting Allport's (1954) seminal work is helpful in this regard. He identified four optimal conditions for positive contact between groups in conflict: one, equal status between in-group and out-group members; two, common objectives or a joint cause; three, mutual cooperation; and four, positive encouragement for contact and cooperation by authority figures of each respective in-group. These conditions have been reaffirmed by a number of scholars (Hammack, Pilecki, & Merrilees, 2013; Brenick & Killen, 2014; Kanol, 2014) while others have discussed the ability of contact to generate positive impacts and reduce prejudice even in the absence of Allport's often unrealistic optimal environment (Pettigrew & Tropp, 2006; Stasiuk & Bilewicz, 2013).

This demonstrated ability to reduce prejudice across groups in conflict makes contact a potential tool for desecuritization. However, existing research on intergroup contact suggests that in order for it to render audiences less receptive to securitization processes, such contact needs to occur within controlled environments, where said conditions exist or can be introduced. This differentiates conditioned intergroup contact from everyday incidental intergroup contact, making the latter less effective in achieving desecuritization. However, even within such a controlled environment, attaining equal status in intergroup contact is particularly challenging given the power asymmetry of groups engaged in conflict – a form of inequality that tends to sustain and encourage prejudice (Dixon, Durrheim, Kerr, & Thomae, 2013). Nevertheless, even in asymmetric power relationships typified by prevailing perceptions of threat, there are approaches that enable contact to be positive. Examples here include the Coexistence Model that was applied among Israelis and Palestinians to emphasize their commonalities (Maoz, 2011), and the re-categorization (RC) paradigm that was again applied among Israelis and Palestinians through dialogue-based contact (Hammack et al., 2013).

A number of research initiatives focusing on intergroup contact as well as reconciliation (Rothman, 1999; Broome, 2005; Pettigrew & Tropp, 2006; Maoz, 2011) have adopted observational methodologies requiring contact between antagonistic groups, subsequently engaging with intergroup participants to report on their reactions and discern attitudinal change. The majority of these initiatives confirm the reduction of prejudice through contact, in the process reaffirming that intergroup contact can enable the reduction of identity securitization, and facilitate reconciliation between identity groups locked in conflict.

One of the major critiques to the Contact Hypothesis is that the most prejudiced members of a societal in-group are the ones least likely to engage in intergroup contact with a rival out-group (Pettigrew, 1998). By extension, the argument follows that the merits of reconciliation through intergroup contact are therefore available only to those experiencing lower levels of societal securitization. Pettigrew's observation is critical for this or any consideration of intergroup contact as a potential desecuritizing move, in that it requires a refined, micro-level approach which disaggregates and distinguishes actors, audiences, and impacts. In other words, which audience or audience's 'public consent' towards securitizing moves (Wilhelmsen, 2016) can intergroup contact effectively influence? Considering that intergroup contact has been positive without all four conditions being applied (Pettigrew & Tropp, 2006; Maoz, 2011; Hammack et al., 2013; Stasiuk & Bilewicz, 2013), what can be considered as effective and meaningful contact?

Acknowledging intergroup contact as an influential factor within the securitization process in intergroup conflict settings will enable us, within this study and beyond, to better articulate its effectiveness by addressing who engages in contact, what counts as effective contact, and which variables make contact catalytic to desecritization. The assumption that members of the same in-group can experience various levels of societal securitization makes the examination of securitization processes even more complex, as one societal in-group can be comprised of multiple audiences with various levels of receptiveness towards a securitization act. Stritzel (2007) states that the audience – or multiple audiences – partaking in a securitization process have the agency to accept or reject a speech act, making the audience an overlooked catalyst in the effectiveness of securitization acts.

In order to effectively examine intergroup contact as a tool for reducing outgroup prejudice and influencing audience resilience towards societal security threats, it is also important to differentiate between pre-emptive and reactive applications of intergroup contact. Pre-emptive intergroup contact can occur between groups that are not in antagonistic terms, or whose relations have not been severely damaged, and enable them to reject future securitized threats against one another. On the other hand, reactive intergroup contact – the type of contact more often used in peacebuilding initiatives – is applied among rival groups with high levels of prejudice in order to eliminate intergroup tension, enable rivals to revisit past societal threats, and potentially downgrade their significance. By doing so, reactive intergroup contact contributes to an issue's desecuritization and at the same time reduces the receptiveness of the targeted audience to future threats.

Examining intergroup contact for its ability to influence the perception of both existing and future security threats posed by rival identity groups widens the scope of securitization scholarship beyond the speech act itself, to incorporate the societal parameters affecting securitization before and after the speech act happens. The chapter proceeds to present the methodology applied and the findings collected for examining intergroup contact between Greek and Turkish Cypriot peacebuilders – and their multi-layered group memberships.

A note on methodology

The research approach employed here emphasizes two overlooked parameters of securitization theory: one, the importance of intergroup contact in processes of (de)securitization, and two, the role of the audience as a catalytic agent in these processes. In addressing these parameters, this study moves beyond discursive methodology to evaluate the ability of intergroup contact to influence the credibility of securitization acts, and does so by focusing on the audience's ability to accept or reject societal threats through ethnography.

Stritzel's work (2011) provides an important impetus, particularly in his recommendation for a reconceptualization of security discourse in ways that better account for the 'localization' of security meanings. He suggests that localizing securitization discourse can reveal the context in which a specific speech act is successful, and embraces the localization of security meanings to allow for a greater focus on the audience(s), and the specifics in which the audience(s) can be persuaded.

Although Stritzel's (2011) approach retains securitization's focus on speech-acts and discourse, the notion of localization and its subsequent focus on the audience as a key actor provides a fresh perspective to securitization research, one reflected in this chapter's methodological design. More specifically, this chapter incorporates a concern with localization by employing ethnographic methodologies that provide insight into the idiosyncrasies of the audience under study, in order to highlight the variables contributing to the audience's stance towards societal security threats. In the case study of the peacebuilding community of Cyprus, the audience examined is predominantly comprised of Greek and Turkish Cypriot peacebuilders, accompanied by additional local and international peacebuilders of various ethnic backgrounds. The Greek and Turkish Cypriot peacebuilders reaffirm the complexity of audience affiliations, as they are members of a single in-group – the peacebuilder group – and at the same time belong to two rival out-groups – their Greek Cypriot and Turkish Cypriot communities.

Exploring the agency of audiences in the securitization process can be more effective if methodological designs move beyond a singular focus on discourse. As Huysmans (2011) states, looking at speech-acts alone leaves little room for critical appraisal of the overall political context enveloping securitization, including the technocratic and technological steps taken to enhance and endorse it. Introducing intergroup contact into securitization research can help redress this problem, by informing the researcher of the audience's level of threat receptiveness towards a potentially threatening actor by providing insight into the audience's knowledge of this actor, their nature of interaction if any, and any perceived insecurities or fears within the audience. This last point is crucial; according to Williams (2011) fear can be a determining factor of an audience's susceptibility to a securitization process, and receptiveness of a speech act in particular. Williams emphasizes the inherent and "intimate relationship between existential threat and fear" (2011, p. 453) and yet, as he points out, fear has remained at the margins of securitization theory research.

As discussed above, much of the prevailing research examining intergroup contact considers its impact(s) to be magnified in controlled environments. To this end, it seems fitting to examine the role of intergroup contact in processes of desecuritization within Cyprus' peacebuilding community – a community whose members have engaged in peacebuilding initiatives within a context reflecting

Allport's conditions for positive intergroup contact. First, the audience involves members of two communities engaged in ethnic conflict, who jointly cooperate for a common goal, under terms of equality and mutual respect, and under the auspices of an international authority encouraging their contact. The intercommunal peacebuilding community therefore provides an organic setting satisfying Allport's conditions for positive intergroup conduct and achieves this for the members of two otherwise securitized communities, Greek Cypriots and Turkish Cypriots. Through the personal stories of local peacebuilders – and myself as a co-performer of the community – the present ethnographic model manages to illustrate how contact has had an immediate effect on these peacebuilders' societal securitization, in a way that eventually differentiates them from their respective community in-groups.

In light of the preceding, the remainder of this chapter features an analysis of intergroup contact in Cyprus which employs a mixed methods approach combining narrative history with autoethnography. The former approach allows for contextualization of the evolution of the examined peacebuilding community, as well as analysis of its practices of intergroup contact in reference to securitization and desecuritization processes. The latter approach is used to connect the community's recorded discourse with insights from members of the community, while at the same time acknowledging my role as the author and, simultaneously, as a member of the audience being examined.

The data subjected to analysis here is a combination of reflective memory and direct ethnographic observations from the period 2012–2017, when I was an active co-performer of the peacebuilder audience, a selection of structured interviews with Greek and Turkish Cypriot members of the identified audience taken during the period 2015–2017, and secondary data informing the evolution of the peacebuilding movement from the 1990s until today. Direct quotations derived from the structured interviews are presented under participant pseudonyms. Secondary data used consist of academic publications, archival records, journal articles, and publicly available surveys, reports, and indices. In light of the first-hand narrative quotations derived from the interviews and the notes collected during the field observation process, the analysis is qualitative in nature. The predominant mode of ethnographic data recording is note-taking (Bryman, 2004; Sanders, 2002), an approach employed both for the recording of field observations, but also for the transcription of interviews, which were not audio-visually recorded.

The remainder of this chapter presents and analyzes the study's findings on intercommunal contact and the conditions enabling it for the intercommunal peacebuilding civil society in Cyprus, as well as the significance of intergroup contact for the movement's members in revisiting and potentially desecuritizing community-based societal threats.

Lessons from Cyprus: findings and analysis

1974–1997: securitization in the absence of intergroup contact

The late 1970s and 1980s were an era of suspicion and fear in Cyprus. Nationalist rhetoric in both communities prevailed, leaving little room for rapprochement and reconciliation initiatives (Jarraud, Louise, & Filippou, 2013). The predecessors of today's peacebuilding movement were isolated confidence-building measures that often occurred under the auspices of international organizations. A prominent example is the collaboration of the Greek and Turkish Cypriot municipal authorities of Nicosia to reconnect the city's sewage system, an initiative that commenced in 1978 and came to be known as the Nicosia Master Plan. The 1970s also saw a number of reconciliation initiatives hosted abroad, as local intergroup contact remained complex and problematic, with Yale University's Leonard Doob hosting informal meetings among political leaders in 1973 and 1979 with the aim of providing conflict resolution trainings (Ladini, 2009).

In 1980, a series of meetings was organized by the British Friends of Cyprus Committee for educators, journalists, politicians, public servants, and architects from both communities. In 1984, Harvard University professor Herbert Kelman organized the Interactive Problem-solving Workshop and in 1985, Leonard Doob organized the Operation Locksmith Workshop (Mahallae, 2015). These first post-war intercommunal gatherings were the only outlet of intergroup contact between two communities that were at the time violently partitioned – and many displaced from their homes – in a political environment of antagonism that failed to provide any solutions. Nevertheless, similar initiatives persisted. From 1988 to 1993, Ron Fisher of the Canadian Institute for Peace and Security organized a series of four workshops on problem solving and conflict resolution. Workshops of a similar nature were also carried out in 1992 and 1994 with Louise Diamond of the Institute of Multi-Track Diplomacy and Diana Chigas of the Conflict Management Group, with the support of USAID and the Cyprus Fulbright Commission.

Over the following three years, 32 foreign and 57 local trainers were involved in 47 workshops and 19 dialogue groups involving locals from a wide age range and diverse professional affiliations. During the same period, Fulbright scholar Benjamin Broome introduced the Interactive Management peacebuilding technique, with his initiative resulting in 15 new local projects involving both communities (Broome, 2005; Mahallae, 2015). Additional mediation trainings including role-play and dialogue were offered by Marco Turk and John Ungerlider, also Fulbright scholars (Mahallae, 2015).

As Laouris (2011) states, conflict resolution workshops that were conducted by the Cyprus Fulbright Commission for local civil society activists were initially delivered separately to the two communities. Nevertheless, the 1990s saw a proliferation of intercommunal contact, both due to the support of international agencies such as Fulbright, the UN, and the British High Commission, but also out of the personal initiative of local peace activists, who were often labeled as traitors by their respective communities (Laouris et al., 2009). These projects involved both local academics and civil society activists (Jarraud et al., 2013), as well as international peace professionals willing to engage with intercommunal dialogue on the island. According to Rothman (1999, p. 177), Cyprus offered "an incubator for conflict resolution scholars as they apply their skills to a relatively non-volatile but none the less deeply intransigent conflict." Rothman himself participated as an action-researcher in the 1994 Cyprus Conflict Resolution Consortium, including a number of foreign conflict management experts and approximately 40 participants from both communities.

The 1990s also saw a few attempts at launching organized peace movements such as the Citizens Joint Movement for a Federal and Democratic Cyprus in 1990 (boycotted by Turkish Cypriot authorities who denied access to the movement's meetings in the Ledra Palace hotel), and the Peace Centre Cyprus, the first registered NGO devoted to the promotion of peace (Ladini, 2009). Arguably, the ability to engage in intercommunal contact under the authority of international organizations provided an ideal environment for a number of locals to join forces with members of the other communities in the pursuit of a peaceful settlement to their politically stagnated conflict. This view, however, remained well outside the public eye, as the two partitioned communities continued to live in isolation to one another and suspicious of the other community's political intentions.

A 1997 decision from the Turkish Cypriot authorities to ban peacebuilding activities made the environment for the local intercommunal peacebuilding movement even more restrictive (Jarraud et al., 2013). According to Laouris and Laouri (2008) this decision was taken in response to the EU's rejection of Turkey's application for accession. The decision abruptly discontinued the work of local and international peace experts, which included the establishment of the Trainers' Group[2] and their active engagement with the political negotiations prior to the 2004 peace settlement (Laouris & Laouri, 2008). Along with the administrative and political challenges in place, the first wave of local peacebuilders had to face the menace of local media, as Greek Cypriot Kyriakos, civil society and technology expert explains:

> The first intercommunal group that met at the Ledra Palace in 1994 was portrayed in the media as traitors. When I saw the news, I realised I knew one of the people 'accused' of being a traitor and was amazed; I said to myself, how can this be? [Maria] is a nice person! Then a month later, Fulbright called me and said that they were having difficulty identifying participants for bi-communal meetings, and asked if I was interested in joining. My response was: What's in it for me? They said that I can cross and see the north. I immediately said OK! And that was a breakthrough experience for me.
>
> (Kyriakos, 2017)

As Kyriakos admits, many of the local peacebuilding neophytes did not consciously identify as peacebuilders, but more as concerned and active citizens.

For many – including myself many years later – intercommunal contact and trans-communal movement was a ground-breaking experience, enough to provoke a strong membership to the intercommunal peacebuilding community.

1998–2013: the birth of the intercommunal civil society

In 1998, the United Nations Development Programme (UNDP) launched the Bi-Communal Development Programme (BDP). This ushered in an era of internationally funded grant-giving peacebuilding projects intended to fund local NGOs to run bi-communal activities (UNDP, 2015). The BDP was an initiative to foster inter-communal contact and support the potential growth of an intercommunal civil society. As Jarraud et al. (2013, p. 49) put it, the BDP, which lasted until 2005, was the cornerstone of the "first concerted external investment in the island's nascent civil society as a force for peacebuilding." The BDP was implemented by the United Nations Office for Project Services (UNOPS) and supported by UNDP and the U.S. Agency for International Development (USAID). Its two primary characteristics were that it provided significant funds to civil society leaders for bi-communal work, and that it refrained from politically controversial activities, focusing more on development projects dealing with infrastructure and capacity-building.

According to Ladini (2009), the efforts of international organizations to strengthen local civil society yielded the establishment of two NGO centers on the island in 2001, the Management Centre in the north and the NGO Support Centre in the south. Intergroup contact among the two communities was now enabled and encouraged in a more structured manner, enabling locals to pursue their socio-political interests jointly with members of the other community. Although the percentage of locals involved was a marginal share of the island's population, participants were able to connect with members of the other community that shared common interests and worked towards a common goal.

Yet, while the launch of the BDP in 1998 marked a new era of international peacebuilding projects in Cyprus, attempts for intercommunal contact and collaboration were challenged by the restriction of intercommunal movement and the partition of the Greek and Turkish Cypriot communities due to a securitized Buffer Zone. Angela reflects on her experience as a professional in one of the BDP projects:

> We were employed as temporary staff to our respective Nicosia local authorities, and were paid by the project funding. We worked in the separate authority offices in the south and north and were escorted by the UN to have our coordinating meetings. We didn't have joint offices, but when we had more formal meetings we would meet at the UN offices close to the airport, otherwise we sometimes met downtown at Heracles.[3] We were discussing of having joint offices but that never really happened.
>
> During the programme, we had escorts for entering and visiting the Buffer Zone and that was a bit intimidating. We couldn't visit all parts of the Buffer Zone because some were controlled by the Turkish military.

At one point into the project, before the opening of the checkpoints, one of the team members lost her father and we wanted to attend the funeral in the north. We got permission and went to Ayia Sophia.[4] It was a very emotional day. And you know, I recently saw her and she mentioned that day. She told me that she remembers wondering, how did we even make it there [to the north]?

(Angela, 2016)

The precarious nature of intercommunal contact during the 1990s due to the security procedures was still evident in the early 2000s as well. Angela clarifies:

I joined the project, which was part of the Nicosia Master Plan, in 2002 after completing my studies abroad. I had no contact with the other community prior to my involvement in the [UNOPS] project. Even after I joined the project, I didn't pay much attention to the bi-communal element. What was different for me was not the fact that I was working with Turkish Cypriots, but the overall project, its structure, its outputs; it was an entirely new concept for me.

(Angela, 2016)

Between 1998 and 2003, the BDP supported approximately 200 peacebuilding initiatives, including primarily cultural heritage and environmental and public health projects, again involving international experts, techniques, and best practices (Mahallae, 2015). Local civil society grew in expertise and, with international financial support, was able to achieve public outreach and initiate joint advocacy efforts aimed at influencing the stagnated political negotiation process. A first step to establishing communication with Track I was the Common Vision document, developed and signed by 86 Turkish Cypriot civil society organizations in 2002, calling for an end to the negotiation stalemate (Khallaf & Tür, 2008; Mahallae, 2015).

Turning points: 2003–2004

During the BDP implementation period, the intercommunal peacebuilding movement saw two historic benchmarks: a promising 2003 and a heart-wrenching 2004. Beginning in April 2003, a partial lifting in restrictions on movement agreed between the two communities was implemented, enabling crossings across the Buffer Zone from designated checkpoints. This has undoubtedly provided a boost to civil society peacebuilding efforts, especially in light of a peace referendum in April 2004 (Jarraud et al., 2013). More intercommunal NGOs started to form, including Hands across the Divide, an intercommunal initiative for the revival of Famagusta, and the Association for Historical Dialogue and Research (AHDR) aiming to provide new perspectives of critical thinking in history education, away from the two communities' nationalist doctrines (Ladini, 2009).

Michalis and Sophia respectively emphasize the impact of being able to cross and interact with members of the other community without the formal security procedures that were in place before 2003:

> 2003 was definitely a benchmark due to the opening of checkpoints. There was a major impact because contact was enabled, contributing to the practical understanding of contact theory and also to the economic balance between the communities and the visualisation of a potential solution.
>
> (Michalis, 2015)

> We had meetings within the Ledra Palace and everything was very structured, but now you just wave at the guards and pass. The Home for Cooperation provides a relaxed atmosphere and the difference is huge in terms of accessibility for intercommunal contact, in terms of perceptions and in terms of the environment and setting.
>
> (Sophia, 2016)

A civil society practitioner in youth projects, Neofytos (2014) described how the optimism of a potential reunification, along with the novel opportunity for transcommunal movement, provided significant momentum to intercommunal initiatives. This occurred in spite of the media's insistence on demonizing peacebuilders. Neofytos recalled some media outlets enlisting the names of local peacebuilders as recipients of bribery from international agents pushing for a reunification agenda. He reflected on his first passage to the north as an experience he was otherwise adamantly against, due to the necessity of showing a passport to cross. He did at the time, however, agree to go to the checkpoint with a group of youth workers from his organization, while being in contact with a Turkish Cypriot counterpart as part of a UNDP-ACT youth partnership. Neofytos described how, due to a combination of circumstances, he was able to cross to the north with his youth group without showing passports, an opportunity he perceived as an unexpected solution to a personal dilemma.

The momentum established in 2003 with increased freedom of movement across the Buffer Zone quickly evaporated with the rejection of the Annan peace plan by the Greek Cypriot community in the parallel referendums of 2004. The peacebuilding movement encountered starkly divergent attitudes in the two communities; the Turkish Cypriot civil society leaders found positive ground in favor of reunification, with the Turkish Cypriot community accepting the plan by 65 percent, while Greek Cypriot civil society activists met strong opposition forces, eventually yielding a staggering 76 percent against the Annan Plan (Jarraud et al., 2013). Evident disappointment was reflected across the civil society activists but particularly among Turkish Cypriot activists, as the peace referendum was viewed as a missed opportunity, as well as confirmation of the weakness of the civil society-led peacebuilding movement to engage the wider public and effectively pursue political advocacy in both communities (Jarraud et al., 2013). At the same time, the period up to the referendum comprised a series of speech acts by authority figures – mainly within the Greek Cypriot community and including the Greek Cypriot president – who presented the Plan as a potential threat to their societal survival. The contradiction between the Greek Cypriot popular vote and the attempt of the Greek Cypriot peace activists to support the Plan highlighted the existence of two separate audiences, with the latter rejecting the government's stance on the Plan as a societal threat.

Despite the 2004 backlash, peacebuilding initiatives on the island continued. The BDP was succeeded by the UNDP-Action for Cooperation and Trust in Cyprus (ACT) program, an initiative that was delivered in three phases over the period 2005–2015, and was implemented by UNDP with the support of USAID (UNDP, 2015). ACT I was implemented between 2005 and 2008, delivering more than 300 intercommunal partnerships and more than 680 knowledge-sharing activities (UNDP, 2015). The second phase of ACT was implemented between 2008 and 2011 and aimed at deepening engagement, with public outreach and advocacy towards the reconciliation process becoming the primary end goals for the various projects within the ACT II framework.

The Home for Cooperation

The year 2011 proved to be another benchmark for peacebuilding in Cyprus, both because the intercommunal peacebuilding movement continued to grow within and beyond UNDP-ACT, and because of the realization of a physical space for intercommunal civil society work, the Home for Cooperation. An initiative that started in 2008, the Home for Cooperation was an anticipated physical space for the coordination of peacebuilding efforts and a vital step towards the empowerment of the civil society-led peacebuilding movement (Hadjipavlou & Kanol, 2008). The Home for Cooperation project included the restoration of a rundown building, found on Marcou Drakou Street a few meters away from the Ledra Palace Hotel and the Fulbright Commission. It was, like the two other buildings, at a part of the street found in-between the two communities' checkpoints, an ideal meeting point in the Buffer Zone accessible by members of both communities.

Ladini (2009) and Hadjipavlou and Kanol (2008) contend that the extensive amount of peacebuilding work that occurred on the island prior to the Home's launch had still failed to make the intercommunal civil society peacebuilding movement influential in the Cypriot peace process, or in providing a channel of political participation for the wider public. In Ladini's (2009, p. 52) words, "despite the high number of workshops that have endowed Cyprus civil society with skilled people in conflict management techniques, such seminars usually host a surprisingly small elite of activists." The same observation was made by Autesserre (2014) during her ethnographic study of peacebuilding efforts in Cyprus, which appeared to be confined to a distinct group of Nicosia elites. From an analogous standpoint, a 2011 CIVICUS report highlighted the disparity between the peacebuilding movement and the wider public by stating that "the attitudes of civil society and external stakeholders towards bi-communal activities and the reconciliation process deviate significantly from that of society at large in both communities" (CIVICUS, 2011, p. 17). This realization suggested that intercommunal contact and cooperation was still considered unconventional for the majority of Cypriots—while at the same time proving a catalytic factor in the lives of the island's peace activists.

The Home was established across from the Ledra Palace Hotel, which previously held monitored intercommunal meetings. The two, along with a German language centre and a community media centre, are found in the Buffer Zone segment of Markou Dracou Street, dividing the two island's northern and southern areas by a few hundred meters. The Buffer Zone segment is marked by a checkpoint on each end operated by the respective communal authority, allowing members of both communities to cross into the Buffer Zone or into the other community. Eleni elaborates on the importance of the physical illustrations achieved in the post-Home era:

> On a local level, the most impactful thing we do is theatre workshops, and when they are well-designed and well-facilitated they are very transformative, because they engage both the body and the emotion. You do it for yourself and it really has an impact.
>
> What is also impactful is the mere presence of people in the Buffer Zone. It creates an incredible impact, both Cypriots and internationals. It's an impact to general, not necessarily political audiences, and it can lead to a shift. The manifestation of a practice creates the most impact. You can put people in a room and present academic findings to them, but unless you physicalize those findings, there will be no significant impact.
>
> Having a conversation with a diverse audience in a conference is also manifestation, and academic research that comes to feed into practices is also impactful. Academic field work [by external peacebuilders] has come to fit into the local culture, for example field work illustrated at the Home has had a great impact, it made its way back. The fact that work by external peacebuilders can potentially return back [in practice] is really important and impactful.
>
> (Eleni, 2015)

Soon after its launch, the Home became a point of reference for locals seeking to engage in intercommunal contact, both on a professional level as implementing partners of peacebuilding projects, such as the ones under the UNDP-ACT umbrella, or on a social level, meeting for coffee at the Home's cafe. In addition to the UNDP-led activities, there were plentiful examples, during 2013 and 2014, of intercommunal groups that treated the Home as a convenient space for meetings, to coordinate and deliver events and conferences, to plan youth camps, to recruit volunteers and activity participants, and to network with foreign experts. Some examples include meetings between teachers' associations from the two communities, recruitment and preparation meetings for the Cyprus Friendship Programme (2017), a Couchsurfers'[5] social gathering among members from across the divide, an intercommunal music group practising instrumental music at the Home's multipurpose room, and informal meetings among friends, including student meetings for issuing an intercommunal newspaper and a weekly gathering of two elderly men – a Greek Cypriot and a Turkish Cypriot – who held regular morning meetings at the Home's café teaching their native language to one another over Cypriot coffee.[6]

The Home soon became a space that normalized everyday intercommunal cooperation and presented a reality that showed no signs of rivalry or securitization between the Greek and Turkish Cypriot communities. This reality, however, was not reflective of the climate existing in the rest of Cyprus, among locals that had no contact with members of the other community. Thus, the emergence of the intercommunal civil society and their consistent and growing contact provides a strong indication of how intergroup contact was able to generate the desecuritization of its members towards the societal threat each community posed to one another. This was achieved as the members of the intercommunal civil society were able to redefine their societal perceptions and objectives collectively, and to stand against the positions of their respective communities – whether this was the Turkish Cypriot authorities during the late 1990s or the Greek Cypriot ones during the Annan Plan period. The emergence of the intercommunal peacebuilding civil society, and along with it a discourse of growing contact and increased resilience to mono-communal societal threats, directly associates contact not only with the reduction of prejudice between Greek and Turkish Cypriot peacebuilders, but also with their desecuritization and collective re-categorization as collaborators towards the common aim of a peace settlement. The following section will further discuss the desecuritization of the intercommunal civil society from an autoethnographic stance, covering the years following the Home's commencement of operations until 2017.

2012–2017: enter the researcher (an autoethnographic analysis)

The historical overview of the intercommunal civil society's emergence provided above enriches the understanding of the intergroup dynamics experienced by the members of this community and how these dynamics evolved to affect their resilience towards securitization processes regarding intercommunal societal threats. In order to more effectively achieve the localization of this research, the chapter proceeds to convey its findings through direct feedback from the community under study, including myself as a member of the examined audience.

Choosing to be a co-performer to the examined audience conforms to Derrida's (1981) take on performativity, allowing the author to escape the subject/object dichotomy and more reflectively merge into the conducted research. This approach is particularly appropriate for the study of securitization processes, due to their intersubjective nature, but more so for the reconceptualization of securitization through the perspective of individual and collective identity. Adopting autoethnographic co-performativity, a critical methodology especially suitable to native researchers (Reed-Danahay, 1997; Foley, 2002) also addresses the author's bias more transparently, which according to Jarvis and Holland (2015) can directly affect the validity of research on security processes. To this end, approaching my analysis from a reflective standpoint enables me to more directly associate with the intersubjective processes linking intergroup contact to notions of societal security threats.

As one of the ACT professionals working at the Home, I soon felt a sense of belonging as a member of a unique community with a common identity; i.e., a peacebuilder. Joining a series of projects that took on the island's intractable conflict from a civil society perspective, and at the same time having a physical environment where intercommunal contact, dialogue, and cooperation was a breakthrough for the locals who experienced it, proved vastly contradictory to the monocommunal experience of everyday life in either Cyprus' north or south. I often felt a sense of privilege in being a member of the peacebuilding community, not by exerting exclusivity towards non-members, but for having discovered a community so ground-breaking and still hidden from mainstream life. Nikolas, a Greek Cypriot project manager in his thirties, who had joined the local peacebuilding community after the launch of UNDP-ACT, gave voice to these sentiments:

> These projects created a new generation that deals with peacebuilding, all the young professionals that were part of these projects and it created a new culture that we were privileged to be part of. These projects helped us get a deeper knowledge of the conflict. In terms of long lasting impact to the general audience we didn't do as much of a good work. So our strongest impact was with the people working within the projects, not the public we outreached to.
>
> (Nikolas, 2016)

Being part of the peacebuilding community provided me with, more than anything else, a sense of empowerment. Perhaps what brought the community together was our ability to empower ourselves and our peers while the rest of the country remained at stalemate, and conduct work that reached beyond political and emotional boundaries. The disparity of the peacebuilder audience with the two communities was often acknowledged by the local peacebuilders, who saw their work's outreach remain weak over the years. Nikolas speaks of the existence of an in-group comfort zone that made outreach within the island's ethnic communities considerably weak:

> We felt that we were marginalized but at the same time we were not concerned about it, which was not a good attitude to have. Towards the end [of the project] I felt that we had become an exclusive, special community and that had hindered our public outreach.
>
> We often said 'oh look, it's the same faces again' and 'oh, those are not really our crowd, we shouldn't be inviting them.' This was really bothering

me. Eventually we started breaking [the group] down a bit and tried to work a bit mono-communally to reconfigure our narrative and be more relevant to our own community.

(Nikolas, 2016)

Despite the challenge of outreach and relevance, sharing unique experiences as a group was a key contributor in strengthening the sense of in-group membership for the local peacebuilders. This in turn enabled ethnically and nationally diverse members of the peacebuilder in-group to prioritize their common identities over their divergent ones. One of these shared experiences was the individual break-through moments of local peacebuilders, whether it was about meeting a member of the other community and discovering their commonalities, was crossing to the other side of the Buffer Zone, or simply having access to insights about both communities on the island rather than just their own. It was the moments of indi-vidual revelation that occurred on a collective scale, both in the early years of peacebuilding as well as more recently. On many occasions, this revelation was about acknowledging the other community's perspective. During our October 2017 discussion at the Home for Cooperation, Yiannis remembered one such experience from 1994:

We were a bi-communal group meeting at the building across the street [the Ledra Palace Hotel], we were discussing about refugees and realized we had reached an impasse. Greek Cypriots and Turkish Cypriots had a different view of who is a refugee. Turkish Cypriots accused Greek Cypriots for being too emotional about the issue and Greek Cypriots accused Turkish Cypriots for being heartless. When we reconvened we asked the two sides to explain the term and it appeared that the two communities had vastly different experiences. Turkish Cypriots had lost their homes, but they had gained security, whereas Greek Cypriots had lost both their homes and their security. When this realisation was out in the open, people cried, because they understood the other community and had moved from a lack of empathy to empathy. This for me was a landmark.

(Yiannis, 2017)

A similar experience happened to me in 2012, when I was on a road trip with my Turkish Cypriot colleague, Eylul, to conduct outreach activities for our project's intercommunal youth events. We were driving to a youth camp site on the Kantara mountaintop, and we made a stop at the Kantara castle ruins. This was a site I was told about repeatedly as a child, and I felt overwhelmed to be there, at a site that I grew up hearing had been captured at war. From the mountaintop, I could also see the northern peak of the island, another landmark that I grew up admiring at a distance, and was now able to see in person. I tried conveying my awe to Eylul, only to hear her confess: "I really don't understand why Greek Cypriots are so emotional over visiting the north. I visit the south all the time, my family was displaced from Peristerona and I have visited many times." I responded: "The north has been projected as an idealised lost territory for generations of Greek Cypriots, through the media, through education, through family. I can't explain why, but I feel overwhelmed to be here." It was a joint reflection we were able to experience, and I felt privileged to have had that insightful discussion on the Kantara mountaintop.

2014–2017: a marginalized de-securitized audience

Today there are safe environments to discuss difficult topics, like conflict. It depends on the participants whether they accept other opinions and show respect. If some participants are unwilling to accept that, then neutral participants are useful to have. [...] Essentially what is important is to create platforms that people come in with their own will and feel safe and are given the space to hear different perspectives, they can challenge their narratives, they can feel inspired, they can change their mind or look things up more, so it helps becoming more critical.

(Savvas, 2015)

Following the completion of the ACT projects by the end of 2013 – with the exception of UNDP's lower-scale CCE initiative – the Home experienced a lower volume of international peacebuilding projects, but a continued inflow of visitors engaging in international or grassroots peace projects, or simply socializing at an intercommunal scale. The venue has fostered the continuation of the local peacebuilding community, which is not so much characterized by the coordination or permanence of its members, but more by their common affiliation with the peacebuilder identity. Mehmet, a young Turkish Cypriot freelance peacebuilder, explains his perception of the local peacebuilder in-group:

There is a peacebuilding community in Cyprus, it's the people who try to create bridges between the two communities, so they are not always together, but they are working on the same vision, they have the same values and when they find common resources and opportunities to work together they do. So I do think these guys are a community.

I am part of this community, I try to support whenever I need, I work on translations, offer technical support. Nowadays I prefer to work independently rather than in projects, I have partners.

(Mehmet, 2017)

At the same time, some peacebuilders have admitted that they don't have the means or time to conduct peacebuilding work and others point to the lack of self-awareness towards the peacebuilder identity. As Markos notes:

I would define myself as a peace educator, which falls under the umbrella of peacebuilder. Peacebuilder is a person dedicating part of his [or] her time either professionally or voluntarily towards the construction of peace culture and non-violence. Being a peacebuilder is a process, no one is the ultimate peacebuilder. It's a way of life. There are people who don't identify themselves as peacebuilders but they do peace work, and the opposite, so there is a multiplicity of identity, like all other identities.

(Markos, 2017)

Even though Cyprus' local peacebuilders carry a diversity of perceptions towards their identity as peacebuilders, their intercommunal engagement and their confidence that members of the island's two communities can cooperate and live in peace have come to shape their shared cognition. This shared belief, which evolved through their positive intergroup contact, and in light of past or current speech acts that demonize the other community, significantly differentiates the peacebuilders' receptiveness in comparison to members of their respective ethnic communities that have had no contact and no point of reference to the 'other.'

The intercommunal peacebuilding community, even during its most popular initiatives, achieved low levels of public outreach in the two communities. Although this was seen as a weakness from both the local and international implementing partners of these projects, the seclusion of the community has provided security researchers with the opportunity to examine it as a distinct audience organically illustrating the effects of meaningful and positive intergroup contact in intergroup conflict, in addition to other key variables in securitization processes discussed below.

Analytical reflections on peacebuilding in Cyprus

As shown from the Cyprus case study, peacebuilding projects provided their participants with a unique insight on intergroup dynamics, a personal experience that was more direct and impactful than speech acts of societal securitization that were reiterated in the media by a variety of authority figures. This has led local peacebuilders to revisit, question, and redefine their understanding of their communities and the perceived threats to which they are exposed. The empowerment of realizing that your own perspective is suddenly informed by additional ones through intergroup contact has been, as Cypriot peacebuilders demonstrate, enough to diffuse constructed societal threats and discredit single-source speech acts through a newly-found multi-perspectivity.

The peacebuilding movement in Cyprus illustrates the evolution of a new group membership formed across the conflict's antagonistic Greek and Turkish Cypriot communities, and re-categorizes its members under a common peacebuilder identity, overcoming the securitization of its members' ethnic identities. As revealed above, local peacebuilders experienced breakthrough moments through intergroup contact, which was for the greatest portion of their lives restricted, and organically adopted a common peacebuilder identity that in turn de-securitized their ethnic one. Looking at the peacebuilding community in Cyprus introduces security researchers to the peacebuilder *incubator*, where intergroup contact can take place under significantly more positive conditions and meaningful relations can be built that can impact one's group membership, identity perceptions, and receptiveness to societal security threats. The controlled environment offered by peacebuilding initiatives reveals how the findings from Cyprus can have a broader applicability across international peacebuilding initiatives, which can serve as incubators for desecuritization for the individuals who choose to engage with these initiatives.

Using international peacebuilding projects as a reference for empirical security research effectively enables the in-depth study of securitization in association with collective identity by building on the constructed nature and interconnectedness of the two. More specifically, the study of securitization processes in reference to intergroup contact allows us to delve deeper into the variable of identity and how perceptions of identity affect an individual's receptiveness of constructed threats against certain identities. As a result, the connection between intergroup contact and processes of securitization introduces the concepts of group membership, shared cognition, and cognitive dissonance as key factors in the study of societal security threats.

Peacebuilding initiatives in Cyprus have applied intergroup contact to address and reduce phenomena of intergroup prejudice in a conflictual environment, often doing so in conditions of intergroup equality, and by emphasizing intergroup commonalities through the collaboration of participants towards a common goal. Peacebuilding initiatives of this character represent supporting evidence for the contact hypothesis. This realization enables security research to consider not only the impact of intergroup contact on one's receptiveness towards threats against a collective identity, but also to consider the significance of social psychological variables in the study of securitization processes. More specifically, perceptions of collective identity, intergroup hostility through category activation (Oakes, 2004), re-categorization (Brewer & Gaertner, 2004), and what Dunn (2004) refers to as the process of reframing collective identity can act as potential (de)securitization indicators for societal security threats in intergroup conflict.

The local peacebuilders in Cyprus achieved their desecuritization through the shared social cognition they had with members of an otherwise rival out-group, and their common experiences and shared goal for peace de-legitimized the security threat reiterated by their ethnic community's respective political leaders. These observations reaffirm the interconnection between processes of intergroup contact and societal re-categorization with societal desecuritization. This however, does not imply that intergroup contact alone, apart from other factors, can cause societal desecuritization. Acknowledging the cognitive dissonance of the audience of Cypriot peacebuilders relative to the island's two ethnic communities indicates the impact intergroup contact can have on matters of identity and societal security perceptions.

At the same time, the peacebuilding community's membership indicates that community members with high intergroup enmity did not engage with the island's intercommunal peacebuilding movement, reaffirming the critique that intergroup contact as a tool cannot always reach the most prejudiced – and potentially the most securitized – members of a society (Pettigrew, 1998). To that end, prolonged and meaningful intergroup contact under Allport's optimal conditions can lead to intergroup social cognition and re-categorization, and thus enable affected audiences to revisit, question, de-legitimize, and eventually reject past or future societal security threats. Nevertheless, in-group members refusing to engage in intergroup contact may remain highly responsive to efforts at securitizing out-groups, especially those toward which they already hold prejudice.

Another qualifying consideration revealed in this analysis of the intercommunal peacebuilding community in Cyprus is that the de-securitizing effect of intergroup contact on the peacebuilding audience, while profound, was hardly total. Although members of this community were open to intergroup contact, many admitted to having been suspicious or unaware of the other community, and highly receptive to societal security threats before their experience with peacebuilding. What the peacebuilders' ground-breaking and revelatory moments reveal is that, despite being open to intergroup contact, they were not fully convinced that the other community posed no threat to their own identity. Therefore, being open to intergroup contact does not necessarily imply that one is not experiencing any level of societal securitization. This observation in turn suggests that intergroup contact can be an effective tool for desecuritization for audiences that are recipients of societal securitization processes, yet are willing to engage in meaningful contact with the perceivably threatening out-group.

Conclusion

Undoubtedly, speech acts have played a pivotal role in securitization processes, including those that have long permeated inter-communal conflict in Cyprus. Nonetheless, the securitization process does not end at the speech act; it only starts there. The second step in the securitization process is for the audience to accept the threat as legitimate, and evaluating the audience's inclination towards accepting or rejecting the threat requires that we look beyond speech acts. As such, this assessment of the impact of non-discursive desecuritizing moves and Allport's contact hypothesis represents an attempt at determining who has benefited and who can potentially benefit from intergroup contact as a tool for (de) securitization. Focusing on peacebuilders (and potentially other less-frequent participants in peacebuilding and rapprochement projects) reveals new terrain for securitization research, by expanding the analytical purview of securitization in reference to factors such as in-group favoritism, out-group hostility, and group membership.

Cyprus' intercommunal peacebuilding movement confirms that re-categorization and, subsequently, desecuritization is possible despite in-group favoritism, as in-groups consist of multiple audiences with diverse receptiveness towards securitization acts. Even though some in-group audiences are highly aware of constructed societal threats, others, such as the members of the Cypriot peacebuilding movement, are able to prioritize a shared identity over their securitized ones, and accordingly de-legitimize constructed threats, becoming less receptive to future ones. Social psychological processes such as intergroup contact, shared cognition, and re-categorization are therefore critical factors requiring further consideration by securitization researchers when examining audience agency in securitization processes.

Notes

1 This conceptualization of identity associated with the Copenhagen School was challenged by, among others, McSweeney (1996), who contended that treating identity as a fixed rather than fluid and contingent entity was limiting with respect to securitization theory. This debate, while important, lies outside the scope of this chapter.

2 The Trainers' Group, also known as the Conflict Resolution Trainers' Group, or CRTG, was a team of six peace pioneers who engaged in intercommunal dialogue and, between 1994 and 1997, they were able to conduct peacebuilding initiatives with the support of international agencies, mobilizing "a few thousand Cypriots to work for peace and reconciliation" (Laouris et al., 2009, p. 46). The team also engaged in official communication with the UN with regards to the organisation's support of local peacebuilding work, an initiative that is believed to have directly contributed to the establishment of the UN's BDP programme (Laouris et al., 2009).

3 Heracles is a local ice cream brand that was founded in the mid-twentieth century, with an ice cream store in Ledras street, within the Nicosia Old City and south of the Buffer Zone.

4 Ayia Sophia, also known as Selimiye Mosque is a cathedral that was converted into a mosque during the Ottoman period. It lies at the heart of the old city, at a walking distance from the Ledra Palace crossing and the Ledras/Lokmaci street at the heart of the old city's commercial hub.

5 Couchsurfing is an online community of travelers, who share their space with one another, providing free accommodation to travelers across the world (Couchsurfing, 2016).

6 It is worthy of note that Turkish nationals residing in the north are legally prohibited from crossing to the Greek Cypriot south and, thus, activities within the Buffer Zone also enabled Turkish nationals to come into contact with Greek Cypriots, with Turkish nationals attending the Couchsurfers meeting, volunteering in various peacebuilding projects, and professionally collaborating with local NGOs.

Bibliography

Allport, G. W. (1954). *The nature of prejudice*. Cambridge: Addison-Wesley.

Autesserre, S. (2014). *Peaceland: Conflict resolution and the everyday politics of international intervention*. Cambridge: Cambridge University Press.

Balzacq, T., Léonard, S., & Ruzicka, J. (2016). 'Securitization' revisited: Theory and cases. *International Relations, 30*(4), 494–531.

Barad, K. (2003). Posthumanist Performativity: Toward an understanding of how matter comes to matter. *Signs: Journal of Women in Culture and Society, 28*(3), 801–831.

Brenick, A., & Killen, M. (2014). Moral judgments about Jewish–Arab intergroup exclusion: The role of cultural identity and contact. *Developmental Psychology, 50*(1), 86–99.

Brewer, M. B., & Gaertner, S. L. (2004). Toward reduction of prejudice: Intergroup contact and social categorization. In R. Brown & S. L. Gaertner (Eds.), *Blackwell handbook of social psychology: Intergroup processes*. Oxford: Blackwell.

Broome, B. J. (2005). *Building bridges across the green line*. Nicosia: UNDP.

Bryman, A. (2004). *Social research methods* (2nd ed.). New York: Oxford University Press.

Buzan, B., Wæver, O., & de Wilde, J. (1998). *Security: A new framework for analysis*. Boulder, CO: Lynne Rienner Publishers

CIVICUS. (2011). *An assessment of civil society in Cyprus: A map for the future*. Nicosia: Management Centre of the Mediterranean and NGO Support Centre.

Côté, A. (2016). Agents without agency: Assessing the role of the audience in securitization theory. *Security Dialogue, 47*(6), 541–558.

Couchsurfing. (2016). www.couchsurfing.com. Last accessed May 9, 2016.

Cyprus Friendship Programme. (2017). http://cyprusfriendship.org/. Last accessed May 15, 2017.

Dannreuther, R. (2013). *International security: The contemporary agenda*. Hoboken, N.J.: John Wiley & Sons.

Demjaha, A. (2017). Inter-ethnic relations in Kosovo. *SEEU Review, 12*(1), 181–196.

Derrida, J. (1981). *Positions* (Trans. A. Bass). Chicago: University of Chicago Press.

Dixon, J., Durrheim, K., Kerr, P., & Thomae, M. (2013). 'What's so funny 'bout peace, love and understanding?' Further reflections on the limits of prejudice reduction as a model of social change. *Journal of Social and Political Psychology, 1*(1), 239–252.

Dunn, J. L. (2004). The politics of empathy: Social movements and victim repertoires. *Sociological Focus, 37*(3), 235–250.

Ellinas, A. A. (2013). The rise of Golden Dawn: The new face of the far right in Greece. *South European Society and Politics, 18*(4), 543–565.

Emmers, R. (2013). Securitization (3rd ed.). In A. Collins (Ed.), *Contemporary security studies*. New York: Oxford University Press.

Foley, D. E. (2002). Critical ethnography: The reflexive turn. *International Journal of Qualitative Studies in Education, 15*(4), 469–490.

Foucault, M. (1984). Of other spaces, Heterotopias. Translated from *Architecture, Mouvement, Continuité*, 5, pp. 46–49. Retrieved from https://foucault.info/documents/ heterotopia/foucault.heteroTopia.en/

Greussing, E., & Boomgaarden, H. G. (2017). Shifting the refugee narrative? An automated frame analysis of Europe's 2015 refugee crisis. *Journal of Ethnic and Migration Studies, 43*(11), 1749–1774.

Habermas, J. (1971). *Knowledge and human interests*. Boston: Beacon Press.

Hadjipavlou, M., & Kanol, B. (2008). *Cumulative impact case study: The impacts of peacebuilding work on the Cyprus conflict*. Cambridge, MA: CDA Collaborative Learning Projects.

Hammack, P. L., Pilecki, A., & Merrilees, C. (2013). Interrogating the process and meaning of intergroup contact: Contrasting theoretical approaches. *Journal of Community and Applied Social Psychology, 24*(4), 296–324.

Howard, J. A. (2000). Social psychology of identities. *Annual Review of Sociology, 26*, 367–393.

Huntington, S. P. (1993). The clash of civilizations? *Foreign Affairs, 72*(3), 22–49.

Huysmans, J. (1998). The question of the limit: Desecuritization and the aesthetics of horror in political realism. *Millennium: Journal of International Studies, 27*(3), 569–589.

Huysmans, J. (2011). What's in an act? On security speech acts and little security nothings. *Security Dialogue, 42*(4–5), 371–383.

Janmaat, J. G. (2007). The ethnic 'other' in Ukrainian history textbooks: The case of Russia and the Russians. *Compare, 37*(3), 307–324.

Jarraud, N., Louise, C., & Filippou, G. (2013). The Cypriot Civil Society movement: A legitimate player in the peace process? *Journal of Peacebuilding and Development, 8*(1), 45–59.

Jarvis, L., & Holland, J. (2015). *Security: A critical introduction*. Basingstoke: Palgrave Macmillan.

Kanol, D. (2014). Social cohesion activities and attitude change in Cyprus. *International Journal of Conflict and Violence, 8*(2), 297–304.

Karyotis, G., & Patrikios, S. (2010). Religion, securitization and anti-immigration attitudes: The case of Greece. *Journal of Peace Research, 47*(1), 43–57.

Khallaf, M., & Tür, Ö. (2008). Civil society in the Middle East and Mediterranean: An exploration of opportunities and limitations. In F. V. Heinrich & L. Fioramonti (Eds.), *Survey of the state of civil society, volume 2: Comparative perspectives*. CT: Kumarian Press.

Ladini, G. (2009). Peacebuilding, United Nations and civil society: The case of Cyprus. *The Cyprus Review, 21*(2), 37.

Laouris, Y. (2011). *Masks of demons: A journey in the discovering and breaking of stereotypes in a society in conflict*. Charleston, SC: CreateSpace.

Laouris, Y., & Laouri, R. (2008). Can information and mobile technologies serve to close the economic, educational, digital, and social gaps and accelerate development? *World Futures, 64*(4), 254–275.

Laouris, Y., Michaelides, M., Damdelen, M., Laouri, R., Beyatli, D., & Christakis, A. (2009). A systemic evaluation of the state of affairs following the negative outcome of the referendum in Cyprus using the structured dialogic design process. *Systemic Practice and Action Research, 22*(1), 45–75.

Mahallae. (2015). www.mahallae.org. Last accessed September 2, 2015.

Maoz, I. (2011). Does contact work in protracted asymmetrical conflict? Appraising 20 years of reconciliation-aimed encounters between Israeli Jews and Palestinians. *Journal of Peace Research, 48*(1), 115–125.

McSweeney, B. (1996). Identity and security: Buzan and the Copenhagen School. *Review of International Studies, 22*(1), 81–93.

Newcomb, T. M. (1947). Autistic hostility and social reality. *Human Relations, 1*, 69–86.

Oakes, P. (2004). The root of all evil in intergroup relations? Unearthing the categorization process. In R. Brown & S. L. Gaertner (Eds.), *Blackwell handbook of social psychology: Intergroup processes*. Oxford: Blackwell.

Pettigrew, T. F. (1998). Intergroup contact theory. *Annual Review of Psychology, 49*, 65–85.

Pettigrew, T. F., & Tropp, L. R. (2006). A meta-analytic test of intergroup contact theory. *Journal of Personality and Social Psychology, 90*(5), 751–783.

Reed-Danahay, D. (1997). *Auto/ethnography*. New York: Berg.

Rothman, J. (1999). Articulating goals and monitoring progress in a Cyprus conflict resolution training workshop. In M. H. Ross & J. Rothman (Eds.), *Theory and practice in ethnic conflict management*. UK: Palgrave Macmillan.

Sanders, E. (2002, April/May). Special section: Ethnography in NPD research. How 'applied ethnography' can improve your NPD research process. *Visions Magazine, 26*(2), 8–12.

Simon, B., Aufderheide, B., & Kampmeier, C. (2003). The social psychology of minority-majority relations. In R. Brown & S. L. Gaertner (Eds.), *Blackwell handbook of social psychology: Intergroup processes*. Oxford: Blackwell.

Stasiuk, K., & Bilewicz, M. (2013). Extending contact across generations: Comparison of direct and ancestral intergroup contact effects on current attitudes toward outgroup members. *Journal of Community and Applied Social Psychology, 23*, 481–491.

Stritzel, H. (2007). Towards a theory of securitization: Copenhagen and beyond. *European Journal of International Relations, 13*(3), 357–383.

Stritzel, H. (2011). Security, the translation. *Security Dialogue, 42*(4–5), 343–355.

Turner, J. C., & Reynolds, K. J. (2003). The social identity perspective in intergroup relations: Theories, themes, and controversies. In R. Brown & S. L. Gaertner (Eds.), *Blackwell handbook of social psychology: Intergroup processes*. Oxford: Blackwell.

UNDP. (2015). Final report: Action for cooperation and trust in Cyprus, October 1, 2005–December 31, 2015. *United Nations Development Programme.*

Vollmer, B., & Karakayali, S. (2018). The volatility of the discourse on refugees in Germany. *Journal of Immigrant & Refugee Studies, 16*(1–2), 118–139.

Wilhelmsen, J. (2016). How does war become a legitimate undertaking? Re-engaging the post-structuralist foundation of securitization theory. *Cooperation and Conflict, 52*(2), 166–183.

Williams, M. C. (2011). Securitization and the liberalism of fear. *Security Dialogue, 42*(4–5), 453–463.

Wodak, R. (2013). *Right-wing populism in Europe: Politics and discourse*. London: Bloomsbury.

8 The role of memory in the desecuritization of inter-societal conflicts

Valérie Rosoux

Introduction

"The dead are invisible, but they are not absent." These words pronounced in 1865 by Victor Hugo (1985, p. 65) enlighten all post-conflict settings of the world. In the aftermath of mass atrocities, emotions such as grief, anger, resentment, shame and/or guilt are widely shared and passed on in family circles. Their impact on the individual, social, and political levels is enduring. In such circumstances, how can former enemies gradually draw a line between the past and the present? How can they engage with postwar memory without 'backsliding' in a highly securitized conflict? In short, under which conditions can memory play not only a role in escalating conflicts, but also – and above all – in desecuritizing them?

To address these questions, two main methodological options are generally chosen. The first one focuses on the political uses of the past and considers the evolution of speeches pronounced by official representatives (Langenbacher & Shain, 2010). The second concentrates on individual memories and intergenerational transmission (Rosenblum, 2009). It gathers individual testimonies and analyses the weight of traumatic events on victims. This chapter explores a third option. It employs a synthetic approach, questioning the interactions between local practices, national policies, and international politics in order to show the significance of postwar memory in securitizing and, most of all, desecuritizing processes.

The nexus between security and collective historical memory is a vital one for the critical exploration of security (C.A.S.E. Collective, 2006). If we consider public remembrance in international politics, a whole range of channels tends to represent the past, the *other* and – ultimately – its own group, producing various forms of 'data,' broadly defined: speech-acts, images, monuments, commemorations, museums, textbooks that refer to the figure of the (former) enemy. Each of them contributes to the elaboration of a specific narrative, one often based on victimhood and/or glory. However, it is worth questioning the efficacy of this narrative. Does it have any impact on individual memories, or vice versa? The analysis carried out so far shows that the tensions and even contradictions that exist between individual memories and strategic narratives are crucial to gaining a better understanding of securitizating – and, crucially, desecuritizating – moves.

In terms of empirical material, the analysis is based on four configurations: the Franco-German case (post-international conflict), the South-African case (post-internal conflict), the Franco-Algerian case (post-colonial conflict), and the Rwandan case (post-genocide). Two main kinds of data were combined to dissect the relevant processes in each of these cases. First, a systematic corpus of official speeches allows for a description of the evolution of the leaders since the end of the hostilities. Second, a comprehensive gathering of testimonies shared depicts the reactions of individuals directly affected by a violent past. The case studies chosen to carry out this research emphasize the scope and limits of the "memory work" that former antagonists may employ in order to promote desecuritizing processes (Ricoeur, 2000, p. 496). The purpose is to analyze whether an adjustment regarding diverging interpretations of the past may function as a long-term, future oriented confidence-building measure. The main hypothesis underlying the paper is that addressing painful questions of the past – at the right moment – is essential to providing a sound foundation for a new relationship, and therefore a progressive process of desecuritization (Wæver, 1995).

The chapter is divided into three parts. The first clarifies the concepts used and the research posture that is adopted in this study. The second focuses on agency. Who are the securitizing and desecuritizing agents who attempt to engage with post-war memory – be it to alleviate historical animosities or to reinstate them? The third part concentrates on time. It stresses that the transformation of the relationships between former enemies, as well as the modification of their understanding of security, cannot start at any time and do not take years, but generations.

Concepts and research posture

Memory is different from history. In its principle, history attempts to reconstitute events in a manner that depends as little as possible on variable perceptions or interpretations. The goal is to attain historical truth – encounter events as they happened. By contrast, memory is inherently associated with social perceptions and representations within a group (Nora, 1984). Its goal is to create or maintain an identity. Therefore, it may probably be defined, with Saint Augustine, as "the present of the past" (1964, p. 269).

Memory: the present of the past

As such, memory is neither positive nor negative. It depends directly on the objective pursued by the parties. As the French novelist Georges Bernanos (1949) wrote in *Les enfants humiliés*, "the future does not belong to the dead, but to those who speak for them, who explain why they are dead" (p. 29). This mechanism has been extensively studied from a sociological and political perspective. Nonetheless, it has not been completely explored from an international relations perspective (Bell, 2010). This chapter focuses on the interaction between official memory (i.e., the collection of official representations of the past), and individual memories (i.e., the individual remembrance of lived or transmitted experiences). The authorized version of the past which is conveyed by the legitimate spokespersons of a particular group is a way of presenting events to the world, of showcasing the country for a domestic and external audience. As such, this method is not a systematic integration of the recollections of group members. It is, therefore, interesting to identify two manifestations of competing narratives of the past: one, discrepancies, and even contradictions, between national narratives (see for instance the French and Algerian representations of the Independence War that took place between 1954 and 1962); and two, the tensions and inconsistencies, within each national group, between the official version and remembered versions, between the public and individual representations of the national past (like in the Rwandan case where some parts of the population do not feel included enough in the official narrative of the past).

One of the main questions that prevails throughout this study concerns the degree of compatibility of these representations. Do the various accounts of the past simply result from a series of different viewpoints, or do they reveal fundamental incompatibilities that sustain conflictual relationships and dynamics – which if reconciled, might help repair such relationships and ameliorate such dynamics? This point is essential since securitizing and desecuritizing moves occur within, and are impacted by, the universe of the audience imagination. The efficacy of images and metaphors selected by the agents is directly dependent on the repertoire of stories and histories that constitute the background of the audience's mindset. Thus, the success of a (de)securitization act cannot be understood without paying attention to a particular memory, which emphasizes in a specific way the events and characters that are the most meaningful and/or emotional in the eyes of the group.

From this perspective, memory and securitization are mutually constitutive, and interact in two ways. On the one hand, individual memories inform securitization. After a war, it does not come as a surprise that vivid memories underline an adversarial narrative of the past and *ipso facto* favor securitization. One can speak of the *weight* of the past, the basic movement between the past and the present going from the past to the present. People (leaders included) undergo the legacy of the past. On the other hand, securitization informs memory. In underlining in a systematic way the most adversarial narratives of the past, securitization influences individual memories as well, at least to some extent. Agents choose to evoke this or that historical episode according to their goals. One can speak of the *choice* of the past, the basic movement going this time from the present to the past. In the former case, the past constitutes above all a burden; in the latter, the past fundamentally appears as a tool (on this distinction, see Lavabre, 1991). These two dynamics will be illustrated in the following sections.

Research posture

The observation of both dynamics (weight *and* choice of the past) implies a particular research posture. Far beyond the statist-militarist assumptions and preoccupations of traditional security studies (see the introduction), the understanding of the articulation between official and individual memories is to some degree reflective of the Copenhagen School's emphasis on 'broadening.' Indeed, a concern with memory forces us to take into account a wide range of actors beside the state: NGOs calling for reconciliation, associations of victims, associations of veterans, religious actors, international donors. This type of 'broadening' also concerns a variety of processes that take place at different levels, thereby at the same time constituting a move toward 'deepening': the national level, which remains essential in defining strategic narratives; the local level, where specific memory entrepreneurs can impact the security agenda; the individual level, in order to hear the "subaltern" voices that were marginalized, silenced, or even excluded from the dominant discourse (Dalsheim, 2014); and the transnational level, since NGOs, international organizations, individual experts and architects favour a globalisation of memory practices.

In terms of security sectors (Buzan, Wæver, & de Wilde, 1998), memory issues mainly affect the societal sector (threats to the identity of the group), and in some cases the political sector (when the stability of the state is impacted). National identities are indeed partly elaborated on the basis of memory. Thus, former French Prime Minister Lionel Jospin explained: "Through the ages, an identity is forged with the memories that are adopted, kept alive, lost and sometimes even repressed by people" (Jospin, 1999). Likewise, Ernest Renan, a celebrated French author, referred in a famous conference (Sorbonne, Paris, 1882) to the "rich legacy of memories" and "heritage" that constitute the "soul" and spiritual principle guiding the nation. According to him, "worshipping ancestors is more than legitimate: they have made us who we are" (Renan, 1882).

From this perspective, the concepts of "memory" and "identity" are indissolubly linked: "Memory makes us, we make memory" (Tonkin, 1992, p. 97).[1] Memory shapes us – we are formed through its action – and we in turn influence its content by our own representations. Several authors qualify this process by describing national identities as "imagined communities" (see Anderson, 1983; Hobsbawn & Ranger, 1992). This description reminds us that identities and representations of the past are constantly being updated and adapted to present circumstances. This fluid and dynamic conception of identity is at the opposite pole to a fixed and reified phenomenon (McSweeney, 1999). Rather than thinking of securitization as a mechanism for mobilizing an identity, it may instead be better understood as a tool eliciting and encouraging an identification with particular ideas, notions, or things subjected to securitization – things such as memory (-ies). If there is no way to modify the events of the past, the meaning given to the past is never fixed once and for all. The purpose of this research is to explore when and how this meaning can progressively be negotiated in order to ameliorate a conflictual relationship rather than to intensify it.

In the Franco-German case, to take an example, it took two generations to change the interpretation given to the battle of Verdun (where nearly 800,000 French and German soldiers were killed or wounded in an inconclusive fight over a few square miles of territory between February and December 1916). Initially depicted as a symbol of the hatred and ferocity of the adversaries, Verdun gradually came to be described as a "common tragedy" and a "shared martyrdom" on both sides of the Rhine. This reinterpretation was expressed symbolically when François Mitterrand and Helmut Kohl stood hand in hand in front of the ossuary at Douaumont (France) in 1984. The wars fought against each other in the past were then presented as a common past of collective suffering. The groups ceased to be identified in the official memory as combatants on opposite sides. They somehow lost their character of groups living separately from each other, and were now considered as brothers – all of whom suffered as a result of a tragedy they all had to endure together.

As this illustration shows, a progressive change of meaning can actually play into the desecuritization of societal conflicts. In insisting on a common tragedy rather than a glorious victory or an unfair defeat, French and German leaders consistently tend to bridge both sides of the Rhine. This open-ended process was emblematized in 2018 at Armistice Day Commemorations in Paris. Facing German Chancellor Angela Merkel and more than 70 heads of States, French President Emmanuel Macron celebrated the centenary of the end of WWII in insisting on the "hell that engulfed [during four years] *all* combatants whatever side they came from" (*Arc de Triomphe*, November 11, 2018). It could be argued that the commemorated past is so old that such consensual narratives do not play a role anymore in terms of desecuritization. However, there is still much at stake. First, the two World Wars still highly resonate with large parts of the European population. Second, the increasing tensions within Europe (between Poland, Hungary, Italy, to name only a few, and the rest of the EU member states, without forgetting the turmoil provoked by Brexit) and the multiplication of misunderstandings and even crises between European, Russian, and American leaders (from the US trade war with the EU to the sanctions imposed on Russia or the crisis provoked by the evocation of a potential "European army") remind us that symbolic moments like commemoration days actually constitute turning points that can precipitate escalation or foster desecuritization.

However, the nature of memory issues show that the analysis cannot be reduced to the content and the impact of speech-acts. Beyond words, it is worth mentioning the crucial importance of silence. In numerous contexts, protagonists cannot simply negotiate a common narrative about the past since the issue is and remains explosive. In such circumstances, the simple act of gathering in silence, without offending the other side, is already a critical step to progressively desecuritizing the conflict. Paying silent tribute to the victims of past crimes and/or to the former combatants from all sides matters. As we will see, the efficacy of silence in this matter depends not only on historiographical considerations (based on the fundamental search for the truth about the past), but rather on the emotional resonance of the souvenirs activated by the commemorations.

Beside words and silences, it is difficult to deny that power matters, and that power relationships are fundamental to securitization (and desecuritization) moves. The transformation of relationships between former enemies can hardly be understood without taking into consideration the symmetry or asymmetry of power that characterizes each case. However, in a Machiavellian and deterministic way, it does not matter, since this study is not limited to the pure strategic uses of the past, but also considers the emotional weight of the past. At the end of international or intercommunity conflicts, mistrust, suspicion, and hatred remain very strong, even many years later. Beside the interests and resources of each protagonist, these emotions are key to understanding postwar dynamics and deadlocks. Thus, even if a rapprochement seems necessary to the representatives of each party, it cannot be imposed by decree. Violent conflicts provoke an infinite series of individual fires that need to be extinguished one by one. The intensity of the violence that was committed in the past plays a large part in the persistence of "existential threats" in people's minds (Buzan et al., 1998). The deep fear of being victimized again justifies the survival dimension attached to these threats. These individual resistances remind that, if the *raison d'état* is a necessary condition to modify the process of desecuritization, it is not a sufficient one (cf. infra).

Agency: official narratives and individual memories

In seeking to understand how official narratives of the past and individual memories interact and relate to securitization and desecuritization, at least three scenarios merit consideration: one, official narratives and individual memories can be similar; two, they can be divergent and even contradictory; three, they can be partially identical. The first scenario refers to a situation where the official narrative of the past that is selected to pursue a securitization or desecuritization objective resonates with the individual memories lived and/or transmitted by the population. This overlap between both representations of past events highly stimulates the efficiency of either process. In the second scenario, individual memories systematically resist the official narrative, which is perceived as a manipulative form of propaganda by the population. That means that a parallel memory, sometimes described as an underground memory (in the case of totalitarian regimes), is transmitted in social and family circles. In this case, the discrepancies between official and individual representations of the past seriously jeopardize the planned securitization or desecuritization moves. The third scenario is the most likely. It refers to all situations where a particular strategic narrative arouses the adherence of certain groups and the strong opposition of others. In this case, the balance of power between the authorities and each specific group determines to a large extent whether the agents of securitization or desecuritization can succeed or not.

Illustrations: a jungle of tensions

Numerous examples could illustrate these scenarios. Among the case studies selected for this research, the Franco-Algerian case is particularly emblematic. Regarding the first scenario, it is worth stressing the transition between the end of World War II and the beginning of the Algerian War. In Algeria on May 8, 1945, just as people were celebrating the Allied victory over Germany (in which native Algerian troops participated), banned demonstrations of Algerian nationalists took place in several towns. In Sétif, the demonstration turned into a riot after the police forces intervened. Ninety French settlers were killed. The severe repression organized by the army left many thousands dead – between 10,000 and 45,000 victims, according to sources. In the view of Algerian writer Kated Yacine, who witnessed "this horrible slaughter" (*Le Monde*, March 9, 2005), the Sétif massacre was the founding moment of Algerian nationalism. Some historians even consider that the Algerian war of independence did not start on November 1, 1954, but on May 8, 1945. From that point forward, the National Liberation Front (FLN) systematically accentuated the colonial oppression that had lasted for more than 120 years.

Although the legitimacy of the FLN was never a topic of uniform agreement among Algerians, their emphasis on a past of systematic scorn and humiliation did strongly resonate with a population that felt the colonial burden on a day-to-day basis. In the personal diary (1955–1962) that he wrote before being murdered, Algerian teacher Mouloud Feraoun explains the gradual expression of suffering and rage between French and Algerians. To him, the intensity of the violence that explodes on Algerian soil cannot be understood without remembering that Algerians "endured servitude and misery," "rulers, bosses, masters, owners, [and] directors" arrived in Algeria "to look at them scornfully and disparagingly" (Feraoun, 2000). His posture towards France illustrates the ambivalence of feelings provoked by the war: "I cannot repudiate your culture, but don't expect that I disown myself, that I admit your superiority, your racism, your anger, your hatred. Your lies. A century of lies" (p. 138). In such circumstances, the narrative stressed to justify violence against the colonial power largely overlapped the individual memories and emotions shared by the Algerian population. Besides the provocative and often violent character of the French reactions to the call for independence, the common representation of an unjust past, undeniably favored a rapid securitization.

The second scenario (official narratives and individual memories do not coincide) is illustrated by the incompatibility that existed between the French official representation of the Independence War (which remained a war without a name for almost four decades), and the individual memories shared and transmitted by the French population. In categorically refusing to recognize the Algerian War as a war, the French government did provoke a progressive gap between the sanitized narrative that was emphasized and the public awareness of the violence that characterized the conflict. From 1962 to the end of the 1980s, all French presidents justified the concealment of this violence in a paradoxical way.

According to Charles de Gaulle, France did not need "the truth," but hope and cohesion. Therefore, the only events that merit mention were "heroic actions and expressions of national unity" (de Gaulle, 1970, pp. 238–239). Ten years later, his successor, Georges Pompidou adopted the same posture:

> Our country; for more than 30 years, went from national tragedy to another one. We had the war, the defeat and its humiliation, the Occupation [...] and then the awful Algerian conflict and its horrors on both sides. [...] Isn't it time now to forget these times when the French did not love themselves, fought against each other and even killed each other?
>
> (Paris, September 21, 1972)

In 1981, François Mitterrand confirmed the duty to pacify these harmful memories. This consistent strategy of occultation could be compared to a long "ellipse." Its aim was to turn the page. However, acting in such a manner required a collective act of feigned forgetfulness. Rather than fostering a desecuritization process, this strategy inhibited it.

The third and last scenario (official narratives and individual memories are partially identical) was particularly tangible when French President Jacques Chirac and Algerian Abdelaziz Bouteflika launched a dramatic rapprochement of the official narratives in France and Algeria in order to negotiate a Friendship Treaty in 2003. In doing so, both underlined the role of Algerian combatants in the French army during both World War I and World War II. Rather than being systematically divergent, the two official narratives focused on a consensual, if not harmonious, past. While experts from both sides rapidly drew up the document to be signed, domestic spoilers constantly interfered. Thus, on February 23, 2005, French MPs passed a law that highlighted certain "positive effects of colonization" (French National Assembly, Law No. 2005–158, Art. 4, para. 2). Initiated by a group of French settlers repatriated after Algerian independence, this unanticipated event was immediately perceived as a scandal in Algeria. The gulf between what Algerians considered to be an unacceptable law and the "memory work" that they expected quickly jeopardized the negotiation of the Friendship Treaty. As this example reminds us, the discrepancies between a relatively new official narrative in France (the term of "war" being eventually recognized, and the massacres of May 8, 1945 – that were denied for almost six decades – being officially presented as "an unforgivable tragedy") and the set of memories underlined by some associations of *Pieds-Noirs* did prevent the desecuritization move that was initially planned by Algiers and Paris.

On the contrary, this missed opportunity led to an escalation that undeniably increased historical grievances on both sides of the Mediterranean. In Algeria, the veterans' "national organisation of the Moudjahidine" and the powerful victims' association "8 May 1945 Foundation" contended that France should not only acknowledge the inhuman acts committed from 1830 to 1962 (i.e., the colonial period) but should also ask for forgiveness, along the lines of the official acknowledgment made by Jacques Chirac in 1995 regarding French responsibility in the deportation of Jews during World War II. Conversely, in France, some associations of *Pieds-Noirs* took to depicting themselves as having been "excluded from history." Testimonies are abundant in this regard: "We are actually the losers, we have been manhandled, misled, humiliated, tortured, imprisoned, broken, rejected, caricaturized"; "We are a dead people. Without geography, there is nothing left"; "Verdun, people will continue to commemorate it for a long time"; "[Our situation] does not interest anybody. [...] We relate to the guilty conscience and we are not from here, [...] we do not exist" (Baussant, 2002, pp. 424 and 433).

The incompatibility of the narratives is even more striking if we consider the way the Algerian Government depicted the *harkis* (the Algerians who fought alongside the French and who were massacred *en masse* when French forces withdrew from Algeria). Surviving members of this group are still treated as "traitors" and left to bear the burden of individual memories shared by the *harkis* who escaped and survived in France. Mentioning the weight of a "double absence" (the absence of the country that they were forced to leave and the absence of the country that they thought they would find in Europe), the *harkis* often considered themselves as second-class French citizens (Sayad, 1999), and representatives of the "wrong side" (Zeniter, 2017). During the negotiation process, Jacques Chirac suggested that the *harkis* be mentioned at the moment of the signature of the Treaty, while Algiers did not want to hear anything about these "collaborators."

These illustrations show that the overlap – or lack of overlap – between official narratives and individual memories results to a large extent from the weight of traumatic events. This point is crucial to understanding the power of some historical references in escalating conflicts. The efficacy of political uses of history depends directly on the emotional resonance of the past. Thus, references to colonial layers of violence, for obvious reasons, activate powerful images that resonate in the mind of former colonized populations. Likewise, references to acts of torture committed during an international or intercommunal conflict can trigger a greater perception of threat and *ipso facto* the fear of annihilation, loss and alienation (Williams, 2011). This fear justifies the absolute need to resist – even by violent means. In this regard, the research carried out so far indicates that the long-term consequences of physical suffering actually impact the possibility, the depth, and the sustainability of any desecuritization process (Brudholm & Rosoux, 2013).

The Algerian case, along with numerous others, demonstrates that the inexpressibility of the pain that systematically characterizes postwar settings has political ramifications that can be critical when seeking to understand resistance towards rapprochement between former enemies (Scarry, 1987). Aside from strategic interests and rhetorical arguments, it seems critical to consider the importance of the concrete experience of individuals who were – and, for some of them, remain – physically and psychologically affected by the past violence. This experience is usually overlooked in securitization theory and research, and more broadly in international relations. Nonetheless, it helps to understand in a subtler way the scope and limits of any desecuritizating "work of memory." First, it calls into question the clear-cut distinction that is often underlined between leaders and ordinary people. Knowing that leaders are made of flesh and blood, it is worth taking into account the effects and, even more so, the after-effects of violence, regarding their own attitudes. Second, this perspective forces scholars who frequently focus on speech-acts and statespersons to pay attention to local practices and rituals as well (Igreja, 2012).

Plurality of agents: who makes memory, and who interprets it?

Official authorities are most often identified as the main securitizing agents. This makes sense in that they are the ones who decide to securitize specific issues on behalf of a population to be protected (securitization) or stimulated towards a progressive rapprochement with the former enemy (desecuritization). However, as the illustrations below indicate, it is worth broadening the picture to also consider the role played by private actors and in particular memory entrepreneurs. In several cases, victims' associations and veterans' associations contribute to the identification of what constitute "existential threats."

For example, during the negotiation process that was supposed to lead to the signature of a Treaty of Friendship between France and Algeria, Algerian victims' associations argued that the passage of a French law (2005–158) emphasizing the positive aspects of the colonial period was equivalent to a denial of past crimes, and could therefore be considered as the tangible signal of an actual threat. In their attempt to target both the Algerian audience and the international opinion, these associations claimed that the French law could not be considered as a "little security nothing" (Huysmans, 2011), but as the expression of a new stage in terms of securitization. After a couple of months, this work of undermining on both sides of the Mediterranean (by these associations *and* by the associations of *Pieds Noirs* who were at the origins of the famous French law) had such a significant impact on the process of rapprochement launched by Jacques Chirac and Abdelaziz Bouteflika that the two leaders, who were extremely motivated to reach a historic agreement (both explained that they wanted to incarnate the "Charles de Gaulle and Konrad Adenauer" of the Franco-Algerian relations), ultimately could not find the compromise necessary in order to turn the colonial page.

The influence of private actors is not only detrimental to desecuritization; it can also be key to it, through alleviation of historical animosities. In this respect, the South African case shows the impact of NGOs such as human rights organizations before, during, and after the negotiation that made possible the transition from apartheid. Unsurprisingly, memory work in post-1994 South Africa was primarily shaped by political constraints such as the balance of power between the parties. The main issue of amnesty for human rights offenders was decided by a political deal between the National Party and the African National Congress (ANC). However, human rights organizations did a great deal of lobbying between the passage of the interim constitution and the National Unity and

Reconciliation Act in 1995. Groups such as the citizenship rights group Justice in Transition, headed by Alex Boraine, and the Centre for the Study of Violence and Reconciliation played a significant role in framing the terms of the Truth and Reconciliation Commission (TRC). Their impact on desecuritization was limited but still decisive (Wilson, 2001, pp. 198–200).

Besides this kind of association, it is worth examining the role played by historians in this field. The scope of their actions is particularly tangible when securitizing or (de)securitizing 'moves' take the form of a revision of textbooks. In this regard, one might argue that the desecuritizing process implies a triple form of reassessment: reassessment of the common past; reassessment of the representation that each party has about the other; and reassessment of the self-image (which remains the most delicate aspect of this process due to the high level of resistances against any kind of weakening in terms of identity). The Franco-German case effectively illustrates this dynamic. In 1950, some French and German historians met in order to pursue the initiative taken in the 1920s by Jules Isaac. Their objective was to critically scrutinize the myths of a 'hereditary enmity' between France and Germany. Their intuition was that a sustainable rapprochement would not only imply new structures, but also new narratives. Years of long and arduous negotiation between historians from each side eventually led to the publication of *one* common history textbook on both sides of the Rhine. This evolution can easily be seen as a long-term mechanism of desecuritization. The accentuation of a common project, and even sometimes a common "destiny," appears as a way to escape competitive victimhood (Chaumont, 1997). Yet, as suggested by the Franco-Algerian case, strategic speeches and updated textbooks can hardly influence individual memories if they contradict the stories shared and transmitted at home.

In this regard, a very important factor of credibility lies in the personal past of the agents (be they official representatives, associations' spokespersons, or historians). Desecuritization will be fostered if it is advocated by a person who is perceived as legitimate and who asks the whole population to undergo a transformation that he – or she – has undergone him/herself – i.e., overcoming resentment towards the former enemy. For instance, the historical legitimacy of Charles de Gaulle probably helped the French people to change their views about wars against Germany. A similar point can be made with respect to Nelson Mandela in South Africa.

The desecuritization – reconciliation nexus

As these cases suggest, most agents involved in desecuritizing a conflict (be they leaders, association members or other memory entrepreneurs) refer to reconciliation as an explicit objective. Accordingly, the notions of desecuritization and reconciliation are closely intertwined. Research has identified them as transformative processes that facilitate sustainable peace. However, they do not systematically refer to identical processes. To better understand the interactions between the two notions, it is useful to explore the plurality of meanings given to the concept of reconciliation. At least three main approaches to political reconciliation can be distinguished: structural, social-psychological, and spiritual (Rosoux, 2008). The first approach gives priority to security, economic interdependence, and political cooperation between parties (Kacowicz, 2000), the second underlines the cognitive and emotional aspects of the process of rapprochement between former adversaries (Bar-Siman-Tov, 2004), while the third accentuates a process of collective healing based on the rehabilitation of both victims and offenders (Tutu, 1999).

Although some structural changes can be implemented relatively quickly after the end of a conflict, the transformation of relationships does not occur in the same way. Studies dedicated to this slow and arduous process largely parallel each other, but their visions of the transformation process are divergent. Cognitive and social-psychological approaches analyse deep changes in the public's psychological repertoire. This evolution results from a reciprocal process of adjustments of beliefs, attitudes, motivations, and emotions shared by the majority of society members. The spiritual approaches go a step further by asserting that reconciliation attempts to lead to forgiveness for the adversary's misdeeds. The interest of this distinction is to show that all protagonists (official representatives, NGO workers, or scholars) position themselves on a continuum between a minimalist vision according to which reconciliation refers to any mutually conciliatory accommodation between former enemies, and a maximalist vision that highlights the transcendent nature of a far more demanding process requiring truth, justice, and forgiveness.

This continuum is important in at least two regards. First, it reminds us of the plurality of the goals being pursued. From a minimalist perspective, the objective is coexistence: former enemies living together non-violently, even though they still hate each other. They tolerate each other, but the situation remains largely explosive. Beyond coexistence, an intermediary goal can be a form of respect. In order to prevent any potential recurrence of the violence, former enemies may continue to strongly disagree, but they do more than simply coexist – they respect each other as fellow citizens. More robust conceptions of reconciliation put the emphasis on harmony as an ultimate goal. Second, the minimalist/maximalist continuum helps to understand the impact of each approach in terms of memory. The minimalist view of reconciliation does not imply any change concerning the representations of the past: former enemies keep their own stories about the war. By contrast, the maximalist perspective presupposes the existence of a shared narrative of the past – which is highly ambitious.

These two remarks allow us to distinguish two options regarding the links between desecuritization and reconciliation. From a minimalist perspective, the two notions can almost be considered as synonymous. Rather than being defined as a joint vision for the future (aspirational horizon), in this view reconciliatory events are thought to take place *during* the conflict resolution phase – in short, it is one of immediate and ongoing significance for desecuritizing. In launching an inclusive "reconfiguration" process, rather than insisting on historical grievances, these events can constitute milestones in the desecuritizing process. The reverse could easily be argued.

In allowing for the return of an issue from urgent and securitized situations to the area of normal negotiations in the political sphere, desecuritization directly favors the reconciliation process. Both dynamics attempt to *normalize* the relationships between former adversaries. Desecuritization and reconciliation processes benefit both from the presence of legitimate leaders and private actors committed to moving from confrontation to some degree of cooperation in resolving historical issues (stakeholder agency) *and* from the existence of robust institutions where parties can work together – at both the governmental and the societal levels (functional institutions). In these particular circumstances, an adjustment regarding diverging interpretations of the past may function as a long-term desecuritizing measure. However, if these two variables (agency and institutions) are necessary conditions, they are not sufficient to ensure the rapprochement between (former) enemies. As we will see in the third section, the acknowledgement of embarrassing events cannot occur at any time (cf. infra).

From a maximalist approach, reconciliation does not refer to structural changes that can be observed on the ground. It is rather perceived as a transcendent process that is so demanding that it becomes a desirable longer-term objective. In this line of reasoning, desecuritization appears as a sine qua non condition of reconciliation. Both notions do not coincide anymore. This distinction has concrete consequences for practitioners. If reconciliation is associated with a long-term process that eventually requires truth, forgiveness, and harmony, we easily understand that it is not always possible. Knowing that the notion of political forgiveness is so controversial, we could even question whether it is always necessary (Brudohlm & Rosoux, 2013). That means that, contrary to desecuritization, reconciliation (at least in its maximalist sense) is not indispensable to ensure an enduring peace.

Time: ripeness and duration

All of the case studies considered here demonstrate that one of the most critical questions regards timing. When are former enemies ready for launching a process of desecuritization based on the acknowledgment of the past violence? Politically speaking, it would be naive to consider the recognition of others' interpretation of the past in a normative way. The work of memory that can be undertaken within the framework of a desecuritization process can only emerge if parties consider that it is in their national interest to commit themselves to this process. It is obvious that all states are reluctant to admit that violence was committed for their sake and in their name. No state easily recognizes errors and/or betrayals attributed to its citizens that are committed during conflicts with other nations.

Not too soon

William Zartman has emphasized the significance of ripeness in the area of negotiation (2000). This issue should also be addressed with respect to desecuritization. As in any negotiation, parties become involved in a desecuritization process when they have to do so. They only join together in this way if each party's efforts to achieve a unilaterally satisfactory result are blocked, and if the parties feel trapped in a costly predicament. Similarly, the notion of a "mutually hurting stalemate" (Zartman, 2000) is relevant for understanding why and how former enemies tend to construct security outcomes. When parties find themselves locked in a situation that is painful for both of them (although not necessarily to the same extent or for the same reasons), the way out they seek can indeed become the starting-point of a desecuritization process.

The post-World War II Franco-German case is telling in this regard. In a devastated Europe, the decision to work towards a rapprochement was not a matter of altruism, but was rather in both the French and German national interests. The complete and radical character of Germany's defeat explains its crucial need for political rehabilitation and a restoration of sovereignty. Moreover, to German leaders, the economic future of their country was an additional reason to pursue the normalization of relationships with their neighbors as quickly as possible. In this particular context, a rapprochement with France was depicted as a vital necessity. As for France, it was also a question of need; after the war, the French economy was reduced by half, its infrastructure devastated, and its demography compromised by the human cost of the conflict. Both countries needed one another.

Aside from these domestic issues, the configuration of the broader international system was decisive in stimulating a rapprochement. Among all the political, economic, and security considerations that promoted the transformation of relations between such so-called 'hereditary enemies,' one was particularly significant: the existence of a common enemy in the USSR, and therefore the external (largely American) support for rapprochement. In such circumstances, French and German leaders perceived an undeniable mutually hurting stalemate and considered the European Coal and Steel Community (ECSC), a six-nation western European economic union, as their way out.

However, this concrete and progressive desecuritization should not be understood as reflective of memory work, at least not initially. In the immediate postwar years, German society showed little guilt regarding the horrors of the war, being above all preoccupied with its own suffering. Germany had lost over 6.5 million soldiers and civilians. Every major city had been reduced to rubble. The vast majority of Germans concentrated on their basic survival, as well as political and economic reconstruction. The dominant narrative emphasized Germany's own torment: the ethnic cleansing of Germans from Eastern Europe, the treatment of German prisoners of war in Soviet camps, and the brutality of the Soviet invasion. Nonetheless, the knowledge of the crimes of the Nazi regime was widespread among the German population thanks to the war crimes tribunals and the determined efforts of the Allies to publicize them.

At the official level, German representatives initially avoided the delicate question of the extent to which all Germans bore a responsibility. All of them actively rejected the notion of "collective guilt" on the basis that the crimes committed in Germany's name emanated from a relatively small group of leaders.

Even though the German army was heavily implicated in the Holocaust, the myth spread that only the SS, not ordinary soldiers, had been involved. In insisting on the country's postwar achievement, rather than in adopting an exclusively contrite stance, Chancellor Konrad Adenauer favored a "partial amnesia" (Lind, 2009).[2]

Many other examples show that the work of memory is hardly undertaken at the beginning of the desecuritization process. Immediately upon the cessation of hostilities, the objective is to move conflict from the arena of violence to the arena of politics – not to settle memory issues. In the framework of the Oslo process, parties initially repeated their past legacies and their demands for reparations and punishment as the basis of their position. But as Abu Ala'a said after the initial exchanges of grievances between the two sides, "let us not compete on who was right and who was wrong in the past. Let us see what we can do in the future." In response, Uri Savir recalls telling him,

> I'm sure we can debate the past for years and never agree. Let's see if we can agree about the future. [...] We had arrived at our first understanding. Never again would we argue about the past. This was an important step, for it moved us beyond an endless wrangle over right and wrong. Discussing the future would mean reconciling two rights, not re-addressing ancient wrongs.
>
> (Quoted in Zartman, 2005, p. 291)

Robert Malley, who participated in the Camp David negotiations, shares this future-oriented perspective. As he said, the objective of any political agreement is not to assess historical realities. "In the Middle East, each side develops a narrative of its own history. But negotiators cannot deal with representations that have been shaping the identities of the parties for decades." His conclusion is sharp: "Firstly the political conditions for peace. Afterwards the work of memory" (Malley, 2001).

Not too quick

The emotional weight of the past can take many forms, from silence to resentment. Can it gradually be lifted? The transformation of the representations that parties have of the past is an ongoing process that generally lasts for decades. Psychologically speaking, events such as particularly traumatic violations of human rights can remain unexpressed for a period of time – a period that psychoanalysts often call "latent" (Weinrich, 1999, p. 189). Some specialists refer to a period of 25 years. However, there does not appear to be any standard time-period in this matter. These words are echoed tragically by the experience of Holocaust survivor Charlotte Delbo. To Delbo, the experiences of Auschwitz existed for her in a "perpetual present." As she wrote, Auschwitz was "there, fixed and unchangeable" (1970, p. 13). In these circumstances, the official narrative of the past that is selected to pursue a desecuritization might be vain or even counterproductive.

After World War II, the variety of reactions by survivors of the Nazi atrocities is striking. Some of them directly chose to speak up even though they were rarely believed or understood. Others remained silent until their death. Between these two extreme cases (immediately versus never), some survivors started elaborating about the past after years, or even decades. According to clinicians, looking back was dangerous, if not fatal (Rosenblum, 2009). Survivors who underwent torture were confronted with a specific difficulty, which is the "unsharability" of physical pain since "physical pain does not simply resist language, but actually destroys it" (Scarry, 1987, p. 4). Beside these psychological and physical dimensions, political and social considerations explain why some memories can remain unexpressed for a long time. However, these obstacles to transmit explicit narratives of the past do not prevent the transmission of emotions such as anger, hatred, resentment, grief, shame, or guilt. This particular transmission directly concerns family circles and is undeniably intergenerational (Thompson, 2002).

Thinking in terms of intergenerational processes is not new. In Greek tragedies, old debts were only paid after three generations (Salles, 2012). The notion of "transgenerational transmission" of trauma (Alexander et al., 2004; Volkan, 2006) is admittedly debatable. However, even if we are not convinced that 'traumatic memories' are literally passed on to one's children and other loved ones, it is difficult to deny that the younger people who live in the presence of survivors of war and genocide feel the emotional pull of their elders' suffering to such an extent that they can appropriate the memories of the first generation as their own (Argenti & Schramm, 2009). Numerous studies in social psychology demonstrate that the second and third generations remain preoccupied with continuing feelings of guilt or victimisation, especially when past injustices have not been adequately addressed by their parents' generation (Klar & Branscombe, 2016).

The Armenian-Turkish case is emblematic in this regard. The persistence of intense emotions has had specific consequences in terms of security. It limits the potential concessions made on each side and partly explains why certain issues have remained non-negotiable for decades. Resistance to recognizing an atrocity can be so strong as to be qualified as "irrational." One way to understand the dynamics that lead to this kind of impasse is to consider the extent to which the process may be "haunted" by the past. In the aftermath of mass atrocities, it is often meaningful to refer to the notion of "ghost." As a former American ambassador to Iran once explained, parties should always realize that after a war, there are always many more protagonists at the table than one might initially have thought (Limbert, 2009).

All these examples remind us that it is worth drawing attention to the gap – in terms of tempo – between official and social processes. In the South African case, the institutional time of the TRC was not similar with the individual time of most victims. Individual healing is a process that necessarily advances at its own pace, and which cannot be pushed or programmed (Hamber & Wilson, 2002). In the space of a few years, truth commissions could only create the conditions in which desecuritization might eventually occur (Garton Ash, 2003, p. 416). This remark suggests that we would be well-advised to differentiate between protagonists not only on the basis of their interests but also according to their respective time frames. The time frames of survivors, perpetrators, and bystanders vary. Similarly, the time frames of peacebuilders, policy-makers, and descendants have little in common.

Furthermore, it is important to remember that a consideration of several points of view does not imply that all perceptions are to be taken as equivalent. A sort of plurality appears to be inherent to the representations parties have of the past. Recognizing this plurality does not imply a questioning of the existence of a reality beyond representations. The idea of a shared language about the past is not based on a theory where everything is presented as relative to a peculiar perspective (relativism). It entails, rather, the hope that alternative futures exist (Olick, 1999). To sum up, desecuritization in the long run implies to live *with* the memories rather than without them or against them (Rousso, 1998, p. 47; Chaumont, 1997, p. 314).

Beside this objective, it is worth recalling the limitations of memory work based on reciprocal empathy. Such an exercise is only possible if wrongs are shared. In the case of atypical conflicts which are not characterized by belligerents on each side, but by clearly identified victims and perpetrators, it would be morally unfair to require a reciprocal effort of empathy to promote rapprochement. Victims and perpetrators are not interchangeable. Innocent people who have been tortured, teenagers who have been raped, and devastated individuals cannot be put on the same level as the criminals, be they repentant or not. In the aftermath of irreversible crimes, the moral responsibility of offenders cannot be taken lightly. This point is crucial if we are not to disregard the victims. The same can be said of their descendants. We must be aware of the irrevocable dimension of past violence and realize that, for some, the mourning process remains and will remain unfinished.

This example shows that the notion of desecuritization can probably not be completely understood without taking into consideration the specific *othering* that characterizes each conflict. In this regard, at least four settings could be distinguished. As we have seen above with the Franco-German and Franco-Algerian cases, the other can be an enemy to fight (traditional war with combatants on each side) or a child to educate, if not a barbarian to civilize (colonial war). In the case of a civil war, the other is often depicted as a traitor to punish. In the case of a genocide, the other is an animal to exterminate. These settings demonstrate that the deconstruction process of the *other* implies a subsequent reframing of the *other* – after the end of the conflict – which is pursued in a specific way. In other words, the particular form and level of violence that characterizes each situation (international, colonial, internal conflicts, and genocide) entail distinctive consequences in terms of emotions, expectations and, ipso facto, desecuritization.

Conclusion

The initial question addressed in this chapter was rather simple: does memory matter in the desecuritization of international and intercommunity conflicts? The

answer is undeniably yes. While memory certainly should not be overempha-
sized at the expense of strategic, geopolitical, economic, or demographic considerations, this analysis shows that the socially constructed nature of memory
presents possibilities for change – even if change is neither easy nor systematic
– and, therefore, opportunities for desecuritization. As a result, the real question
is probably not whether or not the past should be confronted – but rather when
and how it should take place, and by whom.

Changes of representations, beliefs, and emotions take time. The case studies
presented here show that the appropriate unit of measurement with respect to
security in a deeper, 'thick' sense is probably neither years, nor decades, but
generations. From this vantage point, it is worth questioning the notion of "post-
conflict" – which is generally taken for granted. It is defined in handbooks, dic-
tionaries, and encyclopedias. However, the duration of these post-conflict
environments can still be uncertain. What are the basic criteria that determine
when a conflict is over? How long do the notions of victim and perpetrator make
sense? When does the victors/vanquished dichotomy lose its meaning? Until
when are the labels "occupiers/occupied" relevant?

Furthermore, the duration of the process raises several methodological questions. How can we assess the effects and after-effects of a war? If we consider
that the transformation of the Other-Self relationship implies a change in terms
of representations of the past, the evolution of the narratives (both official and
individual) is key. Nonetheless, how can we measure the transformation of representations from one generation to the next? How can we detect emotional and
even unconscious processes? These questions underline the need to work within
interdisciplinary teams of scholars. Political scientists regularly work with
historians, sociologists, and anthropologists, but it would be fruitful to develop
further collaborations with clinicians and social psychologists.

At the end of this reflection, it seems useful to question the role of third
parties, especially scholars, in the aftermath of a war. What is the legitimacy of
outsiders in the eyes of local communities? How much credibility do they have?
To put it a more personal way, what can we say about desecuritization after mass
atrocities if we are not ourselves survivors? What can we say about the war
experience if we are not among the veterans? A brief anecdote allows us to put
these questions into perspective. During my first stay in Rwanda, I visited a
rather poor area of Kigali with a Rwandan PhD student. We were walking down
a deserted alleyway, far from the crowded streets of the city center, when we
saw an old lady who looked at me bitterly and pronounced a couple of words in
Kinyarwanda. Confused by the coldness of her glance, I asked my PhD student
to tell me what she had just said. Hesitantly, he translated: "Go back home, it's
too late." The lady had already disappeared into the surrounding neighborhood,
and there was, anyway, nothing to add. Nonetheless, her voice and her message
remained with me during the whole trip. They forced me to reflect on my intentions, my hopes, and even my own personal story. They provoked a kind of
"low-profile" reaction that was perhaps useful to avoid the syndrome of *Tintin in
the Congo*. From then on, I started thinking about what Susan Sontag calls the

dilemma of the third party facing the pain of others: being either "a spectator," or "a coward, unable to look" (Sontag, 2003, p. 34).

The question is not only an ethical one; it also has a political dimension. Scholars working in the field of conflict resolution can easily position themselves as combatants on a battlefield. They choose sides and become part of the fight that they are supposed to observe from outside. The need to avoid becoming politically involved in favor of one party over the other may seem obvious. It is, however, not always so clear-cut, practically speaking. In a very tense political context (such as the Middle East, the African Great Lakes or the Balkans – to name only a few examples), scholars and practitioners can be bombarded with militant claims, which are mostly incompatible. Thus, the same talk about 'dealing with the past in Rwanda' may provoke the anger of some Rwandans offended that one could call into question certain specific decisions made by the Rwandan authorities, while others bitterly regret the lack of strong denunciations of the same authorities.

This kind of impasse forces us to take some distance and to reflect on our own need for security. Why are we so eager to favor a rapid transformation of the relationships between former enemies? This insistence on the need to turn the page as soon as possible is not new (see Alvarez, 1998). However, the enthusiasm for quick impact projects can in fact be puzzling. This attitude became particularly striking around the time of the commemoration of the twentieth anniversary of the genocide in Rwanda: the feeling seemed to be that a period of 20 years was as such a guarantee that the country had recovered (Montgomery, 2014). This wishful thinking contradicts to a large extent the actual duration of the war's long-term impact.

A final and more provocative question must be raised regarding our own need for security: what if the sequence desecuritization–reconciliation is not on the agenda? The weight of the past is not only emphasized in a nationalistic way in order to lead to an escalation of violence. Families of survivors and victims may quite legitimately be reluctant and skeptical about any rapprochement with those who committed violence. Their resistance underlines the ambivalence of a process that can increase social capital, while decreasing individual well-being, at least for some victims (Ciliers, Dube, & Siddiqi, 2016). This ambivalence raises a crucial question: is the sequence desecuritization–reconciliation always desirable? How can these notions resonate with all the components of the populations of devastated societies, since individual experiences, emotions, and expectations are dissimilar and fundamentally dissonant?

In the aftermath of mass atrocities, the memory work will probably never lead to an "asecurity community" (Wæver, 1998). Rather than expecting a process that entails friendship or forgiveness, I would insist on the importance of being realistic in terms of timing (changes in this area do not take years but generations) and setting achievable aims (coexistence is already a remarkable goal after mass atrocities). The irreversible character of certain wounds cannot be underestimated. The layers of violence that accumulate during a war provoke festering wounds; physical as well as mental. These wounds are at the origin of an intense hatred that must be taken seriously. In most conflict resolution textbooks, hatred is considered as a strictly 'negative' emotion. Might it not be more appropriate to see it as neither positive nor negative? The purpose is neither to call for it, nor to attempt to crush it by all means.

A meeting in Rwanda highlights the importance of this point. A Rwandan survivor who was particularly involved in local reconciliation projects geared toward perpetrators who had killed all her relatives was asked to explain where she could find the energy to go to jail, visit the criminals, and bring them food. After a sigh, she just said: "I took the time for hatred. It took me ten years. I hated the entire world. Now, I can think about reconciliation." This reaction is edifying. It is not, however, systematic. I will always remember the eyes of a Colombian woman who tragically told me: "Don't touch my hatred. That is the only thing that's left. They took all I had – except for my hatred." These reactions confirm that the response to past atrocities is ultimately an individual one.

Notes

1 Here, the notion of identity employed is one that is fluid, evolutionary, and above all constructed rather than fixed; see McSweeney (1996, 1999).
2 Nevertheless, the amnesia was far from being complete. Chancellor Adenauer had no other choice but to acknowledge Germany's wartime aggression and atrocities, spearheading, for example, the efforts to pay reparations to Israel. As he endorsed the policy before the Bundestag in 1951, he said that most Germans were "aware of the immeasurable suffering brought to the Jews in Germany and in the occupied territories in the era of National Socialism" and that the "unspeakable crimes" which were committed required "moral and material restitution." The West German government paid out tens of billions of dollars in compensation to the victims of the Nazi era, beginning with an initial payment of DM3 billion paid to the state of Israel as part of the Luxemburg Agreement of 1952.

Bibliography

Alexander, J. C., Eyerman, R., Giesen, B., Smelser, N. J., & Sztompka, P. (2004). *Cultural trauma and collective identity*. California: University of California Press.

Alvarez, J. (1998). Rush to closure: Lessons of the Tadić judgment. *Michigan Law Review*, *96*(7), 2031–2112.

Anderson, B. (1983). *Imagined communities: Reflections on the origin and spread of nationalism*. London: Verso.

Argenti, N., & Schramm, K. (Eds.). (2009). *Remembering violence: Anthropological perspectives on intergenerational transmission*. Oxford & New York: Berghahn Books.

Bar-Siman-Tov, Y. (Ed.). (2004). *From conflict resolution to reconciliation*. Oxford: Oxford University Press.

Baussant, M. (2002). *Pieds noirs, mémoires d'exil*. Paris: Stock.

Bell, D. (2010). *Memory, trauma and world politics: Reflections on the relationship between past and present*. London: Palgrave.

Bernanos, G. (1949). *Les enfants humiliés, journal 1939–1940*. Paris: Gallimard.

Brudholm, T., & Rosoux, V. (2013). The unforgiving. Reflections on the resistance to forgiveness after atrocity. In A. Hirsch (Ed.), *Theorizing post-conflict reconciliation: Agonism, restitution and repair* (pp. 115–130). New York: Routledge.

Butler, M., & Wolf, Z. (2017). *Problematizing security: Assessing the constructivist turn in security studies*. Unpublished manuscript.

Buzan, B., Wæver, O., & de Wilde, J. (1998). *Security: A new framework for analysis*. Boulder, CO: Lynne Rienner Publishers.

C.A.S.E. Collective. (2006). Critical approaches to security in Europe: A networked manifesto. *Security Dialogue, 37*(4), 443–487.

Chaumont, J. M. (1997). *La concurrence des victimes, génocide, identité, reconnaissance*. Paris: La Découverte.

Ciliers, J., Dube, O., & Siddiqi, B. (2016). Reconciling after civil conflict increases social capital but decreases individual well-being. *Science, 352*(6287), 787–794.

Dalsheim, J. (2014). *Producing spoilers. Peacemaking and the production of enmity in a secular age*. Oxford: Oxford University Press.

De Gaulle, C. (1970). *Discours et messages*. Paris: Plon.

Delbo, C. (1970). *Une connaissance inutile*. Paris: Minuit.

Delori, M. (2016). *La réconciliation franco-allemande par la jeunesse*. Brussels: Peter Lang.

Feraoun, M. (2000). *Journal, 1955–1962: Reflections on the French-Algerian War*. Lincoln, NE: University of Nebraska Press.

French National Assembly (2005). Law No. 2005–158 of 23 February 2005 (*regarding recognition of the Nation and national contribution in favour of the French repatriates*).

Garton Ash, T. G. (1997, December). La commission vérité et réconciliation en Afrique du sud. *Esprit, 238*, 44–62.

Garton Ash, T. G. (2003). *The waters of Mesomnesia; Dans entre Kant et Kosovo*. Paris: Presses de Sciences Po.

Hamber, B., & Wilson, R. A. (2002). Symbolic closure through memory, reparation and revenge in post-conflict societies. *Journal of Human Rights, 1*(1), 35–53.

Hobsbawn, E., & Ranger, T. (1992). *The invention of tradition*. Cambridge: Cambridge University Press.

Hugo, V. (1985). Actes et paroles. Pendant l'exil (1865). *Oeuvres complètes*, Paris: Robert Laffont.

Huysmans, J. (2011). What's in an act? On security speech acts and little security nothings. *Security Dialogue, 42*(4–5), 371–383.

Igreja, V. (2012). Multiple temporalities in indigenous justice and healing practices in Mozambique. *International Journal of Transitional Justice, 6*(3), 404–422.

Jospin, L. (1999). Memory and identity. Speech at Genshagen Castle, Berlin, Germany. September 25, 1999.

Kacowicz, A. M., Bar-Siman-Tov, Y., Jerneck, M., & Elgström, O. (Eds.). (2000). *Stable peace among nations*. Lanham, MD: Rowman & Littlefield.

Kelman, H. (1978). Israelis and Palestinians: Psychological prerequisites for mutual acceptance. *International Security, 3*(3), 162–186.

Klar, Y., & Branscombe, N. R. (2016). Intergroup reconciliation: Emotions are not enough. *Psychological Inquiry, 27*(2), 106–112.

Langenbacher, E., & Shain, Y. (Eds). (2010). *Power and the past. Collective memory and international relations*. Washington, D.C.: Georgetown University Press.

Lavabre, M-C. (1991). Du poids et du choix du passé. Lecture critique du 'syndrome de Vichy. In D. Peschanski, M. Pollak & H. Rousso (Eds.), *Histoire politique et sciences sociales* (pp. 265–278). Brussels: Complexe.

Limbert, J. W. (2009). *Negotiating with Iran: Wrestling the ghosts of history*. Washington, D.C.: U.S. Institute of Peace Press.

Lind, J. (2009). The perils of apology: What Japan shouldn't learn from Germany. *Foreign Affairs*, *88*(3), 132–146.

Malley, R. (2001, January 23). Au Proche-Orient, on en reviendra toujours à l'équation posée par Bill Clinton. *Le Monde*.

McSweeney, B. (1996). Identity and security: Buzan and the Copenhagen School. *Review of International Studies*, *22*(1), 81–93.

McSweeney, B. (1999). *Security, identity, and interests: A sociology of international relations*. Cambridge: Cambridge University Press.

Montgomery, S. (2014, April 1). Rwanda: 20 years later: The burden of survival. *The Gazette*.

Nora, P. (1984). Entre mémoire et histoire. *Les Lieux de mémoire, I, La République*. Paris: Gallimard.

Olick, J. (1999). Genre memories and memory genres: A dialogical analysis of May 8, 1945 commemorations in the Federal Republic of Germany. *American Sociological Review*, *64*(3), 381–402.

Renan, E. (1882). Qu'est-ce qu'une nation? Conference faite en Sorbonne, March 11, 1882.

Ricoeur, P. (2000). *La mémoire, l'histoire, l'oubli*. Paris: Le Seuil.

Rosenblum, R. (2009, December). Postponing trauma: The dangers of Tellin. *International Journal of Psychoanalysis*, *90*(6), 1319–1340.

Rosoux, V. (2004). Human rights and the 'work of memory' in international relations. *International Journal of Human Rights*, *3*(2), 159–170.

Rosoux, V. (2008). Reconciliation as a peace-building process. In J. Bercovitch, V. Kremenyuk & W. Zartman (Eds.), *Handbook of conflict resolution* (pp. 543–563). London: Sage Publications.

Rousso, H. (1998). *La hantise du passé*. Paris: Textuel.

Saint Augustine. (1964). *Les confessions*. Paris: Garnier-Flammarion.

Salles, R. (2012). Oikeiosis in Epictetus. In A. G. Vigo (Ed.), *Oikeiosis and the natural bases of morality: From classical stoicism to modern philosophy* (pp. 95–120). Hildesheim: Georg Olms Verlag.

Sayad, A. (1999). *La double absence. Des illusions de l'émigré aux souffrances de l'immigré*. Paris: Le Seuil.

Scarry, E. (1987). *The body in pain. The making and unmaking of the world*. Oxford: Oxford University Press.

Sontag, S. (2003). Regarding the pain of others. *Diogène 1*, 127–139.

Stritzel, H. (2011). Security, the translation. *Security Dialogue*, *42*(4–5), 343–355.

Thompson, J. (2002). *Taking responsibility for the past: Reparation and historical injustice*. London: Polity.

Tonkin, E. (1992). *Narrating our pasts. The social reconstruction of oral history*. Cambridge: Cambridge University Press.

Tutu, D. (1999). *No future without forgiveness*. New York: Doubleday.

van Ness, D. (1993). New wine and old wineskins: Four challenges of restorative justice. *Criminal Law Forum*, *4*(2), 251–276.

Volkan, V. D. (2006). What some monuments tell us about mourning and forgiveness. In E. Barkan & A. Karn (Eds.), *Taking wrongs seriously: Apologies and reconciliation* (pp. 115–131). Stanford: Stanford University Press.

Uzelac, A. (1997, January 23–29). Apprendre aux petits Bosniaques que leur voisin est un ennemi. *Gazeta Wyborcza – Courrier International*, *325*, 32.

Wæver, O. (1995). Securitization and desecuritization. In R. D. Lipschutz (Ed.), *On security* (pp. 46–87). New York: Columbia University Press.

Wæver, O. (1998). Insecurity, security, and asecurity in the West European non-war community. In E. Adler & M. Barnett (Eds.), *Security Communities* (pp. 69–118). Cambridge: Cambridge University Press.

Weinrich, H. (1999). *Léthé: Art et critique de l'oubli*. Paris: Fayard.

Williams, M. (2011). Securitization and the liberalism of fear. *Security Dialogue*, *42*(4–5), 453–563.

Wilson, R. A. (2001). Justice and legitimacy in South African transition. In A. Barahona De Brito, C. Gonzales-Enriquez, & P. Aguilar (Eds.), *The politics of memory: Transitional justice in democratizing societies* (pp. 190–217). Oxford: Oxford University Press).

Zartman, I. W. (2000). Ripeness: The hurting stalemate and beyond. In P. C. Stern & D. Druckman (Eds.), *International conflict resolution after the Cold War* (pp. 225–250). Commission on Behavioral and Social Sciences and Education, National Research Council. Washington, D.C: National Academy Press.

Zartman, I. W., & Kremenyuk, V. (2005). *Peace versus justice: Negotiating forward and backward-looking outcomes*. Lanham: Rowman and Littlefield.

Zeniter, A. (2017). *L'art de perdre*. Paris: Flammarion.

Conclusion

Securitization, revisited: revealed insights, future directions

Michael J. Butler

From the outset, the ultimate objective of this book was to build on the foundation established by the generation of scholars who first developed, and later applied, securitization theory. Doing so demanded not only that the contributors chronicle the phenomenon of securitization across a wide range of analytical domains and policy issues, but that we do so with a distinctly critical eye. Recognizing and accounting for wide variation by actor, issue, and spatial and temporal context, the guidepost here was reflexivity – in considering the impact of securitization theory as applied across a variety of topics, and in the implications of those applications for the (re)formulation of securitization theory itself.

In pursuit of this objective, as noted in the introduction, this project was oriented around three common concerns: revealing deficiencies in and through application(s) of securitization; considering units of analysis other than speech-acts and discourse; and exposing any latent orthodoxies embedded in the conceptualization of securitization. The findings generated from across the range of analyses featured here are clearly reflective of these three foci. Although not intended to minimize the particular and unique findings contained within each of the preceding chapters – each dealing with prominent, distinct, and in some cases under-examined security domains – this concluding chapter seeks to synthesize and reveal those broader themes which have emerged as a result of our common enterprise.

The utility of malleability

The first of these revealed insights is the challenging, if ultimately helpful, conceptual malleability of securitization. This was a point of emphasis in Roxanna Sjöstedt's opening assessment of securitization theory, and was borne out repeatedly in the various applications that followed. 'Fuzzy' concepts often draw the ire of the social scientist; here one might think of Roland Paris' (2001) famous critique of human security, or Kenneth Waltz's (1979) efforts to equate security with survival. The various applications presented here get us no closer to a parsimonious understanding of securitization; indeed, quite the opposite. Yet it is precisely this malleability that imbues the concept of securitization with such explanatory power, lending it utility across a wide array of actors and phenomena – from monarchs to filmmakers, rising sea levels to weaponized memories.

Our examination of a sweeping landscape of securitizing agents, securitized threats and referent objects, and securitization mechanisms and technologies reflects not only the malleability of the concept of securitization, but also the profound complexity of securitization processes. For example, as Katerina Antoniou demonstrates in her examination of the peacebuilder community in Cyprus, a multiplicity of audiences are in fact embedded within any given securitization process – with each distinct audience typified by the potential for significantly variant responses to speech-acts and other securitizing moves. Likewise, as Jarosław Jarząbek acknowledges in his assessment of RSCT, the constitutive function that the orthodox notion of territorialized 'boundaries' plays in defining a regional security complex may actually work at cross-purposes to the goal of understanding security dynamics by obscuring the de-territorialized political and normative undercurrents of much contemporary securitized (and securitization) activity.

On top of it all, geographic and cultural overlays compound the processual complexity, particularly when we train our focus on securitization processes that concern and/or occur in societies outside of the 'West' or the 'Global North.' The contributions here by Blanca Camps-Febrer, Mark Boyer, and Neil Oculi, and Natalie Hudson and Alexandra Budabin each in their own way speak to this point, while also acknowledging the need for more (and more systematic) forays in securitization research outside of a Eurocentric context, and apart from its common assumptions and analytical foci. This is a path forward in securitization research that we consider absolutely imperative, and one that might especially benefit from the inherent malleability of securitization captured in this volume. At the same time, those engaging in it would be well-advised to explicitly acknowledge their own positionality as scholars – and, in our case, scholars operating in a western, Eurocentric context. Such an acknowledgment represents at least a first step toward mitigating the "dilemma of the third party" (Sontag, 2003) as Valérie Rosoux discusses in chronicling her efforts to grapple with the weight of memory in places like Rwanda, South Africa, and Algeria.

Ambivalent and contingent outcomes

A second insight revealed by the various treatments of securitization here (particularly, but not exclusively, those featured in Part II) stems from their individual and collective efforts to engage with and unpack the 'security trap' (C.A.S.E. Collective, 2006). Whatever one thinks of it, securitization undoubtedly invokes exceptionality and sets a chain of events in motion wherein an issue, problem, or challenge is transformed in particular ways which may – or may not – be security-enhancing or -inducing for affected individuals and societies (C.A.S.E. Collective, 2006). Here, then, we might add to our aforementioned acknowledgment of securitization's malleability a collective sense of ambivalence with respect to the highly variable effects of the securitization process as it unfolds through both discourse(s) and practice(s). In sum, we view the implications of securitizing any given issue(s), actor(s), or behavior(s) – sometimes hazardous, sometimes generative, never neutral – as wholly contingent on the agents, audiences, referents, and technologies involved in the process which plays out within a particular social and temporal context.

In this way, Blanca Camps-Febrer's trenchant critique of the authority-claiming, regime-serving function of the securitization of terrorism in Morocco can in fact co-exist alongside Mark Boyer and Neil Oculi's perceptive rendering of the impact that scientific expertise, funneled through securitizing moves, can play in elevating the issue of climate change to the status of 'first-order threat,' even in the face of widespread climate change denialism. Securitization is a discernible process with some common and recurrent features that nevertheless can and do generate highly variable outcomes. Natalie Hudson and Alexandra Budabin's careful examination of what are rather mixed effects generated by the securitization of sexual and gender-based violence in conflict settings provides a further example of the contingency inherent in securitization outcomes, and by extension our overall ambivalence with respect to the process itself.

Though by definition the contingent nature of securitization outcomes is domain-specific, our engagements with securitization in application across a range of policy and issue domains suggest there are, at a minimum, three considerations – questions – which can be used to structure any attempt to unpack the securitization process whenever and wherever it occurs. The first such question is **'who'** – i.e., who is (are) the agent(s) of securitization? Heretofore they have been largely assumed to be political and social elites, in many cases direct representatives or associates of the state. Here we see a display of latent orthodoxy in the privileging of the state and the presumption that a particular subset of actors is predominantly responsible (in a 'top-down' fashion) for initiating, sustaining, and directing the securitization process. To the contrary, our examination of securitization (and desecuritization, as discussed below) in various applications reveals the increasing relevance of non-state and substate actors of various types in the process, including those situated outside the corridors of power. This is a point of emphasis identified by Jarosław Jarząbek as a crucial deficiency of RSCT, and again with respect to efforts to securitize issues such as sexual and gender-based violence (Hudson & Budabin) or climate change (Boyer & Oculi).

A second question to ask when grappling with the contingent effects of securitization is that of **how** – meaning, how does the process of securitization actually occur, and what mechanisms for securitization are employed and embedded within the process? We are sympathetic to the Paris School's arguments concerning the narrowly restrictive nature of a singular focus on discourse and speech-acts, and the consequences of excluding the many non-discursive securitizing 'moves' and 'technologies' unfolding within a particular policy/issue domain (including the potential for reifying existing power relations by doing so). A narrow preoccupation with the speech-act conveyed through official discourse necessarily translates to an incomplete picture with respect to understanding the process of securitization, but by extension, hinders our ability to gauge the effects of that process. This is demonstrated by Blanca Camps-Febrer through the reproduction and diffusion of insecurity via the use of various technologies in Morocco, and likewise in the use of advocacy platforms such as films or social media by decidedly non-elite (or, at least, non-governmental elites) to amplify attention, and resources, to sexual and gender-based violence in conflict settings, as Natalie Hudson and Alexandra Budabin discuss. If, instead, we ground our assessments of securitization in application through consideration of various types of 'encounters' that do not register in official discourse, we are likely to not only gain a fuller sense of how securitization works in a given domain, but also of its likely outcomes and impacts.

The third question to ask when attempting to navigate through the contingent nature of securitization and its effects is **to whom** – meaning, to whom or what audience or audiences is the securitization process directed? Again, the multiplicity of audiences deserves our consideration. The failure to consider the degree of receptivity and salience of securitizing moves of all types and forms across different audiences leads to analytical omissions (such as that revealed by Katerina Antoniou in chronicling the rejection of securitizing narratives by peacebuilders in Cyprus) or false binaries regarding the success/failure of securitization efforts, as Natalie Hudson and Alexandra Budabin demonstrate in accounting for the panoply of audiences (as well as agents) embedded within the securitization of SGBV. Here we recall Roxanna Sjöstedt's helpful reminder of the importance of constructivism's central tenet of intersubjectivity to securitization processes and mechanisms. Intersubjectivity should never be understood as a mere additive proposition occurring between two parties, but rather an interactive and symbiotic dynamic which co-produces meaning or understanding across 'x' parties. Thus, we see the 'to whom' question asked in the critical interrogation of counter-terrorism technologies in Morocco, in the multi-layered reverberations of securitized memories (across various strata of society) in Franco-Algerian relations, or in the vital distinction between audiences in vast developed countries versus those in Small Island Developing States (SIDS).

Operationalizing desecuritization

The third revealed insight – or, really, set of insights – emerge primarily from Part III of the book, in the selections expressly dedicated to operationalizing desecuritization. Prompted in part by the underspecified nature of desecuritization (Aradau, 2004), the contributions from Katerina Antoniou, Siniša Vuković, and Valérie Rosoux each individually and collectively follow Hansen's (2012) admonition to think of desecuritization as something more than the inverse of securitization. Rather, desecuritization is a distinct and equally complex (and malleable) societal process calibrated toward a return to 'normal politics' (Wæver, 1995) through a variety of mechanisms (replacement, re-articulation, fading, silencing).

As noted above, expanding one's analytical frame concerning securitization actors, audiences, mechanisms, and even timelines – as we have attempted to do throughout the book – enhances the prospects for a fuller appreciation of securitization as both a process and a concept. This is no less true with respect to desecuritization, as the three chapters specifically concerned with it demonstrate. So, in the same way that Hudson and Budabin and Boyer and Oculi convey the catalytic role that non-state and substate actors and public audiences play in the securitization process of SGBV or climate change (respectively), so too are these actors and audiences pivotal in efforts to de-securitize group identity in Cyprus (as Antoniou chronicles) or memory in various contexts, including that of Franco-German reconciliation after World War II (as elaborated by Rosoux).

To the extent that a narrow concern with discourse hinders our ability to assess the securitization process and its impacts, it is equally limiting with respect to desecuritization. To this end, consider Siniša Vuković's extensive discussion of the many and varied non-discursive practices and mechanisms available to, and employed by, third-party mediators in their efforts to de-securitize protracted and intractable social conflicts through signaling, institution building, and the like. As Katerina Antoniou characterizes it, like securitization, desecuritization neither begins nor ends at the speech-act, and may very well require engagement with and dismantling of 'facts' (histories) and affective dispositions toward them (memories) that are deeply embedded in conscious or even unconscious processes, as Valérie Rosoux suggests. Thus, we would be well-advised to consider a range of mechanisms of and for desecuritization, including phenomena that heretofore have not been given much consideration within the realm of security studies such as intergroup and inter-personal contact (Antoniou), memory (Rosoux), and incentive structures (Vuković).

An additional finding specific to the investigations of desecuritization here concerns that of time horizons and their importance to the analyst and, for that matter, the policymaker. Regardless of the policy/issue domain of concern, our ability to understand the process of desecuritization – and seek to gauge outcomes derived from that process – is likely to be restricted if we employ an overly narrow time horizon. This is essentially true of securitization processes; as Blanca Camps-Febrer points out, the embeddedness of power-relations within securitizing discourse and technologies necessitate consideration of the 'longue durée.' Yet the edifices created by securitization – and their institutionalization and normalization – only magnify and underscore the need for viewing desecuritization processes through an elongated temporal lens. This was a point made especially clear in Siniša Vuković's discussion of the role of the mediator in desecuritization.

If we are to capture what might very well be non-discursive de-securitizing 'moves' emanating from non-elite agents far from the channels of official power at their earliest stages, as well as their possibly quiet – but not insignificant – reverberations over time, then thinking differently about our time horizon for analytical purposes is essential. The narrative histories provided by Antoniou and Rosoux are revealing in this regard. Indeed, with respect to 'time,' as Rosoux argues, the appropriate unit of measure with respect to desecuritization may be generations rather than months or years. This is a compelling insight, and one which indirectly reveals the rather orthodox way in which securitization research has dealt with temporal considerations – one consequence of which has been the privileging of securitization (which, by dint of its exceptionality, can unfold more rapidly and dramatically) at the expense of desecuritization. We have little alternative but to resist replicating this orthodoxy, lest we continue to train our analytical efforts disproportionately on securitization at the expense of advancing our collective understanding of desecuritization processes and mechanisms and their attendant possibilities.

Concluding reflections

Ultimately, our inquiries here affirm the profoundly dynamic and elastic quality of securitization and desecuritization. In this way, they resemble the field of security studies from which they have emerged, and to which they have made such a significant contribution. They are also clearly concepts that bear fruit when applied across a wide range of phenomena – including topics and concerns not always viewed through the lens of security. Not unlike the larger field of security studies itself, securitization theory and its adherents and critics (which perhaps ought to be one and the same) would be well served to examine the securitizing and desecuritizing moves of a wider range of actors, and to consider a wider range of actions and behaviors as securitizing (or desecuritizing) moves.

In addition to the particular findings of each of the preceding investigations, these insights speak not only to the many contributions of securitization research to the field of security studies, but also to the critical pathways which scholars would be well-advised to pursue if the explanatory power of securitization as a concept is to be sustained into the future. In that vein, where else might scholars of securitization devote their energies? Certainly, a concerted and systematic effort to refine and improve securitization as a concept by applying it more extensively to non-Western security and social contexts is essential. Further, we would be wise to think more, and more deeply, about the normative implications of securitization – including and especially for traditionally marginalized populations. In our efforts to widen the purview of securitization theory and analysis, we would be wrong to forget the stakes involved, and the stakeholders. Finally, and perhaps most fundamentally, we must strive to develop our capacity to better comprehend and diagnose scenarios and stages in which either securitization or, conversely, desecuritization is warranted – and work actively as citizen-scholars to facilitate the appropriate process, in whatever way(s) possible. This latter task would seem especially imperative in light of the consequences of failing to do so.

Bibliography

Aradau, C. (2004). Security and the democratic scene: Desecuritization and emancipation. *Journal of International Relations and Development 7*(4), 388–413.

C.A.S.E. Collective. (2006). Critical approaches to security in Europe: A networked manifesto. *Security Dialogue, 37*(4), 443–487

Hansen, L. (2012). Reconstructing desecuritisation: The normative-political in the Copen-hagen School and directions for how to apply it. *Review of International Studies, 38,* 525–546.

Paris, R. (2001). Human security: Paradigm shift or hot air? *International Security, 26*(2), 87–102.

Sontag, S. (2003). Regarding the pain of others. *Diogène 1,* 127–139.

Wæver, O. (1995). Securitization and desecuritization. In R. D. Lipschutz, (Ed.), *On security* (pp. 46–86). New York: Columbia University Press.

Waltz, K. N. (1979). *Theory of international politics.* Reading, MA: Addison-Wesley.

Index

For Product Safety Concerns and Information please contact our EU
representative GPSR@taylorandfrancis.com
Taylor & Francis Verlag GmbH, Kaufingerstraße 24, 80331 München, Germany

www.ingramcontent.com/pod-product-compliance
Lightning Source LLC
Chambersburg PA
CBHW070402270326
41926CB00014B/2668

*9 7 8 0 3 6 7 7 8 5 2 3 9 *